# Frontiers of Classroom Research

*Edited by Gabriel Chanan
and Sara Delamont*

*NFER Publishing Company*

Published by the NFER Publishing Company Ltd.,
Book Division, 2 Jennings Buildings, Thames Avenue,
Windsor, Berks SL4 1QS

Registered Office: The Mere, Upton Park, Slough, Berks, SL1 2DQ

First Published 1975

85633 075 2

Printed in Great Britain by
King, Thorne & Stace Ltd., School Road, Hove, Sussex, BN3 5JE

Distributed in the USA by Humanities Press Inc.,
Hillary House-Fernhill House, Atlantic Highlands,
New Jersey 07716 USA

# CONTENTS

Chapter 1 Introduction  *Sara Delamont*  5

Chapter 2 The first generation of British 'interaction' studies  *E. C. Wragg*  13

Chapter 3 Microteaching: research and developments  *G. A. Brown*  25

Chapter 4 A conceptual map for interaction studies  *Jim Eggleston, M. J. Galton and Margaret Jones*  52

Chapter 5 Teaching styles: a typological approach  *S. N. Bennett*  89

Chapter 6 Teacher-centred strategies in interaction research  *A. Morrison*  109

Chapter 7 'Showing them up' in secondary school  *Peter Woods*  122

Chapter 8 The problem of the 'unmotivated' in an open school: a participant observation study  *Andrew Hannan*  146

Chapter 9 In cold blood: Bedside teaching in a medical school  *Paul Atkinson*  163

Chapter 10 Systematic observation in informal classrooms  *Deanne Boydell*  183

Chapter 11 Teachers' questions and reactions: a microteaching study  *Gordon MacLeod, Donald MacLennan and Donald McIntyre*  198

Chapter 12 Developing pictures for other frames: action research and case study  *Clem Adelman and Rob Walker*  220

Chapter 13 Teaching and talking: a sociolinguistic approach to classroom interaction  *Michael Stubbs*  233

Chapter 14 The classroom setting as a unit of analysis in observation studies  *Pamela K. Poppleton*  247

Chapter 15 A Scottish alternative to interaction analysis  *John Powell*  255

# ACKNOWLEDGEMENTS

We would like to thank the Social Science Research Council for sponsoring the seminars for which the original versions of these papers were prepared, as explained in the introduction.

# CHAPTER 1

# Introduction

*Sara Delamont, Leicester University School of Education*

This book presents a wide variety of papers on contemporary British research into classroom processes. It grew out of two seminars funded by the Social Science Research Council, to discuss the state of classroom research, which were held in Leicester in 1973 and 1974. This introduction presents an historical account of the research area and relates the papers to an overall structure.

## Background

Classroom research in Britain is booming. In 1972, when I took over the mailing list of the infant British Classroom Study Group it contained thirty-odd names, of whom twenty or so were actively engaged in projects. There are now over eighty people on the list who claim to be working on classroom phenomena, and new inquiries reach me every week. There are probably as many more researchers struggling alone with the problems of understanding classroom life, and this book may be of particular interest to them.

Five years ago, when the group began, studies undertaken in classrooms were a very minor part of educational research in Britain. Most workers were dependent on borrowing American techniques and theories. Now research in classrooms is an important enough speciality to be chosen as one of the two topics for the inaugural conference of the British Educational Research Association, and the work is developing along specifically British lines. The present volume is the first attempt at displaying the spectrum of this developing work away from the shadow of the American giants.

The British Classroom Study Group was founded by John Garner in 1970, when he was himself involved in some fascinating work on teacher expectancy and behaviour in infant classes (Garner and Bing, 1973). Feeling the lack of any suitable forum for discussing classroom phenomena, he circulated higher education institution asking if anyone wanted to join a group on the 'Study of Classroom Behaviour'. Enough people responded for Garner to run two work-shops in Lancaster – and it is those workshops which form the background to this book. The Lancaster meetings were informal and honest; the participants were still junior enough to be sitting in classrooms themselves and were mainly working without large grants. A pioneering spirit was abroad, and the atmosphere of those gatherings is often recalled with evident nostalgia.

When John Garner went to Australia in 1972, he left the study group in my hands. Soon afterwards the Social Science Research Council, who were expanding their policy of funding small seminars on specific research topics (ssrc, 1973; 1974a and 1974b), asked me to run a series of meetings on classroom research; and it is on these meetings that this book is based.

The most famous tradition in American classroom research is a social-psychological one, stemming from Anderson, Bales, and Lewin, Lippitt and White (see Amidon and Hough, 1967, for further details). This research tradition involves coding classroom events into pre-determined categories, and then using the codings to place teachers on a stylistic continuum according to the limits they place upon the pupils' freedom of speech. Good all-American teachers are integrative not dominating, democratic not authori-tarian, or in the terminology of Ned Flanders (the best known living exponent of the approach) they use indirect rather than direct influence. This variety of systematic classroom research is generally referred to as *interaction analysis*. The majority of observation systems in the classroom researcher's 'pharmacopoeia' (Simon and Boyer, 1970) are direct offshoots from this social-psychological tradition. Given this dominance in the usa – so great that 'classroom research' and 'interaction analysis' are often used interchangably – it is not surprising that many early British studies were strongly influenced by the work of Flanders and his disciples. The first seminar in the ssrc series was, therefore centred on interaction analysis, and Flanders himself attended it.

Although the social-psychological tradition has dominated class-room research on both sides of the Atlantic, other research per-spectives have always existed alongside it, and a variety of these were presented at the second seminar. Some of the researchers in the usa drew their inspiration from other branches of psychology and some from psychiatry, sociology, anthropology and linguistics.

There, the workers in these various traditions do not work together – indeed they hardly attempt any dialogue between approaches. Flanders does not mention Louis Smith's work, Philip Jackson ignores Arno Bellack's. In Britain, adherents of approaches other than interaction analysis do know of each other's existence, and the second seminar was deliberately arranged to foster this communication. However, interdisciplinary meetings are never trouble-free, and it is rare for any *rapprochement* to occur. The reader will find contradictory views expressed in the various papers which follow, and may wonder if they can be reconciled. To understand the issues underlying these differing views some discussion of the intellectual context of classroom research in Britain is necessary, and this is presented in the following section.

**Intellectual context**

British classroom researchers have always tended to meet at conferences, regardless of the disciplines from which they approach their research. It is the interdisciplinary mix which gives British work its greatest strength – particularly when compared with the segregated American variety. But when one considers that the authors in this volume come not only from four disciplines – anthropology, sociology, psychology and linguistics – but also from a wide range of different 'schools' within those disciplines, it is not surprising that mutual incomprehension or even hostility, frequently characterize classroom seminars. While most of the leading figures now pay lip-service to the need for interdisciplinary, or multi-disciplinary, approaches to classroom phenomena, few are prepared to settle down to the hard work involved in immersing themselves in the literature and methodology of stances other than their own. This book, like the seminars on which it draws, is dedicated to building an interdisciplinary perspective for studying classroom phenomena.[1]

The empirical investigation of classroom processes does not fit clearly into mainstream psychology or sociology. In the USA, where social psychology has a much more clearly defined territory between sociology and psychology, it was natural for much classroom investigation to be done by researchers with a background in social psychology. In Britain social psychology is much less developed

[1]In this section I have drawn heavily on ideas presented elsewhere by David Hamilton (1973).

and lacks autonomy and was not strong enough to annex the study of classrooms. Thus, while classrooms are now recognized as an important topic for educational research, they do not 'belong' unambiguously to any one group of specialists. British researchers in the sociology and psychology of education discovered classrooms in the late sixties, starting from very different premises. They now confront each other in an uneasy state of truce.

The traditional concerns of psychology of education were learning theories and psychometrics. By the late sixties it was clear to perceptive psychologists that such research had contributed all it was likely to, and that new approaches must be tried.[1] Educational problems existed which the traditional concerns did not reach, and these had to be tackled. One such problem was the classroom. Psychological studies had treated the classroom as a black box for input-output studies, or replaced it altogether by developing programmed learning, teaching machines and computer-assisted instruction. This neglect of classroom interaction may have been one reason for teachers' widespread neglect of research findings. This disenchantment among educational psychologists was mirrored by wider discontent among members of the psychological profession specializing in other fields – as the calls for a more 'relevant' and 'humane' discipline in Brown (1973) and Armistead (1974) testify. Gradually, following the American lead, British psychologists began to look at classrooms. Many were afraid to abandon their traditional methodology – they added observation to questionnaires, inventories and tests. But, although they were still clasping their respectable garments of reliability and validity about them, they did begin to observe human behaviour in natural, rather than laboratory, settings. Still concerned to be 'scientific', they used systematic observation techniques (i.e. schedules of pre-determined categories), at first imported American ones, but soon their own. (There are at least thirty 'home-grown' classroom observation schedules in Britain today.)

The sociology of education was facing its own particular problems. In the sixties some leading figures had predicted that 'the sociology of the school' would supplant, or at least rival, studies of social mobility and opportunity. By the end of the decade it was clear that this had not happened. Little work had appeared and one of

[1]The re-emergence of public debate about the 'Race and IQ' question reinforces this conviction. The debate is now a political and not an academic concern.

the most vaunted projects was an embarrassing fiasco. The focus became the curriculum instead and it is the sociology of knowledge, rather than of the school, which has grown to rival stratification studies in importance. However, a handful of younger sociologists, inspired by Goffman, Becker, Strauss and Cicourel, rather than by the organization theorists who had been expected to lead the change, stayed inside schools and headed for the action – into the classroom.

Relatively few psychologists or sociologists actually undertake classroom research, but enough of them do so to dwarf the few linguistics and anthropologists who have become interested. The linguists were also regarded as rebels within their discipline, because they had the strange notion that their job was to study language in contexts where it occurred – to collect real speech acts in real settings. (Traditionally linguists had studied utterances of their own making such as the famous 'Flying planes can be dangerous'.) Classrooms were both theoretically interesting and convenient as a source of sociolinguistic data (see Stubbs, *q.v.* for further details). The handful of anthropologists who looked at classrooms may have been inspired by the increasingly multiracial nature of urban schools, or by the desire to apply the technique of participant observation to face-to-face groups in their own society. Finally, it should be noted that many of those who pioneered classroom studies were 'method' tutors in teacher training departments, whose backgrounds were in Modern Languages, Chemistry, English and so on. These researchers were often inexperienced in any particular social science, and were especially vulnerable to pressures for academic respectability. For them too, the sense of isolation described by Wragg (*q.v.*) was at its most acute – in the early days everyone felt isolated, but those with a clear discipline behind them were at least partially protected.

Researchers from all these groups had begun classroom studies by the time Garner circulated his invitation. His respondents came from all the various disciplines, and all the fundamental disagreements to be found in this volume were present at the first meeting in Lancaster. Such disagreements are caused by the head-on collision of disciplines, and they will not be resolved until one group can collar all the research funds, or ban the others from schools or from publication – or until a new social science of interactive processes has been evolved.

At one level the issues are trivial. One powerful education professor suggested to Garner that his classroom group operate within the education section of the British Psychological Society, thus restricting membership of the group to qualified psychologists. Similar territorial bids were recognizable during the British Educational Research Association's inaugural conference in 1974. However, more fundamental issues in social science are also raised by the disagreements. Should social science attempt to measure and predict in the manner of the physical sciences? Or should we be asking how it is that observers can maintain presence in classrooms? How do we understand everyday life?

Such rhetorical questions may seem remote from the classroom 'chalk-face'. However, whether they acknowledge it or not, all the authors in this book are faced with these fundamental issues. One example is the researchers' reaction to the 'open' classroom. As schools become increasingly open, in both the architectural and the social meanings of the term, established techniques of classroom research become unworkable. We have to decide whether there can be conventional classroom research without conventional classrooms. The interaction analysts have always placed their major emphasis on the coding of 'public' talk, believing it to be the most salient feature of classroom life. Now that there are classrooms in which public talk is obviously *not* the most salient feature, researchers who might never have questioned the basic premise of interaction analysis are forced to do so. The consequent rethinking may bring them into agreement (or sharp dispute) with those who have always disliked that approach. A group of papers showing various strategies for studying such classrooms is a prominent feature of this volume (see Hannan, Adelman, Walker, Boydell and Poppleton, *q.v.*). These papers are, however, contradictory. Boydell, for example, opts for low-inference schedules, while Hannan has chosen to study teachers' definitions of the situation.

### About the book
The papers in this collection fall into three main types: research reviews (Wragg and Brown), theoretical and polemical contributions on the 'state of the art' (Eggleston, Galton and Jones, Morrison, Poppleton, Walker and Adelman) and accounts of specific research projects and approaches (Stubbs, Hannan, Boydell, Bennett, Atkinson, Woods, MacLeod, McLennan and MacIntyre, and Powell).

The two reviews are slightly different in focus. Wragg's paper covers the development of classroom research in Britain and is a revised version of the introductory paper to the first ssrc seminar. It was specifically designed to provide an introduction to British work for Professor Flanders, and incidentally, to remind the natives of the diversity of British research. While Wragg concentrates upon studies done in classrooms, Brown deals with an 'applied' aspect of classroom research – microteaching. Practitioners of microteaching, the miniaturization of teaching situations for training purposes, have their own informal communication networks, but many of those involved with it have also used interaction analysis techniques. Brown's review of British work on microteaching parallels Wragg's paper. Together they form an essential background to the rest of the book for newcomers, as well as making interesting reading in their own right.

The second category of papers is more diverse. Eggleston, Galton and Jones present the first British attempt to develop a taxonomy of observation strategies (see Simon and Boyer, 1970 for an American typology of schedules.) This was presented at the second seminar and proved to be highly controversial. In particular the taxonomy was attacked for its relegation of all the most interesting studies – such as Jackson (1968) – to the category 'inductive'. This category was, as Professor Eggleston acknowledged in discussion, an unanalysed 'bucket'. There was also criticism of the way the taxonomy is based on the researcher's intentions, which may or may not have been explicated. The model proposed by Adelman, on the other hand, is grounded in sociological theory. Walker, Adelman, Poppleton and Morrison present arguments about the interrelationships between the researcher, the teacher and the changing education system. These are all accessible to the newcomer, and raise issues which anyone contemplating classroom studies should consider.

Finally, the accounts of specific research projects, which form the major part of the book. Boydell, Bennett and Powell deal with the primary age-range; Stubbs, Hannan and Woods with the secondary; and Atkinson and McLeod, MacLennan and MacIntyre with aspects of higher education and professional training. Atkinson writes on social interaction at the bedside – the 'classroom' of clinical medical education, and the Stirling authors on training student teachers.

Just as the various sectors of education are represented, so are the various disciplines discussed above. Stubbs explicitly sets out to show how sociolinguists might study classrooms. Hannan's paper is explicitly sociological, drawing directly on Basil Bernstein's curriculum theory, and thus ultimately on Durkheim. Atkinson, too, is sociological in his approach, but uses American writing on 'information games' as his jumping-off point. In complete contrast, Bennett starts from a questionnaire to teachers, proceeding to cluster analyses of their responses, while McLeod and his colleagues have adapted the American psychological tradition embodied in microteaching. In short every paper represents a different approach to classroom phenomena, and the reader must decide which approach is most relevant to him. In the last analysis, every researcher and teacher has to choose his own strategy, but we hope this book will inform the choice.

**References**

AMIDON, E. J. and HOUGH, J. B. (Eds) (1967). *Interaction Analysis*. Reading, Mass.: Addison-Wesley.
ARMISTEAD, N. (Ed.) (1974). *Reconstructing Social Psychology*. Harmondsworth: Penguin.
BROWN, P. (Ed.) (1973). *Radical Psychology*. London: Tavistock.
GARNER, J. and BING, M. (1973). 'The elusiveness of Pygmalion and differences in teacher–pupil contacts,' *Interchange*, **4** (No. 1), 34–42.
HAMILTON, D. (1973). *At classroom level: studies in the learning milieu*. Unpublished PHD Thesis, University of Edinburgh.
JACKSON, P. (1968). *Life in Classrooms*. New York: Holt, Rinehart & Winston.
SIMON, A. and BOYER, G. (Eds) (1970). *Mirrors for Behavior*. Philadelphia: Research for Better Schools Inc.
SOCIAL SCIENCE RESEARCH COUNCIL (1973). Newsletter, **18**, p. 17.
SOCIAL SCIENCE RESEARCH COUNCIL (1974a). Newsletter, **22**, p. 14.
SOCIAL SCIENCE RESEARCH COUNCIL (1974b). Newsletter, **23**, p. 28.

CHAPTER 2

# The First Generation of British 'Interaction' Studies

*E. C. Wragg, Nottingham University*

## Early investigations

An analysis of British journals publishing educational research articles prior to the mid 1960s produces almost nothing about teaching/learning processes based on live observation of classroom events. Indeed most studies of learning outcomes tended to ignore process variables and investigate the predictive power of such presage variables as social class, intelligence and the personality and attitudes of teachers and pupils.

Where writers of research theses reported live observation techniques, these were usually modest in scope. Emmett (1964) using a systematic verbal analysis schedule to study a small group of student teachers, and Poole (1964) who analysed tapes and time-lapse photographs taken in ten Manchester schools, identifying seven major classroom activities, are amongst a tiny number of investigators in this category.

After 1965 several studies were initiated, usually by investigators working in isolation and frequently drawing inspiration from research in the United States by such as Flanders, Goffman, Jackson, Smith and Meux, Medley and Mitzel, and Good and Brophy. Many took as their initial inspiration Medley and Mitzel's seminal article 'Measuring classroom behaviour by systematic observation' in Gage's *Handbook of Research on Teaching* which is still amongst the best analyses of problems facing the classroom investigator to be found in the literature. It was not until 1970, when those engaged in classroom observation studies began to meet as a group and exchange information, that the phenomenon of the isolate working without support began to disappear, or rather become a less frequent occurrence.

An inevitable consequence of scattered *ad hoc* inquiries was that no single British style of inquiry emerged. The various projects

became as different from each other as were the background and
motivation of their initiators. There were larger scale studies of
over a hundred teachers as well as intensive scrutinies of single
classrooms. Methodological approaches were also of many kinds,
and time samplers, event counters and notebook scribblers hummed
happily at opposite ends of the country.

### The teacher's day

Outside the framework of largely university-based, small-scale
research were two more substantial descriptive accounts of the
daily transactions of the primary school teacher, one in Scotland,
the other in England. The main focus of Duthie's (1970) description
of teaching in thirty-seven primary schools in a varied and carefully
selected sample from all over Scotland was on teacher activities
which could be performed by an auxiliary helper. It was difficult
for him to restrict his account to such activities and ignore other
important teacher and pupil behaviour. Consequently, he produced
a well documented analysis of Scottish primary schools in which he
attempted, among other things, to define the critical behavioural
differences between what are commonly called 'traditional' and
'progressive' teaching methods. This involved the construction of
two macro-paradigms which preserved the sequence of observed
classroom events. The *instructional* paradigm, resembling what is
popularly called traditional primary school teaching, contained
behaviour such as 'teacher structures information or question',
'pupil answers' and 'teacher gives positive feedback'. The *self-
instructional* paradigm, the predominant style of what is often known
as progressive primary school teaching, showed activities such as
'pupil plans project', 'pupil checks progress against a plan', 'pupil
asks for teacher's help' and 'teacher interprets'.

After a feasibility study in the Slough area in 1967, the NFER
conducted a survey of the daily activities of one hundred and
twenty-nine teachers in sixty-six junior schools in the county of
Surrey during 1969. Hilsum and Cane (1971) did not confine their
attention to formally scheduled class hours, as their intention was
to construct a picture of the whole of a teacher's professional
activities, which included morning, afternoon and lunch breaks as
well as such out-of-school time as evenings, weekends and vacations
used for planning, marking and reading.

There are numerous findings of professional interest. It was found, for example, that about a quarter of the day was spent on instruction, though forty per cent was spent on the related activities of organizing pupils, consultation, marking, planning and lesson-related reading. A further quarter of the day was consumed by clerical and mechanical chores and supervision. Class size and ability mix were said to have little effect on the balance between individual and whole-class teaching, though teachers of large classes, not unexpectedly, did most of their marking in their own time rather than during lessons. The writers concluded their report by re-emphasizing the importance of non-classroom work and asking whether pupil contact time is currently being used as effectively as possible.

In their analysis of actual teaching sessions, Hilsum and Cane used a category recording system developed from teachers' self-reports and tested on videotapes of thirty lessons from the feasibility study. Three observers were trained to a high degree of inter-observer reliability.

## University-based projects

Almost all the other research projects prior to the early 1970s were begun in various universities, although most were supported by national funding bodies. There is some difficulty in deciding how to report these as they do not lend themselves easily to grouping. One might distinguish, for example, between studies of primary and secondary teachers, or students and experienced teachers, or on the basis of methodological criteria between those using category systems and those adopting the approach of the ethologist or social anthropologist. In the end it is probably much easier to describe what was happening in each locality and simply tour, in alphabetical order, the universities where classroom study was being undertaken.

At *Birmingham University* it was linguistic theory which formed the basis of the analysis of classroom discourse by Sinclair and Coulthard (1972). They used transcripts of lesson tape recordings to study transactions between teacher and pupil, as well as boundary markers between transactions, and metastatements, that is lesson-structuring remarks used to summarize past learning or delineate matters of future concern. When teacher questions were analysed, a sandwich structure was frequently discovered, whereby a teacher's question was followed by a pupil answer and a teacher reaction, similar to the $4-8-3$ or $4-8-2$ sequence often reported by investigators using the Flanders system. Additional matters of concern included the fit or lack of fit between grammatical form and discourse function, the use of commands, general patterns and sequences of classroom exchanges, and the identification of the larger linguistic units.

Walker and Adelman (1972), working from the *Chelsea College of Science and Technology* used a participant observer technique as well as time-lapse photography (Adelman and Walker, 1974) to study life in classrooms in a way similar to that employed by Jackson (1968) in the United States. The principal focus has been on schools which have carried through organizational change, and in class-rooms where particular curriculum projects have been adopted and developed. Data analysed have involved film and audio recordings, as well as the notes of observers and teachers, lesson plans and interview material.

*Edinburgh University* fostered a number of studies which were mainly the work of SSRC sponsored PhD students. The projects were almost all completed in the period 1969-1973. Hamilton (1973) worked within an anthropological framework, and over a sixteen week period he studied children following the Scottish Integrated Science Scheme. He showed how objectives were fulfilled which were directly opposed to those originally intended by the curriculum planners, clearly a matter for some concern when national schemes are implemented in a wide variety of classroom contexts. From his unusual vantage point as both teacher and observer with some of the classes, he was able to consider not only the effect of an observer's presence but also the interactional nexus between himself and the objects of his scrutiny.

Torode (1974) drew his inspiration from Garfinkel and the ethnomethodologists. He used pencil and notebook to record conversations in a class of forty-one fourteen-year-old boys in a large Scottish comprehensive school. He recorded the utterances of both teacher and pupils. This novel study was based initially on the views of Sartre and Garfinkel. Sartre believes that, in conversation, people try to reassert certain central preoccupations they have chosen for themselves, and to identify themselves deeply with certain concepts which, if seriously challenged, could undermine their whole identity. Garfinkel argues that people interacting with each other wish to show one another that their actions are both intelligible and worth copying. Torode investigated the differential skill of the boys in his sample at talking both to their peers and their teachers. One group of middle-class boys identified readily with teachers, spending a great deal of time discussing, mimicking and sometimes ridiculing them. A second group, largely of working class background, rarely discussed teachers, preferring instead to talk about sport. In addition, Torode has considered teachers able and unable to sustain order in the classroom, and looked to their own speech for elucidation of the reasons for classroom disorder in the light of the writings of a number of phenomenologists.

A third *Edinburgh* project was an intensive study by Delamont (1973) of teacher-pupil interaction in a private fee-paying girls' school. She used a study-habits inventory to identify groups of girls who were 'syllabus-bound', that is happiest working to a clearly-planned, externally defined syllabus, and those who were 'syllabus-free', preferring to follow their own interests and instincts. The 'syllabus-bound' group tended to be worried by indirect teachers as categorized by Flanders' i/d ('indirect/direct') ratio, preferring the stable routine of the more direct teachers, and even the 'syllabus-free' group tended to choose subjects taught by more directive teachers. The twenty-nine teachers in the sample were observed to be more indirect than the teachers described in the American literature. This study was a methodological hybrid, using systematic analysis of the Flanders type as well as the conventional weaponry of the social anthropologist. The writer finally produced a symbolic interactionist model for the classroom.

In a further project at *Edinburgh*, Nash (1973) studied children in six primary schools which fed the same secondary school. He used personal construct theory to assemble information about teachers' perceptions of children in both their schools, and field notes based on live observation of what happened in the various classrooms. He compared the roles which children adopted in their new secondary schools with those they had played in their primary schools and highlighted both differences and similarities. This is a unique study in Britain, documenting the period of primary to secondary transfer by reference to teachers' perceptions and observed classroom events.

In a final project commenced at *Edinburgh* and continued from *Dundee*, Morrison (1973) considered a group of four hundred children studying the same International Affairs syllabus. Teacher behaviour was measured by the Flanders system, and although broad differences in style were detected amongst the twenty-five teachers these were not related to differences found amongst the classes in tests of knowledge of the area covered.

Cameron-Jones and Morrison (1973) of *Dundee University* looked at teachers' assessments of their pupils in six comprehensive schools in Eastern Scotland. Live observation of the seventeen teachers involved was used to analyse the processes of assessment employed by teachers in their classrooms, and an observation schedule specifying sixty-eight kinds of assessment act was constructed to enable tape-recordings to be coded. Two classes of assessment act were formulated, namely solicitations and reactions, terms not synonymous with those used by Bellack (1966). A series of tabular data showed differences between teachers in their use of the various kinds of classroom assessment, and a factor analysis was performed in a supplementary process-product study from which relationships between achievement means and teacher behaviour emerged.

At *Exeter University* the present writer (Wragg, 1972, 1973) conducted an inquiry, sponsored by the Social Science Research Council, into the teaching behaviour of 102 graduate student teachers being trained at Exeter University Department of Education. A team of observers collected Flanders data and wrote field reports on 578 lessons given by the 102 student teachers in 41 schools in the South-West of England.

Comparison of data obtained with those produced by Flanders (1970) showed that the British student teachers tended to have a lower Teacher Question Ratio (British student teachers=21, American teachers=26) than the figure estimated by Flanders. Other comparisons showed a higher Pupil Initiation Ratio (British=43, American=34), a higher Steady State Ratio (British=59, American=50), a higher Immediate Teacher Response Ratio (British=80, American=60), and a lower Content Cross Ratio (British=50, American=55).

The students in the sample also completed the Cattell 16PF test, the Allport-Vernon-Lindzey Study of Values (Richardson's British Form), the Torrance Tests of Creative Thinking (Verbal Test B) and the Alice Heim AH5 test of high grade intelligence. These scores, along with ratings of teaching effectiveness, by supervising tutor and teaching practice school, were then analysed along with the classroom data. Among correlations between presage and process variables found to be significant at the one per cent level were the following:-

| | |
|---|---|
| *Cattell Factor A (warmth)* | and Flanders category 3 (r=·25) |
| | and Teacher Question Ratio (r=·31) |
| *Cattell Factor I (sensitive)* | and category 8 (r=·27) |
| | and % Teacher Talk (r=—·37) |
| | and Pupil Steady State Ratio (r=·32) |
| *Cattell Factor O (insecure)* | and category 6 (r=·27) |
| *Allport-Vernon-Lindzey Aesthetic Value* | and category 1 (r=·25) |
| | and category 8 (r=·30) |
| | and category 9 (r=·25) |
| | and % Teacher Talk (r=—·42) |
| *Torrance Fluency score* | and category 3 (r=·27) |
| *Alice Heim AH5 Intelligence Test* | and category 6 (r=·26) |

Comparison of the ratings of effectiveness and classroom data showed a negative correlation (r=—·27) between use of criticism and and tutor's rating and a correlation of r=·25 between occurrence of solicited pupil talk and ratings by the teaching practice school.

A factor analysis of a selection of the presage, process and product variables showed no very strong factors. Two of the main factors produced were: an 'academic' factor which loaded on use of lecture, use of praise, political value and class of degree (Bachelor degree), and a 'warm accepting' factor which loaded on Cattell Factor A, acceptance of feelings and ideas, questioning, pupil talk and flexibility (i.e. variety of lesson pattern).

Evans and Wragg (1969) also adapted the Flanders system to enable the interactions between teachers and individual children to be identified. When the technique was used in a school for severely subnormal children they found that the teachers tended to spend most of their time interacting with children who had scored lowest on speech tests. Although the children who scored higher on speech tests made more spontaneous contributions, they were asked fewer questions and received less praise.

In their study at *Lancaster University* of five first-year junior school classes, Garner and Bing (1973) made contacts between teachers and individual children the primary target of their concern. Classrooms were visited on several successive days and the whole day's activities were coded so that the differential nature of teachers' contacts with individual pupils could be described. In addition teachers' ratings of pupils on characteristics such as conduct, attitude to work, independence and sociability were secured and compared with the nature and extent of interpersonal contact between teacher and pupil. A cluster analysis with a six cluster solution was produced from the individual pupils' scores on twenty-two ratings and classroom observation measures. There were several interesting findings, including the one that children not especially distinctive according to either rated personality or observed classroom behaviour received fewer contacts than average. In addition, as might be expected, highest contacts were experienced by children found to be most active in either a constructive or a destructive way. This neat study did more than simply confirm what many teachers might instinctively report by highlighting more precisely via cluster analysis the kinds of activity and passivity which produce high or low interaction rates between pupil and teacher.

Two projects were undertaken at *Leicester University,* one concerned with primary schools, the other with science teaching in the secondary school.

In the first of these, directed by Professor Brian Simon, there was a two year feasibility phase during which the classroom organization of a number of junior schools was studied (Bealing, 1972). Subsequently two observational techniques were developed to be used by classroom observers, one concentrating on teacher, the other on pupil, behaviour. Six pairs of observers (one using the pupil instrument, the other the teacher schedule) field tested the systems in junior schools mathematics classes (Boydell, 1974). The teacher record is designed to preserve information about the teacher's conversation (or silence), the size of audience and the nature of the activity involved at twenty-five second intervals. The pupil record, based on a personal recording system devised by D. M. Medley at Princeton, is also based on a sampling act every twenty-five seconds. A child is selected and studied for two and a half minutes, permitting approximately twenty-four children per hour to be observed. The system permits coding of pupil-pupil as well as teacher-pupil interaction and no interaction at all.

The second *Leicester* study by Eggleston and Galton (Eggleston, 1973) involved live observation of ninety-five teachers of science using the twenty-five category Science Teacher Observation System (STOS) developed by the investigators. Trained observers recorded Biology, Chemistry and Physics lessons given to classes of pupils preparing for 'O' level examination. A cluster analysis process identified three discrete groups of teachers. Group I showed high incidence of teachers' questions and other teacher-dominated transactions with a correspondingly low incidence of pupil-initiated and maintained activities. The emphasis in teachers' statements was on science as a problem-solving activity. Group II on the other hand showed low incidence of teacher questions except to elicit recall or application of factual information. There was high incidence of teacher statements of factual information and the group's lessons as a whole were characterized by fact-acquisition and less emphasis on practical laboratory work. Group III teachers achieved highest pupil participation and practical work, and the climate within their classrooms is described as 'pupil-centred inquiring'. A process-product analysis related classroom behaviour to scores on tests of achievement and other measures. Usually differences in initial ability rather than teaching style accounted for most of the variance in post-test scores.

At *Sussex University*, pupil-pupil interaction was investigated by Burgess (1973). Sixteen small groups of girls, eight homogeneous in cognitive capacity, eight heterogeneous, were observed performing a number of tasks. Some of the observed process variables were significantly related to outcomes, and there were qualitative differences between the heterogeneous and homogeneous groups.

**Other studies**

The research described in the preceding section was almost entirely based on regular, live observation of classroom behaviour in naturalistic settings, and it has been the writer's intention to concentrate on these. There are other pieces of British work, however, which must be mentioned, including the extensive research into microteaching at the Universities of Ulster and Stirling. In a series of linked experiments Brown (1973), for example, has investigated the effects of training in interaction analysis and other experimental treatments on the behaviour of student teachers in microteaching sessions. Further reference to some of these studies can be found in Stones and Morris (1972), Brown (1973) and Wragg (1974).

Equally, the excellent work of people like Barnes *et al.* (1969) should not be overlooked. They studied language and classroom learning, generally by making intuitive interpretation of what was recorded in naturalistic settings. Hargreaves (1972) has achieved similar penetrating insights into classroom phenomena, but rather more from a symbolic interactionist perspective.

### Future prospects

It is perhaps timely to take stock of classroom research in Britain now that the first wave of studies has been completed, for the descriptions of these given above constitute a catalogue rather than a critical review. Probably the unevenness of the first generation will be smoothed out and gaps filled with attention to inadequately or unresearched areas such as open plan schools, classroom unruliness and studies of the teaching of integrated subjects like environmental studies, humanities and other interdisciplinary fields.

Certainly the first few British studies have triggered several further inquiries, still *ad hoc* and highly localized, but nevertheless replicating, extending and developing what has been achieved so far, and these largely descriptive studies are helping establish some picture of life in British classrooms.

If there is one single criticism of British research so far, it is probably that the payoff has been disappointingly small. Few publications have been produced and findings from many projects turn out to be elusive, even illusory. Nor is it clear how the research has affected current practice in schools. Perhaps it is as yet too early to hope for such tangible outcomes.

One looks forward to a number of developments if the interesting, but self-indulgent and somewhat flaccid research to date is to be stiffened, have a better chance of influencing practising teachers and arouse excitement about improving classroom learning. First of all we should move towards accepting the validity of the viewpoint expressed by Rosenshine and Furst (1973) about the inadequacy of purely descriptive studies. These writers formulate a descriptive-correlational-experimental loop model, wherein the findings of descriptive and correlational studies are used to design and evaluate experimental work. Secondly, major curriculum projects need associated classroom observation monitoring, so that one knows to what extent the behavioural objectives of the designers are being adhered to, modified or rejected. Thirdly, pre-service and in-service teacher training procedures need to take greater cognizance of what is known about classroom dynamics, and teachers should be trained to analyse their own teaching so as to gain a better understanding of what it is they do which achieves pupil learning, attitude change, co-operative behaviour or whatever other outcome is said to be desired. Fourthly, the transatlantic umbilical cord should be severed, thereby reducing what to date has been excessive dependence on American methodology and ideology.

Given some of these conditions, the considerable energy and enthusiasm generated by the early British investigators can be a sound basis for healthy development in the coming decades.

## References

ADELMAN, C. and WALKER, R. (1974). 'A technique for recording long-term sequences in school classrooms,' *Journal of Society and Motion Picture Engineers* (March issue).

BARNES, D., BRITTON, J. A. and ROSEN, H. (1969). *Language, the learner and the school.* Harmondsworth: Penguin.

BEALING, D. (1972). 'The organization of junior school classrooms,' *Educational Research*, **14**, 3, 231.

BELLACK, A. A. *et al.* (1966). *The Language of the Classroom.* New York: Teachers' College Press.

BOYDELL, D. (1974). 'Teacher-pupil contact in junior classrooms,' *British Journal of Educational Psychology* (November).

BROWN, G. A. (1973). *The Effects of Different Forms of Training upon the Performance of Students in Teaching Situations.* DPhil Thesis. Coleraine: New University of Ulster.

BURGESS, J. (1973). 'The development of cognitive processes.' Paper read at British Psychological Society Annual Conference, Liverpool, April 1973.

CAMERON-JONES, M. and MORRISON, A. (1973). 'Teachers' assessments of their pupils.' In: CHANAN, G. (ed.). *Towards a Science of Teaching.* Slough: NFER.

DELAMONT, S. (1973). *Academic Conformity Observed: Studies in the Classroom.* PhD Thesis, Edinburgh University.

DUTHIE, J. H. (1970). *Primary School Survey.* Edinburgh: HMSO.

EGGLESTON, J. F. (1973). 'Action and reaction in science teaching.' Inaugural Lecture, Nottingham University.

EMMETT, R. G. (1964). *An Experimental Study of Personal Interaction in the Classroom, with Special Reference to the Self-concept of Student Teachers.* PhD Thesis, London University.

EVANS, D. and WRAGG, E. C. (1969). 'The use of a verbal interaction analysis technique with severely subnormal children,' *Journal of Mental Subnormality*, December (1969).

FLANDERS, N. A. (1970). *Analysing Teaching Behaviour.* New York: Addison Wesley.

GAGE, N. L. (1963). *Handbook of Research on Teaching.* Chicago: Rand McNally.

GARNER, J. and BING, M. (1973). 'Inequalities of teacher-pupil contact,' *British Journal of Educational Psychology*, **43**.

HAMILTON, D. (1973). *At Classroom Level: Studies of Learning Milieu.* PhD Thesis, Edinburgh University.

HARGREAVES, D. H. (1972). *Interpersonal Relations and Education.* London: Routledge and Kegan Paul.

HILSUM, S. and CANE, B. S. (1971). *The Teacher's Day.* Slough: NFER.

JACKSON, P. W. (1968). *Life in Classrooms.* New York: Holt, Rinehart and Winston.

MEDLEY, D. M. and MITZEL, H. E. (1963). 'Measuring classroom behaviour by systematic observation.' In: GAGE, N. L. *Handbook of Research on Teaching.* Chicago: Rand McNally.

MORRISON, A. (1973). 'The teaching of international affairs in Scotland,' *Journal of the Modern Studies Association,* No. 2, May (1973).

NASH, R. (1973). *Classrooms Observed.* London: Routledge and Kegan Paul.

POOLE, J. (1964). *Operational Research in the Classroom in Relation to Educational Theory.* MSc Thesis, Manchester University.

ROSENSHINE, B. and FURST, N. (1973). 'The use of direct observation to study teaching.' In: TRAVERS, R. M. W. (ed.). *Second Handbook of Research on Teaching.* Chicago: Rand McNally.

SINCLAIR, J. A., COULTHARD, R. M., FORSYTH, I. J., ASHBY, M. C. (1972). 'The English used by teachers and pupils.' SSRC Final Report.

STONES, E. and MORRIS, S. (1972). *Teaching Practice: Problems and Perspective.* London: Methuen.

TORODE, B. (1974). *Constituting the Classroom Context.* Mimeograph. Dublin: Trinity College.

WALKER, R. and ADELMAN, C. (1972). 'Towards a sociography of classrooms.' SSRC Final Report.

WRAGG, E. C. (1972). *An Analysis of the Verbal Classroom Interaction between Graduate Student Teachers and Children.* PhD Thesis, Exeter University.

WRAGG, E. C. (1973). 'A study of student teachers in the classroom.' In: CHANAN, G. (ed). *Towards a Science of Teaching.* Slough: NFER.

WRAGG, E. C. (1974). *Teaching Teaching.* London: David and Charles.

CHAPTER 3

# Microteaching: Research and Developments

*G. A. Brown, University of Nottingham*

## Microteaching and measuring teaching

Microteaching may be described as a scaled down teaching encounter. A trainee (student or teacher) plans and teaches a small group of pupils for between five and twenty minutes. The proceedings are usually videorecorded. The trainee then observes his own performance usually with a supervisor. He then replans the lesson and reteaches the lesson to another group of pupils. The basic microteaching cycle is Plan — Teach — Observe/Analyse — Replan — Reteach — Reobserve. Each cycle may be devoted to the practice of skill such as questioning or a cluster of skills such as those required to promote discussion. The rationale underlying the procedure is described in learning theory terms by Meier (1968). It is also possible to describe it in terms of Argyle's Social Skills models (Argyle, 1970, Brown, 1975a) or in terms of symbolic interaction (Gregory, 1972).

The original microteaching model was developed at Stanford in 1963 (Allen and Ryan, 1969) and it focused almost exclusively on the performance of the teacher. Since then there have been so many variations in the approach that the term microteaching is generic rather than specific. For example, the groups may vary in size, the pupils may be school children or one's peers, the length of teaching time may vary, the proceedings may be videorecorded, audiotaped, analysed using a category system, rated on a rating schedule or merely observed live—as in demonstration lessons which were popular thirty years ago in Colleges. The trainee may discuss his lesson with his peers only, a supervisor, supervisor and peers or with no one at all. The content and range of skills may vary from practice of a simple technique such as asking drill questions to the complexities of promoting discovery learning. The interval between teach and reteach may vary from twenty

minutes to ten days and in some programmes reteach is not used
at all. The video playback may show the teacher, the pupils or both.
In fully fledged microteaching programmes the trainee may attend
lectures, skill demonstrations and take part in role playing sessions.
Videotaped, audiotaped or tapescript examples of teaching skills
may be examined, the skill practised and compared with the model.
Finally, the video equipment may vary from the simple to the
sophisticated. For example, a one fixed camera set up which focuses
on the teacher may be used, two fixed cameras and a mixer which
allows practice of teachers, pupils or both to be recorded, or very
sophisticated remote controlled camera and lenses which can track
the teacher or particular pupils. A simple set up consisting of one
camera, a videotape recorder and a monitor costs approximately
£800 (in 1974); a two camera set up with three monitors (one each
for teacher, pupils and for recording) costs about £1200 and sophisticated systems cost upwards of £5000. For teaching and most
research purposes a two camera set up in well-equipped carpeted
rooms (to reduce noise) is sufficient. Separate viewing rooms
containing a videotape recorder and monitor are also useful if
large numbers of students are involved. Brown (1975a) contains
further details. Clearly there are wide variations in the types of
microteaching, so one needs to be cautious in generalizing results
from one set up to another, nor can one readily isolate the effects
of the microteaching component from the teacher education programme of which it is a part.

    To complicate matters further, the measurement of the effective-
ness of microteaching is no less complex than the measurement of
teaching itself. And measurement of teaching pivots on notions of
the good and the successful. The latter are usually based upon
pupil achievement measures (Rosenshine, 1971); and attempts to
use them in microteaching settings have not as yet proved satisfactory (Foster, Heys and Harvey, 1973; MacClennan, 1973). The
former are usually based upon ratings of teaching performance by
trained or untrained observers. The rating may be the conventional
global 15 point scale or rating schedules such as the Stanford
Competence Appraisal Guide or the Lesson Appraisal Guide used
at Ulster (see Fig. 1). In addition, rating schedules of various
component skills such as Teacher Liveliness or Pupil Reinforcement may be used or sign and category systems of teacher-pupil
behaviour. Rosenshine and Furst (1973) contains an excellent

discussion of these methods of observing teaching. The advantages and disadvantages of these methods in microteaching are currently being explored at the Northern Ireland Polytechnic by D. Whittington and O. Hargie and at Stirling by D. McIntyre. It may be that one needs to use some instruments for feedback of information to trainees and others for evaluating microteaching programmes.

Reports on microteaching during its first decade have been predominantly descriptive and hortatory rather than research based. Descriptions of some microteaching programmes in Britain may be found in Perrott and Duthie (1969), Unwin and McAleese (1970), Gibbs (1974a) and Trott (1974). The first five years of research in microteaching are reviewed by McAleese and Unwin (1971) and McKnight (1971). This review will emphasize recent research in Britain, Sweden, Israel and Australia and draw upon the substantial contributions of researchers in the United States. The research has been divided into three sections: microteaching and other modes of teacher preparation; changes in teaching behaviour attributable to microteaching; and experience and studies of various elements of microteaching programmes.

**FIGURE 1: Examples of ways of measuring microteaching**

STANFORD TEACHER COMPETENCE APPRAISAL GUIDE
*7 point scales*

1. Clarity of aims
2. Appropriateness of aims
3. Organization of lesson
4. Selection of content
5. Selection of materials
6. Beginning the lesson
7. Clarity of presentation
8. Pacing the lesson
9. Pupil participation and attention
10. Ending the lesson
11. Teacher-pupil rapport

LESSON APPRAISAL GUIDE
*7 point scales*

1. Gaining pupils' attention
2. Explanation and narration
3. Giving directions
4. Asking and adapting questions
5. Recognizing difficulties of understanding
6. Voice and speech habits
7. Non-verbal cues

*continued overleaf*

8. Encouraging appropriate responses
9. Holding pupils' attention
10. Gaining pupil participation
11. Pupil control
12. Use of aids
13. Allocation of time for pupil learning
14. Lesson planning and structure

FLANDERS INTERACTION ANALYSIS SYSTEM
*Basic categories\**

1. Accepts pupil feeling
2. Praises
3. Uses pupils' ideas
4. Asks questions
5. Lectures
6. Gives directions
7. Criticizes, justifies authority
8. Pupil response
9. Pupil initiated response
10. Silence or confusion

\*Categories recorded every third second.

## Microteaching and school practice

There are two major questions one can ask about micro-teaching and school practice. Is performance in microteaching related in any way to performance in subsequent school practice? And are students trained by microteaching methods judged to be better teachers than those trained by school practice methods? Analyses of variance are usually used to directly compare different modes of training. Correlations between ratings of performance in microteaching and school practice are used to examine the first question. These are usually based upon the total scores derived from rating schedules such as the Lesson Appraisal Guide completed by supervisors or from the final marks awarded by supervisors for a student's performance in microteaching and school situations. A more rigorous, but rarely used, procedure is to obtain ratings by independent observers who have been trained to use a particular rating schedule and have high inter-observer reliability.

Table 1 sets out some typical results of correlational studies. The first three were carried out at Stanford, the fourth also in California and the last two in Ulster. In all the studies the students microtaught school pupils and the microteaching programmes were based upon practice of component skills with videotape feedback with a final session of microteaching in which the students are asked to teach a lesson which displays all the skills that they have learnt. Supervisors' ratings were used in all the studies. The final column of Table 1 indicates the form of rating used. In none of the studies did the school practice supervisors know the marks or ratings that their students received in microteaching. In the Kallenbach study, school practice scores were obtained nine months after microteaching, and in the studies by Brown and Spelman, fifteen months later.

**Table 1: Microteaching and school experience**

| Source | Sample | Stat. test and Sig level | Instrument Microteaching School experience |
|---|---|---|---|
| Aubertine (1964) | 30 students | Chi-square 0·0001 | STCAG/Global |
| Allen and Fortune (1966) | 60 students | Chi-square 0·0001 | STCAG/Global |
| Allen and Fortune (1966) | 114 students | Chi-square 0·0001 | STCAG/Global |
| Kallenbach and Gall (1969) | 27 students | Correlation ($r = 0·51$**, pre-test $r = 0·28$, post test) | STCAG/Global |
| Brown (1973) | 34 students | Correlation $r = 0·74$** | Global scores |
| Spelman (1975) | 60 students | Correlation $r = 0·5$** $r = 0·35$** $r = 0·43$** | Global scores LAG/Global scores Ryans Scale/ (1960). |

STCAG = Stanford Teacher Competence Appraisal Guide
LAG = Lesson Appraisal Guide
Global = Teaching practice mark given by a supervisor on a 15pt scale.
** = 0·01 sig. level.

The Kallenback study yielded a lower correlation between the final score of microteaching and the school experience score than between the initial score and school experience. Spelman's study showed global assessments to be more useful predictors of school experience than rating schedule totals. All the correlations were higher than those usually obtained in factorial studies of personality, achievement and teaching skills (Warburton, Butcher and Forrest, 1963; Garner, 1973). But such correlations merely tell us that students who score highly in microteaching tend to score highly in teaching. They do not measure the efficacy of the programme itself. However, multiple stepwise regression analysis of data collected from the thirty-four students in Brown's study suggest that

the scores derived from the latter stages of an eight session programme were the best predictor. The regression equation he
derived accurately predicted 11 of the 34 cases and yielded a
calculated score within one of the actual score for 21 cases. The
results suggest that the cumulative effects of microteaching do
influence subsequent classroom performance.

Direct comparisons of students who have been trained by microteaching methods and school practice are rare—the tangle of
uncontrolled variables is daunting. Both Ward (1970) and Schuck
(1971) in their reviews of pre-service microteaching programmes in
the United States report the general impression that microteaching
students are at least equally competent to those taught in conventional programmes. In an early experiment Allen and Fortune (1966)
randomly assigned sixty teachers to an experimental group for
microteaching practice and a control group for school practice.
Post-training performance in a micro-lesson yielded significant
differences in favour of the microteaching students. Unfortunately,
the supervisors and the microteaching pupils were paid volunteers
and they had previously been in contact with students who had had
microteaching experience. In their replication, Kallenbach and
Gall (1969) used performance in school classrooms as the criterion.
There were no significant differences between the two groups. The
pay-off was that microteaching students achieved these results in
one fifth of the time; the programme used fewer pupils; it was
easier to organize; and the system was under the control of the
course organizers.

Microteaching may change perceptions of teaching as well as
performance. Legge and Asper (1972) report a comparison of
students who had given five micro-lessons (with videotape feedback)
to pupils during fourteen weeks and those who had been on school
practice for fourteen weeks. Both groups saw the same videotaped
lesson at the beginning and end of the time. The microteaching
group was more critical of the videotaped lesson as revealed by
their comments and the lower scores they gave to the lesson on the
rating schedules.

More recently an interim report of a large scale investigation at
Macquarrie University, Sydney by Levis *et al.* (1973) shows that
microteaching students performed at a significantly higher level in
questioning techniques than students who had conventional school
practice. Gibbs (1974) is completing his analyses of a comparison of

traditional methods, interaction analysis and microteaching at Callender Park College of Education, and P. Kelly of Coventry College of Education is embarking upon a comparison of school practice and microteaching.

It would be rash to assume from these studies that all forms of microteaching are as good as or better than conventional school practice programmes. Nonetheless one can tentatively conclude that teaching small groups of pupils followed by videotape feedback and discussion of the lesson is at least as effective as school practice in producing changes in teaching behaviour. And these forms of microteaching are certainly more efficient in terms of time and numbers of pupils involved than school practice. Part of this apparent success is due to the *inefficiency* of existing school practice programmes (Stone and Morris, 1972a, 1972b; Shipman, 1966). Future researchers need to look critically at the precise relationship between skills which have been acquired and refined in microteaching and their use in normal classrooms. Microteaching based on component skills may enlarge a student's skill repertoire. He also needs to learn when to use the skill appropriately. Herein lie problems of improving and measuring effectiveness. As Morrison and McIntyre point out (1973): 'While one may be confident that a specified skill is of value in teaching, the decision as to whether or not it is appropriate to use that skill in the content of any particular lesson must generally be highly subjective'. Further, if microteaching is to be used as a preliminary to school practice. it may be that it should include some teaching practice intermediary in lesson length, size of class and range of skills. Berliner's (1969) notion of multiple skill practice is relevant here. So is the report of Foster, Heys and Harvey (1975) on the Sydney Teachers' College project and the new developments in the Ulster microteaching programme (Brown, 1975a). Such programmes require a close relationship between personnel involved in microteaching, school practice and the development of school practice observation and feedback instruments which relate back to skill practised in microteaching. White (1972) of Stirling has carried out an exploratory study in this area.

*Microteaching and methods courses*

In a detailed study based on Flanders interaction analysis (Flanders, 1970; Wragg, 1973), Davis and Smoat (1973) compared the performance of eighty-five students who had microtaught their peers (with videotape feedback) with those of fifty-five students who discussed in small groups the problems of teaching. There were significant differences on seventeen of the twenty-two measures taken. The microteaching group asked more probing and divergent questions and clarified pupils' statements more than the conventionally trained group. The microteaching group not only changed their behaviours but also increased the variety of their teaching repertoire. Similarly, a study by Harris *et al.* (1970) concluded that microteaching produced more significant changes in intending science teachers than conventional practice teaching. The microteaching experience increased the students' use of background information, experimental materials and the children's own observations, and they more frequently helped children to develop and verify conclusions.

Peck and Tucker (1973) discuss a well-designed study by Emmer and Millett (1968) in which an experimental group of twenty-seven students took part in a ten week peer group teaching programme involving supervisor and 'pupil' feedback in ten 15 minute lessons. The control group took pre- and post-test micro-lessons and followed a traditional methods course. The final lessons were audiotaped and coded. The results indicated that the experimental group made greater use of pupils' ideas, used more questioning and elicited more pupil response than the control group. Reed *et al.* (1970) in a small-scale study compared the effects of microteaching/ no microteaching in combination with demonstrations and hints on the skills and general discussions. Microteaching, in combination with skill demonstrations, yielded the best results.

Not all studies have shown distinct superiority of microteaching over other modes of teacher preparation. Minicourse one, which is discussed below, was field tested on pre-service teachers. The experimental group completed the whole course of self-instructional materials, observations of films and model tapes and practised microteaching with videotape feedback. The control group read the materials. The experimental group improved on six of the eleven measures but on only two of these were they significantly different from those of the control group. (Kallenbach, 1968.)

A similar result was reported by Peterson (1973) who used ratings of performance in school practice as his criterion. The same mini-course yielded significant differences on all eleven measures when it was field tested with experienced teachers (Borg *et al.*, 1970). The researcher suggests that the differences may be accounted for by weaknesses in the experimental treatment in the pre-service experiment. It may also be that the absence of supervisors and an intensive, detailed component skills approach is more appropriate for experienced teachers than beginners.

Comparisons of microteaching and training in interaction analysis techniques such as Flanders (1970) have also not yielded significant differences in favour of microteaching. Hough, Lobmann and Ober (1969) compared the final, thirty minute lessons of 168 students who had been taught Flanders systems with 232 students who had unstructured microteaching without videotape. Not surprisingly, the careful attention to the FIAC programme was more effective than microteaching experience. The experimental group used significantly more praise and encouragement, more acceptance and clarification of pupils' ideas and less criticism. In a follow-up study of thirty students from each group in schools, the experimental group continued to use more praise and encouragement, to clarify and use pupils' ideas and to lecture and criticize less. Clearly, the values implicit in Flanders system of analysis had operated successfully. Perlberg *et al.* (1973) compared microteaching and training in the category system developed at the Technion, Haifa in a $2 \times 2$ factorial design involving 128 students. Microteaching on its own effectively reduced the time devoted to lecturing and increased the proportion of time devoted to discussion, but the interaction analysis training condition yielded highly significant changes on seven of the measures used. This condition appeared to be better than the combination of microteaching and interaction analysis. Neither of these studies compared fully-fledged microteaching programmes with interaction analysis training.

## Changes in teaching skill attributable to microteaching

The studies described so far have compared microteaching with school practice and other forms of teacher preparation. The studies in this section compare changes in teaching which may be attributable to microteaching.

The early Stanford studies (Allen and Fortune, 1968) used positive changes in supervisor and pupil ratings on the Stanford Teacher Competence Appraisal Guide (see Fig. 1) as the criterion for improvement between the first and last experience of microteaching. The changes reported were highly significant on planning, teacher-pupil rapport and several other items. They were not rigorous proofs of changes for no control groups were used, the supervisors and pupils were paid volunteers and as Allen and Fortune (1968) admitted, there was:

'no evidence which tells us how much the rater's criteria and judgement changed during the course of the summer . . . we have no evidence that their criteria did change . . .' (p. 20).

Nonetheless these were promising lines of inquiry and they were replicated with some modifications at Ulster (Brown, 1973). Independent observers' ratings of the initial and final microteaching lesson of a group of sixteen students were compared using the Lesson Appraisal Guide (see Fig. 1) and the lessons were also analysed using categories of FIAC (Flanders, 1970). The independent observers' ratings yielded significant differences between the initial and final lesson. The FIAC analysis yielded significant changes on nine of the ten basic categories shown in Fig. 1. There was an increase in the use of pupils' ideas (3) and a corresponding increase in voluntary contributions by the pupils (9), a decline in simple reinforcement (2) and direct pupil responses (8). The student teachers asked fewer questions (4), spent more time on giving directions and used silence more frequently. Further analyses showed that the number of silences within teacher talk decreased and the number of silences after questions increased. Intra-lesson variability may account for some of these changes; nonetheless they are in line with those described by similar research carried out in classrooms (Moskowitz, 1967, Furst, 1965, and Wragg, 1973).

*Minicourses*

Perhaps the most important evidence for microteaching has come from the work of Borg and his associates at the Far West Educational Research Laboratory (Borg *et al.*, 1970). These are self-instructional courses in which a trainee reads a manual, views a model tape, plans a lesson and teaches it to a small group of pupils in his school. The lesson is videorecorded, the teacher then replays the lesson, and then replans, reteaches and reviews it before moving on to the next part of the programme.

The results have been most promising. Experimental and control groups' pre- and post-course videotapes have been analysed for at least five minicourses and all have shown significant changes in teaching behaviour. For example, Minicourse one improves the skills of promoting discussion. The teachers who took the course used more redirection, prompting and clarifying statements, less repetition of questions and pupils' answers. They allowed more time for pupil answers, and the length and cognitive levels of these answers increased. Minicourse three (Effective questioning) yielded similar results. Minicourse two (Developing language skills) and Minicourse eight (Organizing the kindergarten for independent teaching and small group instruction) yielded significant changes in teacher and pupil responses. Minicourse nine (Thought questions in intermediate grade) also changed the level and frequency of questioning (Acheson and Zigler, 1971).

More recently Flanders (1973) has been developing a minicourse of microteaching with interaction analysis (Minicourse twenty-four, Interaction analysis) in which trainees are taught to analyse their own videotapes. They can then choose to change their teaching styles, if they wish. Field studies of this course have just begun. In Britain, the earlier minicourses are being developed and modified for the use of teachers in British schools by Professor Perrott and a team of researchers at the University of Lancaster. Similar projects are being carried out in Sweden by Professor K. G. Stukat at the University of Göteborg, Professor H. O. Krumn at the University of Tubingen, Germany and Dr C. M. Geerans in the Frans Kieviet Pedagogical Institute, Leiden, Holland. Professor Büsch of the University of Baroda, India has also begun a modest field study of the minicourse materials.

It is worth noting that the minicourses do not require the use of supervisors. They are perhaps the most extreme form of 'mastering the teaching model' rather than 'modelling the master teacher' (Stolurow, 1965), and they have proved to be successful with experienced teachers, but not as successful with beginners (Kallenbach, 1969). Researchers might like to explore this question further. More important questions arise out of the implicit notions of good teaching enshrined in the minicourses, their relationship with pupil achievement and with the values of the organizations and communities adopting existing minicourses. It may be that what is appropriate for Texas is not necessarily appropriate for Thailand.

**Elements of microteaching programmes**

*Peers, pupils and class size*

Ward's (1970) survey revealed that in secondary teacher education programmes in the United States, fellow students were used as
pupils more frequently than school pupils. Fifty-two per cent of the
institutions used peers 76-100 per cent of the time and only 12 per
cent used pupils 76-100 per cent of the time. In Britain, Stirling
rarely uses peers and at Ulster peer teaching is used only during
the first three sessions of microteaching when students are learning
to operate the vtr equipment and to plan lessons. Stirling uses
different pupils in each week of microteaching whereas at Ulster
the same pupils are taught each week by the same students. The
size of microclasses also varies between the institutions. Ulster now
uses ten to twelve pupils—on the grounds that the dynamics of a
group of twelve is likely to be more similar to the dynamics of a
classroom group than a group of six is.

The use of peers and pupils and the optimum class size have not
been studied intensively. Staley (1970) investigated the effects of
different numbers of peers used in microteaching upon subsequent
performance in a lesson given to four school pupils. Four, eight or
twelve to sixteen peers were taught three times. There were no
significant differences. But peer teaching does bring about more
changes in teaching behaviour than seminar discussions. Morse,
Kysilka and Davis (1970) compared the audiotapes of the final
performance of two groups of students who had either followed a
teaching laboratory course on questioning or discussed questioning
skills. Steinbach and Batts (1968) compared the performance of
students who in preliminary training had taught peers or pupils.
The findings indicated several significant differences between the
students who had taught children and those who had taught peers
'suggesting at the elementary level, at least, some skills can only be
learnt by teaching children' (p. 14). Similar results were reported
by Nuthall (1972). Lewis *et al.* (1973) found that in the skills of
questioning, students who taught micro-lessons to high school
pupils rather than peers were more skilful at higher order questioning but there were no differences in fluency in the use of probing
questions. Incidentally, the students who taught peers had a 'more
marked lessening of interest as the programmes continued than
students who taught high school pupils' (p.15). A similar diminution
of interest was noted by Wood and Hedley (1968).

It may be that interest in teaching 'real' pupils accounts for the results of Emmer's (1971) experiments. Forty-four subjects taught eight micro-lessons, seven consisting of peers and one of pupils. The performance of the students increased significantly during the second session with peers and then increased significantly again during the lesson with pupils. Collofello *et al.* (no date), Hoerner (1969) and Doty (1970) in their comparisons found no differences in teaching performance in microteaching situations of those who worked with peers or children, but in all the studies the students expressed preferences for work with pupils.

The evidence cited suggests there is positive transfer from teaching peers to teaching children. There may also be advantages in giving students the opportunity to play the role of pupils so that they gain some understanding of 'the other'. Peer teaching is almost completely risk free and easier to organize than pupil teaching. Nonetheless, since students will be teaching children, it would seem sensible to design a programme which begins with the relatively simple task of teaching a small group of peers and leads on then to teaching larger groups of school pupils and culminating eventually in pupil teaching in schools.

*Supervisors and supervision*

The highly structured minicourses described earlier (Borg *et al.*, 1970b) are powerful evidence that supervisors may not be necessary for experienced teachers. The evidence of the necessity for supervisors and the most effective forms of supervision in microteaching for pre-service teachers is scant and conflicting. Parry and Gibbs (1974) list all the important studies on supervision in teaching and microteaching and Griffiths (1972, 1974) has critically reviewed some of the experiments in this field. The suggestions of Fortune, Cooper and Allen (1969), Horan (1969) and Olivero (1970) are discussed elsewhere (McAleese and Unwin, 1971).

Certainly it seems that a focused review session is more effective than general discussion (Rezler and Anderson, 1971). The supervisor should see the lesson before the review session, select sections of the videotape for particular emphasis, stop the videotape at selected points in the lesson and draw the attention of the students to specific points.

McIntyre and Duthie (1972) in a study of supervision and observational learning versus practice found that discussions between supervisor and single student were more effective than either peer group supervision or team supervision in which students worked in threes with a supervisor. The peer group and team only taught two in six lessons, and observed other peers teaching the remainder whereas the students working with supervisors taught all the lessons. One cannot assume therefore that the one-to-one conference was the prime cause. Indeed, Medley's (1971) results shows that the experience of teaching itself may be more effective than supervisor's comments. In a school practice programme he compared supervisor discussion only, live observations by supervisor followed by the supervisor and student observing the videotape and discussing it, and discussion of the videotape with a supervisor who had not seen the lesson live. No significant differences were reported between the groups but *all* the groups improved significantly during the programme.

Most earlier studies compared 'expert' supervision with other possibilities. Berliner (1969) in a study of reinforcement in supervisory sessions and microteaching compared (1) self-analysis, (2) supervisor reinforcement each time the student had used the skill and (3) supervisor reinforcement and discrimination training (pointing out instances when the student could have used reinforcement, suggesting ways of providing reinforcement and explaining the rationale). Method 3 was significantly superior. Similar results were obtained with the skills of probing and questioning. On the other hand, Waimon and Ramseyer (1970) found no differences in self-evaluation skills between students who had supervisors only and those who had audio-visual feedback only. Harrington (1970) on the basis of his experiment considered that self, peer and expert supervision were equally effective, and Young (1970) concluded that peer group supervision was more effective than one-to-one supervision. Kremer and Perlberg (1971) compared group supervision and individual supervision in a programme of questioning skills. Both groups improved but group supervision yielded significant changes on nine out of twelve variables whereas individual supervision yielded only six significant changes.

Kremer and Perlberg's findings are likely to be confirmed in other studies, for group supervision enables students to plan lessons together, to see each other teaching and to discuss the lessons with a supervisor, whereas in individual supervision a student sees only his own performance and perhaps a model tape. Group supervision is also easier to organize and it is more economical of supervisors' time (Brown, 1975a).

Whilst the value of supervisors may be equivocal, the attitudes of the students to microteaching supervision is not. McIntyre and Duthie (1972), Brown and Gibbs (1973) and Levis *et al.* (1973) all report strong preferences for supervisory assistance. Brown (1975a) and Levis both report preferences for group supervision. Johnson and Knaupp (1970), Foster, Heys and Harvey (1973), Brisling and Tingsell (1973) and Brown (1975a) all report that students expect supervisors to help them learn to develop their own teaching styles.

Although the research evidence is limited and inconsistent, a number of things seem clear. Microteaching supervisors and students require training in perception. Supervision should be positive, supportive and focus sharply on the skills under review. The supervisor is perceived as an important source of feedback and he may need to encourage self-analysis by students so that they continue to improve their own skills. The use of microteaching team supervision has not yet been shown to be consistently superior to other forms of supervision, but it is likely to be. Research on categories of personnel labelled as 'supervisors' or 'students' has not yielded clear findings. It may be more profitable in future to focus on the processes of supervision and subsequent teaching by students. Category systems which permit comparisons between supervisory discussions and a student's teaching performance in classrooms have already been developed (Blumberg, 1970), and Dr B. McGarvey is developing a system at Ulster based on the interaction analysis system used in the microteaching programme.

*Videotape or audiotape in modelling and feedback*

Most researchers prefer videotape recordings, for they provide the most complete permanent description of the teaching situation, and the same data may be analysed in several ways. For example Gage *et al.* (1972) report three separate studies of effectiveness in explaining, based on the same videotapes and pupil achievement scores. Videotapes are also preferred by most microteaching programme organizers. Ward (1970) reported that fifty-nine per cent of the institutions which use videotape replay more than seventy-five per cent of the time whereas only five per cent of those who use audiotape replay more than seventy-five per cent of the time.

Despite the predilection for videotapes, there is little clearcut evidence that it is necessary for improving all teaching skills. Hoerner (1969), Doty (1970), Klingstedt (1970) and Gall *et al.* (1971), found no consistent significant differences between video- tape and audiotape feedback. Leonard *et al.* (1971) found video- tape feedback more effective, whereas Shively *et al.* (1970) found audiotape more effective than videotape for the skill of questioning. P. M. Ward (1970) compared the effectiveness of self videotape, self audiotape, a combination of self videotapes and model tapes and reflective evaluation without any equipment. The largest mean difference in the number of probing questions asked by teachers between pre- and post-course lessons was found in the audiotape group. Ward explains this result as due to the fact that 'the necessity to listen intently without visual concentration provides stimulation sufficient to affect the questioning skill ability of teachers. It is possible that audiotape recorders are grossly underrated . . .' (pp. 93-96).

It is likely that the effectiveness of the type of mechanical feedback depends on the nature of the skill being practised. Predominantly verbal skills such as questioning might effectively be changed by audiotape. Skills involving non-verbal cues such as teacher live- liness would obviously require videorecordings and some skills such as use of blackboards and overhead projectors may require no mechanical feedback. The economic implications of the use of VTR and audiotape recorders clearly require exploration and already a study of the cost effectiveness of existing types of microteaching has begun at Stirling (Kennedy, 1974).

A difficulty facing the Stirling team is that most early investi- gations used videotape and audiotape in different modelling and feedback procedures so it is not possible to say which is the more effective. One can say only that Model X combined with Feedback X appears more effective than Model W combined with Feedback Z. For example, Orme (1967) assigned students to six training conditions (17 to 20 students per group) involving viewing of model tapes, reading of tape scripts, self-viewing and self-viewing with a supervisor. Claus (1969) and Berliner (1969) carried out similar experiments on higher order questioning and Young (1968) on pupil reinforcement. In all but Berliner's study, videotaped models were effective, and in conjunction with supervisor's cueing were the most effective experimental treatment.

Modelling and feedback procedures which show the teacher only, pupils only and both together have also been compared. Waimon and Ramseyer (1970) found no difference in the feedback procedures but Koran *et al.* (1972) found that the most effective models showed the teachers and pupils on a 'split' screen.

It also seems certain that unguided solitary self confrontation with reinforced feedback is ineffective whether that feedback is audio (Morse, Kysilke and Davidson, 1970) or audio-visual (Acheson, 1965). Salomon and McDonald (1970) and Bierschenk (1972) have also shown that unguided self-confrontation produces more comments related to self-image than to teaching skills. A similar result is reported by Macleod (1973).

Clearly whether to videorecord or audiorecord is a question still requiring exploration. It is unlikely to prove simple for it is not the use of videotape or audiotape *per se* so much as the use to which they are put which determines their effectiveness.

*Interaction analysis in microteaching situations*

Interaction analysis and allied methods such as sign or rating systems have long been used in teacher education (see Amidon and Hough, 1967, Simon and Boyer, 1967, and Rosenshine and Furst, 1973). In microteaching, interaction analysis techniques may be used to describe teaching behaviour, to give structured feedback and as a form of discrimination training. Rating schedules evaluate teaching, give structured opinions and may also be used as discrimination training. As indicated earlier, the relative merits of interaction analysis and rating schedules in microteaching have not been explored, but increasingly researchers are using or developing interaction analysis category systems. Flanders (1970) describes some of the microteaching programmes using his system. Traill (1970), Brisling and Tingsell (1973) and Stukat (1972) have reported their modifications. McIntyre *et al.* (1972) and Miller (1972) have developed systems based on Bellack *et al.* (1966). Brown (1974) has developed a time-line system derived from Flanders system.

But there is little work as yet on the use of interaction analysis or discrimination training and feedback in microteaching. Studies of interaction analysis training in classrooms (for example Bondi, 1970) show that descrimination training improves performance but Tuckman *et al.* (1970) claim, on the basis of their experiment, that this was not due merely to learning the system. At Ulster these views were explored in two related experiments (Brown, 1975b).

In the first, an experimental group received six hours' training in
FIAC. Both the experimental and control group were asked not to
read books on interaction analysis. They rated a videotaped lesson
at the beginning and end of a semester of microteaching. In the
second experiment, the experimental group were given feedback
derived from FIAC categories immediately after each teaching
session. Again both groups were asked not to read about interaction
analysis and they rated the same standard lesson at the beginning
and end of the microteaching experience. Independent observer
ratings and FIAC analyses of pre- and post-course videotapes were
carried out. In the first experiment, there was a significant change
in the FIAC trained group's perception of teaching but no difference
between their performance and that of the control group. In the
second experiment, the FIAC feedback group's perception of the
videotape lesson did not change significantly but their performance
did.

The studies were based on small samples (16 and 19) and so
should be treated cautiously. But the results do suggest that if the
intention is to change students' perceptions of teaching, they should
be trained in interaction analysis. If the intention is to change their
teaching performance then feedback from interaction analysis is
sufficient. In the writer's view both discrimination training and
feedback are necessary so that students can continue to analyse
their own teaching without the aid of supervisors. As Davis (1971)
points out, 'since most teaching occurs isolated from other adults,
training in self-analysis is an important objective of teacher education programmes' (p. 82).

*Studies of attitudes and personality*

Students' reactions to microteaching have been largely favourable
regardless of the type of programme or its value. For example, the
peer group microteaching programme at Brigham Young University received very favourable comments (Webb *et al.*, 1968).
Turney (1970) and Levis *et al.* (1973) describe the favourable
reactions of Australian students, Naesland (1972) of Swedish
students and McIntyre and Duthie (1972) and Brown and Gibbs
(1973) of British students. Ward (1970) in his survey of United
States institutions gives favourable but indirect evidence on students'
attitudes to microteaching.

Such studies are important as feedback devices for course

organizers and, as Stones and Morris (1972b) suggest, 'in the absence of evidence that positive student attitudes are deleterious to student performance, student acceptance of training methods is greatly to be desired' (p. 96).

Polling participants is important but it presents methodological problems. If unstructured questionnaires are used it is difficult to decide whether respondents mean what they say; if structured questionnaires are used it is difficult to decide whether respondents are saying what they mean. If the respondents have no other relevant experiences, their reactions to microteaching may be no different from their reactions to other forms of training. It was partly for these reasons that Brown and Gibbs included students who had experienced both microteaching and school experience in their survey. Over seventy per cent of such students considered microteaching a valuable preliminary to class teaching. The most commonly expressed reason for favouring microteaching was 'the opportunity to see oneself teach'.

In the initial stages, self-confrontation might evoke some anxiety in participants, but in this writer's experience only three out of over five hundred students have reacted very strongly against seeing themselves microteach. In all three cases sympathetic help and encouragement reduced their fears. Bloom (1969), Kohn (1970) and Perlberg's (1971) studies of university teachers all report favourable reactions to videotape as a means of behavioural change but Kearney (1970) claimed, on the basis of her study, that audiotape was just as efficient and less threatening to self-esteem. Fuller and Manning (1973) end their comprehensive review of self-confrontation with the wry conclusion that it is 'more promising than we had hoped and more dangerous than we knew to fear' (p. 512).

Supervisors' and pupils' reactions to microteaching have received little attention. Guelcher *et al.* (1970) report that pupils found the Stanford model of microteaching a meaningless activity whereas Naesland (1972) and Bloom (1969) report favourable pupil reactions when the pupils had the same student teachers each week. Naesland also reports favourable reactions from co-operating teachers and supervisors involved in the programme.

These generally favourable reactions to microteaching are encouraging but there is an urgent need to explore more deep rooted attitudes, particularly of supervisory tutors. The success or

failure of an educational innovation often lies in the attitudes of
the users (Gross *et al.*, 1971; Barker-Lunn, 1970). The studies cited
have usually taken place in institutions committed to new developments in teacher education and so they cannot be taken as generalizable to institutions firmly committed to conventional methods of
school experience. Even within innovating institutions there are
likely to be tensions between those who are skills-oriented and those
who are content-oriented. Perhaps the resolution of such tensions
may yield even more effective microteaching programmes.

*Personality studies in microteaching*

   Studies of personality characteristics and teaching performance
have long been the hunting ground of researchers (Garner, 1973;
Getzels and Jackson, 1963; Rabinowitz and Travers, 1953). The
yield has not been high so it is no surprise that there are few studies
of personality correlates with microteaching performance. Hughes
(1969) found no significant difference between students who had
microtaught or received a conventional method course on anxiety
change. Gall, Borg *et al.* (1969) found no correlation between personality correlates and performance of women teachers before and
after Minicourse 1, but they did find that the more male teachers
talked in pre-course discussions, the more likely they were to be
aggressive, achievement-oriented and authoritarian. After the
minicourse, the influence of these personality characteristics was
less marked. Austad (1972) found only chance correlations between
personality variables and teaching performance. Spelman (1975)
has however found significant correlations between sets of personality correlates and various models of teacher effectiveness in microteaching. For example, students who are rated highly on the Lesson
Appraisal Guide (see Fig. 1) tend to be socially extroverted, high on
logical thinking and pragmatic, whereas students rated highly on the
Classroom Creativity Observation Schedule (Denny-Ives, 1968)
tend to be introverted, imaginative and tenderminded.

   Such studies are important for they point to the limits of the
effects of training within teacher education courses. Students begin
learning values and the basic skills of communicating long before
entering such courses and they continue to learn about teaching
during their professional careers. An effective training programme
can nevertheless give demonstrable help and help which students
welcome in improving teaching behaviour. This is surely no mean

feat in a field of endeavour—teacher education—that has hitherto been dogged by the difficulty of knowing when it was or was not succeeding.

## Conclusion

This review has brought together important work carried out on the research and development of microteaching during the past few years. The evidence clearly indicates that microteaching does change teaching behaviours, and performance in microteaching appears to be closely related to classroom teaching. Microteaching seems, therefore, to be a useful preliminary to school practice for intending teachers, a valuable tool for inservice education and a worthwhile research strategy for the study of teaching behaviours and their relationship to pupil learning.

There are however several questions which require further exploration. In particular, the use of components skills versus 'whole' learning, videotape versus other modes of feedback and the relative effectiveness of videotaped, audiotaped and written (symbolic) models. The precise relationship between skills acquired and refined in microteaching and those practised in school teaching merits further attention, as does the relationships between supervisors and students in microteaching.

These questions are amenable to classical methods of statistical inquiry. In addition, there is a need to explore, perhaps by means of case studies and ethnomethodological techniques, the problems of incorporating microteaching programmes into traditionally-based institutions. Ultimately, the success of microteaching as a mode of teacher preparation depends not so much upon studies of research and development as upon the way it is perceived and valued by participating supervisors, students and pupils.

## References

ACHESON, K. A. (1964). *The Effects of Feedback from T.V. Recording and Three Types of Supervisory Treatment on Selected Teacher Behaviours.* Stanford University, USA (mimeo).

ACHESON, K. A. (1971). *Audio Tape and Video Tape Feedback : Review of Related Literature.* Report No. A71-24, Teacher Education Division Publication Series. Far West Laboratory for Educational Research and Development, Berkeley, California.

ACHESON, K. A. and TUCKER, P. E. (1971). *Videotape versus written transcripts and videotape versus audiotape feedback in a Minicourse on Higher Cognitive Questions.* Far West Laboratory of Educational Research and Development, Berkeley, California, Report A71-18.

ACHESON, K. A. and ZIGLER, C. J. (1971). *A Comparison of Two Teacher Training Programs in Higher Cognitive Questioning.* Report No. A71-19 Teacher Education Division Publication Series. Far West Laboratory for Educational Research and Development, Berkeley, California.

ALLEN, D. W. and CLARK Jr., D. W. (1967). 'Microteaching: its rationale,' *The High School Journal,* **51**, 75-9.

ALLEN, D. W. and FORTUNE, J. C. (1966). 'An analysis in microteaching: new procedure in teacher education,' *Microteaching: A Description.* School of Education, Stanford University, USA.

ALLEN, D. W. and RYAN, K. A. (1969). *Microteaching.* New York: Addison Wesley.

AMIDON, E. J. and HOUGH, J. B. (eds.) (1967). *Interaction Analysis: Theory Research and Applications.* New York: Addison Wesley.

AUBERTINE, H. E. (1964). *An experiment in the Set Induction Process and its Application in Teaching.* Unpublished Doctoral Thesis, Standford University, Berkeley, California.

AUSTAD, C. A. (1972). 'Personality correlates of teacher performance in a microteaching laboratory,' *J. Exper. Educ.* **40**, 3, pp. 1-5.

ARGYLE, M. (1970). *Social Interaction.* London: Methuen.

BARKER-LUNN, Joan (1969). *Streaming in the Primary School.* Slough: NFER.

BELLACK, A. (1966). *The Language of the Classroom.* New York: Teachers College, Columbia University.

BERLINER, D. C. (1969). *Microteaching and the Technical Skills Approach to Teacher Training.* Technical Report, No. 8, Stanford University, California, USA.

BIERSCHENK, B. (1972). *Self Confrontation via closed circuit Television in Teacher Training.* University of Malmo, Sweden (mimeo).

BLOOM, J. M. (1969). 'Videotape and the vitalization of teaching,' *The Journal of Teacher Education,* **20**, 311-15.

BLUMBERG, A. (1970). 'Supervisor-teacher relationships: a look at the Supervisory conference. *Administrator's Notebook 19,* September.

BLUMBERG, A. (1967). 'A system for analysing supervisor-teacher interaction.' In: SIMON A. and BOYER, E. *Mirrors for Behaviour,* **8**. Philadelphia: Research for Better Schools.

BONDI, J. C. (1970). 'Feedback from interaction analysis, some implication for the improvement of teaching,' *Journal of Teacher Education,* **21**, 189-196.

BORG, W. R., KALLENBACH, W., MORRIS, M. and FRIEBEL, A. (1969). 'Videotape feedback and microteaching in a teacher training model,' *Journal of Experimental Education,* **37**, 9-16.

BORG, W. R., KELLEY, M. L., LANGER, P. and GALL, M. D. (1970). *The Minicourse: A Microteaching Approach to Teacher Education.* New York: Collier Macmillan.

BROWN, G. A. (1973). *The effects of training upon performance in teaching situations.* Unpublished DPhil. Thesis. Coleraine: New University of Ulster.

BROWN, G. A. (1974). 'Organising a microteaching programme.' In: TROTT, A. (ed.) (1974) *Microteaching Conference Papers.* APLET Occasional Papers, No. 3, pp. 39-51.

BROWN, G. A. (1974). *BIAS: Systematic Method of Observing Microteaching.* Coleraine: New University of Ulster (mimeo).

BROWN, G. A. (1975a). *Microteaching: Programme of Teaching Skills.* London: Methuen.

BROWN, G. A. (1975). 'Some case studies of teacher preparation,' *British Journal of Teacher Education,* **1**, 71-85.

BROWN, G. A. and GIBBS, I. (1973). *Some Students' Reactions to Microteaching.* Coleraine: New University of Ulster (mimeo).

BRUSLING, C. (1972). *Effects of Cued Modelling Procedures and Self Confrontation in a Microteaching Setting aimed at developing non-verbal behaviour*. Paper presented at the International Microteaching Symposium, University of Tabergen.

BRUSLING, C. and TINGSELL, J. (1973). *Self Observation and Self Analysis in Teacher Training*. Department of Educational Research, University of Gothenburg (mimeo).

CLAUS, K. E. (1969). 'Effects of modelling and feedback treatments on the development of teachers' questioning skills,' Technical Report, No. 6, Stanford Centre for Research and Development in Teaching, Stanford University, ERIC ED: 033 081.

COLLOFELLO, P. *et al.* (n.d.). *The Relative Effectiveness of Two Sources of Feedback on Teachers in the Microteaching Situation*. Minnesota Research Coordinating Unit in Occupational Education, Minneapolis. ERIC ED: 044 490.

DAVIS, A. R. (1971). 'Microteaching in a small liberal arts College,' *Audiovisual Instruction* **16**, 81-2.

DAVIS, O. L., Jr. and SMOOT, B. R. (1970). 'Effects on the verbal teaching behaviours of beginning secondary teacher candidates,' Participations in a Programme of Laboratory Teaching. *Educational Leadership* (research Supplement), **28**, 1970, 165-9.

DENNY, D. A. (1968). 'Identification of teacher classroom variables facilitating pupil creative growth,' *Amer. Educ. Res. J.*, **5**, 365-383.

DOTY, C. (1970). 'In-service education with microteaching and videotape feedback of actual classroom and laboratory teaching.' Annual Vocational Technical Teacher Education Seminar, Leadership Series, No. 25.

DUGAS, D. G. (1967). 'Microteaching: a promising medium for teacher retraining.' *The Modern Language Journal*, **51**, 161-6.

EMMER, E. T. (1970). *Transfer of instructional behaviour of performance acquired in simulated teaching*. RHD Report No. 50, Centre for Teacher Education, University of Texas.

EMMER, E. T. (1971). 'Transfer of instructional behaviour of performance acquired in simulated teaching.' *J. Educ. Res.*, **65**, 178-182.

EMMER, E. T. and MILLETT, G. B. (1968). *An Assessment of Terminal Performance in a Teaching Laboratory*. Centre of Teacher Education, University of Austin, Texas (mimeo).

FLANDERS, N. A. (1970). *Analysing Teaching Behaviour*. New York: Addison Wesley.

FLANDERS, N. A. (1973). *Interaction Analysis*. For West Lab. for Educ. Res. and Development. Berkeley, California (Restricted circulation).

FORTUNE, J. C., COOPER, J. M. and ALLEN, D. (1967). 'Stanford summer microteaching clinic 1965,' *J. Tchr. Educ.*, **181**, 389-93 Winter.

FOSTER, J., HEYS, T. and HARVEY, J. (1973). *Microteaching: A Review and a Study of the Effects of Microteaching upon Teaching Effectiveness*. Forum of Education, Sydney Teachers' College.

FRIEBEL, A. C. and KALLENBACH, W. W. (1969). *Effects of Video-tape Feedback and Microteaching as Developed in the Field Test of Minicourse with Student Teachers*. For West Laboratory, Berkeley, California, USA, March.

FULLER, F. F. and MANNING, B. A. (1973). 'Self confrontation reviewed: A conceptualisation for video playback in teacher education,' *Rev. Educ. Res.* **43**, 469-528.

FURST, N. A. (1967). *The Effects of Training in Interaction Analysis on the Behaviour of Student Teachers in Secondary Schools*. In: Amidon and Hough, *op. cit.*

GAGE, N. L. (1972). 'Exploration of teachers' effectiveness in lecturing.' In: WESTBURY and BELLAK (Eds.) (1972) *Research in Classroom Processes: Recent Developments and Next Steps*, pp. 75-224.

48 *Frontiers of Classroom Research*

GALL, M. D., BORG, W. R., KELLEY, M. L. and LANGER, P. (1969). *The Relationship between Personality of Teaching Behaviour before and after Inservice Microteaching Training.* For Educ. Res. and Development, Berkeley, California (mimeo).

GARNER, J. (1973). 'The nature of teaching and the effectiveness of teachers.' In: LOMAX, D. (1973). *The Education of Teachers in Britain.* London: J. Wiley & Sons.

GETZELS, J. W. and JACKSON, P. W. (1963). 'The teacher's personality and characteristics.' In: GAGE, N.L. (ed.) *Handbook of Research on Teaching,* 506–82.

GIBBS, I. (1974). Conference Papers on Microteaching and Interaction Analysis, Collender Park College of Education, Falkirk. (mimeo)

GIBBS, I., (1974). *Alternative Methods of Teacher Preparation.* Collendor Park College of Education Research Project (in progress).

GREGORY, T. B. (1972). *Encounters with Teaching.* Englewood Cliffs: Prentice Hall.

GRIFFITHS, A. (1972). *The Role of the Tutor in Microteaching Supervision: A Survey of Research Evidence.* Dept. of Education, Sterling University (mimeo).

GRIFFITHS, R. (1973). *The Future Developments of Microteaching: Some Possibilities.* Paper presented at the APLET Conference on Educational Technology, Brighton, Sussex.

GRIFFITHS, R. (1974). 'The contribution of feedback to microteaching technique.' In: TROTT, A. (1971) *Microteaching Conference Papers,* APLET Occasional Paper No. 3.

GROSS, N., GIACQUINTA, J. B. and BERNSTEIN, M. (1971). *Implementing Organisational Innovationes.* New York, London: Harper International Edition.

GUELCHER, W. et al. (1970). *Microteaching and Teacher Training: A Refined Version.* Graduate School of Education, Chicago University, ERIC ED : 050 017.

HARRINGTON, F. W. et al. (1971). *Assessment of Microteaching and Videorecordings in vocational and technical teacher education.* Phase VI, Natural Centre for Educational Research and Development. State University of Ohio.

HARRIS, W. N., LEE, V. W. and PIGGE, F. L. (1970). 'Effectiveness of microteaching experiences in elementary science methods classes,' *Journal of Research in Science Teaching,* 7(1), 31–3.

HOERNER, J. (1969). *An Assessment of Microteaching as a Means of Improving the Effectiveness of the Pre-Service Trade and Industrial Teacher Education Workshop.* Unpublished doctoral dissertation, Ohio State University, ERIC ED: 039 318.

HOUGH, J. B., LOHMANN, E. E. and OBER, R. (1969). 'Shaping and predicting verbal teaching behaviour in a general methods course,' *The Journal of Teacher Education,* **20**, 213–224.

HUGHES, K. A. (1969). *The Effect of Microteaching and Student Teaching on Scales of Dogmatism, Anxiety and Attitudes of Prospective Elementary Teachers.* Unpublished doctoral dissertation, University of Dakota, Dissertation Abstracts International, 30/A/3831-2.

JOHNSON, W. D. and KNAUPP, J. E. (1970). 'Trainee role expectations of the microteaching supervisor,' *Journal, Tchr. Educ.,* **21**, 396-401.

KALLENBACH, W. (1968). *The Effectiveness of Microteaching in the Preparation of Elementary Intern Teachers.* Washington, DC: AERA Conference Report.

KALLENBACH, W. W. and GALL, M. D. (1969). 'Microteaching versus conventional methods in training elementary intern teachers,' *Journal of Educational Research,* **63,** 136-141.

KEARNEY, M. (1971). *A Comparison of the effects of videotapes, interaction analysis, and regular classroom observation in programmes of elementary teacher preparation.* Berkeley: University of California.

KENNEDY, K. (1974). *The Costs of Microteaching.* Paper read at the Microteaching Research Seminar, School of Education, University of Liverpool.

KLINGSTEDT, J. (1971). *Effectiveness of three microteaching feedback procedures.* Houston: Texas Tech. University. Unpublished dissertation.

KOHN, D. A. (1970). 'Videotaping large numbers of prospective student teachers. Can it be effectively accomplished,' *Audiovisual Instruction,* **15**, 105-7.

KORAN, J. J. (1969). 'Supervision: an attempt to modify behaviour,' *Educational Leadership*, **26**, 759-7.

KORAN, J. J., KORAN, M. L. and MCDONALD, E. J. (1972). 'Effects of different sources of positive and negative information on observational learning of a teaching skill', *J. Educ. Psychol.*, **63**, 136-141.

KREMER, L. and PERLBERG, A. (1971). *The use of Microteaching Techniques to Train Student Teachers in Stimulating Learners' Questions.* Technion, Haifa, Israel (mimeo).

LEGGE, W. B. and ASPER, L. (1972). 'The effect of videotaped microteaching lessons on the evaluative behaviour of pre-student-teachers,' *The Journal of Teacher Education*, **23**(3), 363-6.

LEONARD, B. C. *et al.* (1971). 'The effect of selected media feedback upon the interactive behaviour of student teachers,' *The Journal of Educational Research*, **64**(10), 478-80.

LEVIS, D. *et al.* (1973). *A Progress Report of the Study to Investigate the Effects of Alternative Techniques to Practice Teaching on the Development of Teaching Skills by Student Teachers.* Sydney: School of Education, Macquarie University.

MACLEOD, G. R. (1973). *A Study of Student Self Viewing.* University of Stirling. Presented at the BPS Education Section Annual Conference.

MACLENNAN, D. (1974). *The Effects of Teacher Questions upon Pupil Attitudes and Achievement: A Study in the Microteaching Content.* MSC Thesis, University of Sterling.

MEDLEY, D. M. (1971). 'The language of teacher behaviour: communicating the results of structured observations to teachers,' *J. Teacher Education*, **22**, 157–165.

MEIER, J. H. (1968). 'Rationale for and application of microtraining to improve teaching,' *J. Teacher Education*, **19**, 145–157.

MILLAR, F. J. (1972). *A Procedure for Analysing evaluations of observed teaching and its application in measuring outcomes of professional education.* Unpublished Thesis. University of Sterling.

MORRISON, A. and MCINTYRE, D. (1973). *Teachers and Teaching.* Harmondsworth: Penguin (2nd Edition).

MORSE, K. R. and DAVIS, O. L. Jr. (1970). *The effectiveness of teaching laboratory instruction on the questioning behaviours of beginning teacher candidates.* R and D Report, No. 43. Houston: Centre for Teacher Education, The University of Texas.

MORSE, K. R., KYSILKA, M. L. and DAVIS, O. L. (1970). *Effects of different types of supervisory feedback on teacher candidates' development.* R and D Report, No. 48. Houston: Centre for Teacher Education, University of Texas.

MOSKOWITZ, G. (1967). 'The attitudes and teaching patterns of co-operating teachers and student teachers trained in interaction analysis.' In: AMIDON, E. J. and HOUGH, J. B. (eds.) (1967) *Interaction Analysis.* Reading, Mass: Addison-Wesley.

MCALEESE, W. R. and UNWIN, D. J. (1973). 'A bibliography of microteaching,' *Programmed Learning and Educational Technology*, **10**, 1, 40–54.

MCALEESE, W. R. and UNWIN, D. J. (1971). 'Microteaching: A selective survey,' *Programmed Learning and Educational Technology*, **8**, 8-24.

MCINTYRE, D. and DUTHIE, J. (1972). *Students reactions to Microteaching.* University of Sterling (mimeo).

MCKNIGHT, P. (1971). 'Microteaching in teacher training: a review of research,' *Res. in Educ.*, **6**, 24–38.

NAESLUND, J. (1972). *Experiments with closed circuit television.* Department of Educational and Psychological Research, University of Stockholm (mimeo).

NUTHALL, G. A. and PATRICK, J. M. (1972). *A comparison of the use of Microteaching with two types of pupils – 10 yr. old pupils and peers acting as pupils.* University of Canterbury, Christchurch, New Zealand. (mimeo)

OLIVERO, J. L. (1970). Microteaching: Medium for improving Instruction. Foundations of Education Series. Ohio: Bobbs-Merrill.

ORME, M., MCDONALD, F. J. and ALLEN, D. W. (1967). *The Effects of Modelling and Feedback Variables on the Acquisition of Complex Teaching Strategy.* School of Education, Stanford University, USA.

PARRY, G. and GIBBS, I. (1974). 'A bibliography of supervision,' *Programmed Learning,* **11**, 2, 97–112.

PECK, R. F. and TUCKER, J. A. (1973). 'Research on teacher education.' In: TRAVERS, R. W. *Second Handbook of Research on Teaching.* Chicago: Rand McNally.

PERLBERG, A. *et al.* (1971) *Studies on the use of video tape recordings and microteaching techniques to improve University Teaching.* Paper presented Amer. Educ. Res. Assocn., New York.

PERLBERG, A., BARON, E., LEVIN, R. and ETROG, A. (1973). *Combined use of Micro-teaching and Category Observation System: Help or Hindrance in Improving Teacher Training – A Three Year Study.* The Technician, Haifa, Israel. (mimeo.)

PERLBERG, A. and THEODORE, E. (1975). 'Patterns and styles in the supervision of teachers.' To be published in the *British Journal of Teacher Education,* 1.

PERROT, E. and DUTHIE, J. H. (1969). 'Microteaching,' University of Sterling, *University Television Newsletter,* No. 7, September.

PETERSON, T. L. (1973). 'Microteaching in the preservice education of teachers: time for a re-examination,' *J. Educ. Res.,* **67**, 34-36.

RABINOWITZ, W. and TRAVERS, R. M. W. (1953). 'Problems of defining and assessing teacher effectiveness,' *Educational Theory,* **3**, 212-19.

REED, C. L. *et al.* (1970). *Effect of Microteaching, Directive and Non-Directive Lectures on Achievement and Attitudes in a Basic Educational Psychology Course. Effect of Mode of Feedback in Microteaching.* (Two documents combined). Papers presented at American Educational Research Association Convention, Minneapolis, Minnesota, ERIC ED: 037 791.

ROSENSHINE, B. (1971). *Teaching Behaviours and Student Achievement.* IEA Studies, No. 1. Slough: NFER.

ROSENSHINE, B. and FURST, N. (1973). 'The use of direct observation to study teaching.' In: TRAVERS, R. W. (Ed.) *Second Handbook of Research on Teaching.* Chicago: Rand McNally.

SADKER, M. and COOPER, J. M. (1972). 'What do we know about microteaching?,' *Educational Leadership,* **29**, 547-51.

SALOMON, G. and MCDONALD, F. J. (1970). 'Pre-test and post-test reactions to self viewing one's teaching performance on video-tape,' *J. Educ. Psychol.,* **61**, 280-286.

SCHUCK, R. F. (1971). 'Microteaching in teacher education programmes.' In: *Microteaching – Selected Papers,* Association of Teacher Educators, Washington.

SCHMUCK, R. (1971). *Self Confrontation of Teachers.* ERIC ED. 062-700.

SHEA, J. J. (1971). *The Relative Effectiveness of Student Teaching Versus a Combination of Student Teaching and Microteaching.* Report No. A71-21, Teacher Education Division Publication Series, Far West Laboratory for Educational Research and Development, Berkeley, California.

SHIPMAN, M. D. (1966). 'The assessment of teaching practice,' *Ed. for Teaching,* No. 70, May, pp. 28-31.

SHIVELEY, J. E. *et al.* (1970). *The Effect of Mode of Feedback in Microteaching.* Paper presented at the annual meeting of the American Educational Research Association, Minneapolis. ERIC ED: 037 391.

SIMON, A. and BOYER, G. E. (Eds.) (1967). *Mirrors for Behaviour: An Anthology of Classroom Observation Instruments.* Philadelphia Research for Better Schools.

SPELMAN, B. (1975). *Contrasting Models of Teacher Effectiveness.* DPhil Thesis (pending). Coleraine: New University of Ulster.

STALEY, F. A. (1970). *A Comparison of the effects on pre-service teachers presenting one or two microteaching lessons to different sexed groups of peers.* Unpublished Thesis. Michigan State University.

STOLUROW, L. M. (1965). 'Model the master teacher or master the teacher model.' In: KRUMBOLTZ, J. D. (Ed.) *Learning and the Educational Process.* Chicago: Rand McNally, 223-247.

STONES, E. and MORRIS, S. (1972a). *Teaching Practice, Problems and Perspectives.* London: Methuen.

STONES, E. and MORRIS, S. (1972b). 'The assessment of practical teaching,' *Educ. Res.*, **14**, 2, 110. In: STONES, E. and MORRIS, S. *cit. op.*, 145-164.

STUKAT, K. G. (1972). *Microteaching.* Department of Educational Research, University of Gothenburg (mimeo).

TROTT, A. (Ed.) (1974). *Microteaching Conference Papers.* APLET Occasional Publication No. 3.

TURNEY, C. (1970). 'Microteaching – a promising innovation in teacher education,' *Aust. J. Educ.*, **14**, 125-141.

TURNEY, C. and CLIFT, J. C. *et al.* (1973). *Microteaching: Research, Theory and Practice.* Sydney University Press.

UNESCO (1972). *Selected Project Reports on New Methods and Techniques in Teacher Training.* Paris: Division of Methods and Materials, UNESCO.

WAIMON, M. D. and RAMSEYER, G. C. (1970). 'Effects of video feedback on the ability to evaluate teaching,' *Jn Tchr Educ.*, **21**, 92-95.

WARBURTON, F. W., BUTCHER, H. J. and FORREST, G. M. (1963). 'Predicting student performance in a university department of education,' *Brit. Jr. Educ. Psychol.*, **33**, 68-79.

WARD, B. E. (1970). *A Survey of Microteaching in Secondary Education Programmes of all NCATE Accredited Colleges and Universities.* Memorandum No. 70, Stanford Centre for Research and Development in Teaching.

WARD, P. M. (1970). *The Use of the Portable Videotape Recorder in Helping Teachers Self-evaluate their Teaching Behaviour.* Stanford: University of California.

WEBB, C. *et al.* (1968). *Description of a Large-Scale Micro-Teaching Programme.* Provo, Utah: College of Education, Brigham Young University.

WHITE, D. (1972). *The Stirling lesson sampling instruments: the preparation and testing of a battery of instruments for sampling teaching.* Unpublished Thesis, University of Stirling.

WOOD, C. C. and HEDLEY, R. L. (1968). 'Training instructional practice (TIPS): observation on student reaction to the use of video-tape recordings (VTR) in simulated classroom situations,' *Canadian Education and Research Digest*, 8, 46-59.

WRAGG, E. C. (1973). 'A study of student teachers in the classroom.' In: CHANAN, G. (ed.) (1973). *Towards a Science of Teaching.* Slough: NFER.

YOUNG, D. A. (1970). *A Preliminary Report on the Effectiveness of Colleague Supervision on the Acquisition of Selected Teaching Behaviours in a Microteaching Series.* Paper presented at the annual meeting of the American Educational Research Association, Minneapolis, ERIC ED: 038 330.

YOUNG, D. A. (1970). *A Preliminary Report on the Effectiveness of Colleague Supervision on the acquisition of selected teaching behaviours in a microteaching situation.* Presented at Amer. Educ. Res. Assoc. annual meeting, Minneapolis ED 038-330.

YOUNG, D. B. (1968). *The Effectiveness of Self instruction in Teacher Education Using Modelling and Videotape Feedback.* Stanford University, USA (doctoral dissertation).

CHAPTER 4

# A Conceptual Map for Interaction Studies

*Jim Eggleston, University of Nottingham School of Education,*
*M. J. Galton and Margaret Jones, University of Leicester, School of Education*

Observations of and researches into the relationships between events
which take place in classrooms and laboratories have been undertaken for a variety of purposes. Many such studies could properly
be called *interaction studies*. The distinctive feature of such studies is
that the data collected, while they may include descriptions of the
learning environment, always include an account of what pupils
and teachers say and do in it. We have found it profitable to classify
interaction studies into five major categories according to their
purpose. These are (1) inductive studies, (2) prescriptive studies,
(3) reflective studies, (4) matching studies and (5) process-product
studies. We will begin by describing the essential features of each
class of research and then go on to consider the common methodological problems which researchers have attempted to solve in ways
that are characteristic of each study.

Case studies of interaction analysis systems will then be described
to exemplify these five categories. It is necessary to outline our interpretation of these systems in some detail, since reports of their
development and use are often far from definitive. Finally, we offer a
tentative cross classification or conceptual map which relates the
development, purpose and use of interaction analysis systems.

## 1. *Inductive studies*

It is at least theoretically possible to free the mind of all pre-
suppositions about the relationships between events in the classroom
and the correlation between these events and possible outcomes. Such
observations of classrooms and their inhabitants can be dealt with
as Darwin dealt with observations during his voyage on the *Beagle* —
that is to say, to make no prior value judgements about phenomena
and allow no theory to determine the selection of phenomena to be

observed. Ideally every aspect of the classroom and the behaviour of its inhabitants is observed and recorded objectively. Data thus obtained are studied in order to induce empirical laws describing relationships between phenomena, which may lead further, to the development of causal theories. No researcher has pursued this *tabula rasa* approach in quite the fashion implied by the above description, but some have approached it. In practice most researchers find it necessary to limit their attention to a restricted range of phenomena within which the above conditions apply. Thus Biddle and Adams (1967) attended to a broad spectrum of socially significant events while Smith and Meux (1970), with their concern for the logic classroom discourse, made the tasks of data collection and a study of their data manageable by restricting their area of interest to cognitive exchanges. It is clear that wherever such constraints are imposed there is the danger that the research takes on board a theoretical structure which could restrict the range of induced laws and theories. In other words, the data collected may be subject to a systematic distortion determined by the perceptions of the researchers.

Even when such constraints as those instanced above are not used, there is usually some existing body of established relationships which may be used as analogues for induced theories. Thus Bellack *et al.* (1966) used concepts from the games theory developed by Wittgenstein to analyse fifteen lessons on *Problems in Democracy*.

Inductive studies are by their nature exploratory; they involve the collection of a more comprehensive array of data than most other types of study and are rarely concerned with measuring the growth of student learning. Such studies form part of a category of researches called *process* studies, in contrast to *process-product* studies where learning outcomes are always measured.

## 2. *Prescriptive studies*

We have coined the term prescriptive for those studies which attempt to put on a firmer footing the task of supervising teachers, particularly student teachers. Students are observed and supervisors collect observational data on which to base their diagnosis of pedagogical ills and their prognosis of the student's potential as a 'good' teacher. The term prescriptive is meant to imply that in the absence of any empirical support for hypotheses about effective teaching behaviour, supervisors, in varying degrees, subscribe to value-laden prescriptions of 'good' teachers and 'good' teaching behaviour. Medley and Mitzel (1963, p. 252) in their excellent review in Gage's *Handbook of Research on Teaching*, exclude 'procedures for obtaining ratings or assessments (of teaching performance) based on direct observations of classroom behaviours', which they do not regard as observation techniques suitable for interaction analysis. Their reason for so doing is that such procedures require the observer to 'rate or weight behaviours on a quantitative scale'. A precise definition of the function of the observer in interaction studies is seen by Medley and Mitzel to be crucial to the development of an effective research methodology. The use of what have been called *high inference* observations, where the link between the observed and the recorded behaviour involves one or more inferential steps, while not totally eschewed, are rejected by Medley and Mitzel when rating is involved. One could regard observation systems as falling at points on a spectrum from primitive to advanced. Primitive observation would involve observing without an explicitly formulated theory or its equivalent. Another characteristic of a primitive system would be a confusion between recording and judging. Advanced systems will seek to differentiate between component procedures and as far as possible to simplify them in accordance with set rules which relate to an accepted or emerging theory.

3. *Reflective studies*

The anthology of classroom interaction systems by Simon and Boyer was aptly entitled *Mirrors for Behaviour*. Many of the seventy-odd systems described by these authors have been used reflectively. A disparity can exist between the way a teacher wants to teach or thinks he does, and his actual classroom performance. It is possible for a teacher to be made aware of this disparity by use of interaction analysis systems. This presumes that the categories of behaviours observed are related to components in the teacher's perception of his 'style'. Thus, for example, a teacher who believed that, say, fifty per cent of his questions put to the class demanded factual answers, could be informed if his belief matched his performance. Similarly, a teacher who thought that of a given lesson half of it was essentially pupil-directed – the teacher's influence being indirect – could again be informed of any disparity between perceived and actual performance.

The relationships between theory and categories in which observations are made in this kind of study is interesting and potentially sinister. Presumably the researcher who devised the observation categories is guided by his own prescriptions or theories, possibly including his own notion of 'good' teaching. It is only in these categories that the teacher under investigation receives any information. It must therefore be, wittingly or otherwise, that the teachers who use these systems are subject to doctrinal influences.

### 4. Matching studies

Many recent curriculum developments, in science particularly, have included statements of behavioural objectives. Where objectives are described in these terms it is possible to infer some teaching behaviours which may be consistent with their attainment. Where, for example, curriculum objectives emphasize the processes of science one would expect intellectual skills related to those processes to be represented in the intellectual transactions which take place in classrooms and laboratories where such a curriculum was in use. For instance, the Nuffield 'O' level chemistry *Handbook for Teachers* includes the objectives of 'skill in devising an appropriate scheme and apparatus for solving a practical problem' and 'ability to interpret information with evidence of judgement and assessment'. Both these objectives, it may be reasonably inferred, are more likely to be achieved when pupils engage in behaviour related to them. Some teacher utterances will be of a kind which defines a practical problem, some pupil responses will contain statements about experimental design.

Observation schedules could be used, even if not exclusively designed, for the purpose of comparing a teacher's actual performance with that consistent with a curriculum development. The categories of teachers' and pupils' behaviour to which attention is given are those related to theories held, not by the teachers involved, nor the researchers who devised the schedule, but by the curriculum developers.

### 5. Process-product studies

The last group of classroom interaction studies contains those that include investigations most nearly related to evaluation of curriculum developments. These studies alone involve the measurement of pupils' intellectual attainment and attitudes. Process-product studies are essentially hypothetico-deductive in character. The process defined in terms of teacher and pupil behaviour observed and recorded by means of classroom interaction is hypothesized to bring about measurable changes in student growth. This hypothesis may be tested when the process is accurately specified and when the products are measured.

## Observing, recording, judging
*Observing*

All classroom interaction studies involve three major methodological problems. The first concerns what to observe, the second how frequently to observe and the third under what circumstances to observe.

If an untrained observer is placed in a science laboratory and given the general instruction to observe and report on the events which take place it will lead to results which are predictable from theories of perception and the empirical data which underpin these theories. The observer will 'see' only a selection of events. He will perceive only those elements of the process he thinks he is observing which relate to his mental constructs or schema. Of these perceived events he will later remember only a proportion. Philosophers of science such as Karl Popper make the assertion that there is no such thing as *theory-free* observing. An observer with an interest in social psychology will in a class see evidence of groupings and relationships; another with an interest in pupils' hygiene will observe unguarded sneezes, pencil sucking and sharing, ambient temperatures and classroom ventilation; a subject matter specialist might note the logical development of a teacher's exposition, errors of fact and so on.

Even when we focus the observer's attention on the learning process, although this would limit the range of phenomena reported, there is in the absence of an established theory of learning, a tendency for an observer to attend selectively to those events which relate to his own 'theory' of learning, however crudely formulated this may be. One way of overcoming this problem is to ask observers to look for particular classes of events and record only these events when they occur. Thus the investigator employs observers whose task is now limited to recognizing instances of predetermined classes of behaviour and recording them. The observer is no longer allowed the luxury of his own 'theory'; instead he attends only to events which relate to the investigator's schema. Thus, for example, Gallagher (1970) who used Guilford's factorial model of the mind asked his observers to attend to those behaviours of teachers and pupils which related to this model.

The nature of the relationships between observations and theory is complex and it varies with the purpose for which the observations are made. Thus inductive studies, which hopefully end rather than begin with a formulated theory, necessitate observing a wide range of very different kinds of phenomena, without any presumption as to what is or might be initially significant or important. Prescriptive studies may have no theoretical base at all, but they do have what is operationally an alternative, that is a prescription for what is held to be good teaching behaviour. When this prescription is analysed into behavioural components, it may be used as a means for concentrating the observers' attention on behaviours which are consistent with this prescription. Essentially, the same arguments apply in reflective studies. Ideally the teacher has his own prescription for the way in which he wishes to teach, and providing he can find an observing system which contains categories consistent with his own expected behaviour, he can employ an observer or an observational system to feed back data on which he can act. In a rather similar way *matching* researches, where a comparison is made between a teacher's behaviour and that behaviour which is consistent with a prescribed curriculum development, can limit the observer's task to attending only to those behaviours which are relevant to this purpose.

Prescriptive, reflective and matching researches are, in a sense, potentially the basis of experimental designs where the teacher's behaviour is the dependent variable.

In process-product studies, however, the dependent variable is either the growth of pupils' intellectual skills and/or changes in pupils' attitudes. In both correlational and experimental studies the investigator may examine certain components in the learning environment or the way in which pupils and teachers behave in it, and relate these to pupil growth. He may deliberately manipulate teacher and pupil behaviour under experimental conditions. Hopefully, such correlational or experimental studies will where possible be based on or contribute to learning theory.

*Recording*

The second series of problems centres around the methods and techniques of recording observations. Lessons are unique events.

While we may, by observing the same teacher teach the same class on a number of occasions, discern patterns of teacher and class behaviour, there is an obvious need to produce some record of the events observed on each occasion. The type of recording procedure used is largely determined by the purpose of the research in which interaction is observed. Inductive studies which, in the days before the ready availability of electronic tape recording devices, demanded the use of very complicated observation schedules and shorthand verbatim reports of teachers' and pupils' statements, now use sound and video tape. The aim is to achieve as comprehensive a record as possible of the events taking place. Later, with or without the aid of transcripts, the events can be subjected to repeated examination and alternative systems of analysis in the search for patterns and empirical laws. In practice the record can never be comprehensive; some selectivity is inevitable because of the physical limitations of the systems used. Moreover, information obtained in this way is subject to a further selection when it is conceptualized.

It is in prescriptive studies where *rating* has been most frequently used. The rating of a teacher's performance on a single literal scale, e.g. A to E, in a single lesson, if not totally misconceived, is too crude for research purposes, but it is not unusual to find researches in which different properties of a teacher's performance or pupils' response are inferred from observed behaviours and recorded on a series of 5- and 7-point scales by observers after the event. The work of Ryans (1960) and the attendant problems defined by Medley and Mitzel (1963) have been referred to previously.

More recently attempts have been made to differentiate the task of observing from that of judging; to define the observer's task as that of identifying certain classes of behaviour as they occur; and to simplify his task of recording by making a tally mark on paper when the behaviour occurs. Central to this recording system is the restriction of events observed and the construction of a classification system into which observed behaviours must fit. Such systems can be grouped under two headings: *category systems* and *sign systems*. In the former, at fixed, usually brief, time intervals, the behaviour, for example, the verbal behaviour occurring at that time, is classified in one of a number of mutually exclusive and comprehensive categories. Sign systems record a noncomprehensive list of behaviours more or less as they occur. Either system can yield measures of the relative frequency with which certain behaviours occur.

Reflective and matching studies have been evolved where either sign or category systems have been used. The category system devised by Flanders (1965) is a popular front runner in the field of reflective studies while Parakh's (1969) category system has been used in a matching study.

Process-product studies are distinguished from other studies mainly by the need to specify and measure accurately the independent variables in teacher-pupil interaction to which dependent pupil growth measures are hypothetically related. The observations of classroom interactions and the record made of them must in such studies lend themselves to quantification. Either sign or category systems may be used.

*Judging*

The third set of problems is associated with the different kinds of judgement that observers can be called upon to make during a study of classroom behaviours. It is important to consider carefully how the nature of these judgements will vary with the type of interaction study, as well as with alternative systems of observing and recording. Not least is the need to assure teachers and pupils who are observed that they are not being judged.

Inductive studies are directed to a search for pattern and empirical laws describing observed events. The final judgements made here are those involving the use of criteria characteristic of inductive logic. Examples of such judgements might be, 'Was the number of cases observed adequate to justify the formulation of the law? Are any apparent exceptions explicable without falsifying the law?' and 'Is the law logically related to the cases?' There may well be other judgements to make in inductive studies, where, for example, conceptual models are borrowed from other fields. In this case, 'goodness of fit' criteria would be used.

Prescriptive studies are by far in the most difficult position with respect to judging. If fashion or some individual tutor dictates what is considered to be 'good' teaching or even some behavioural concomitants of good teaching, and spells these out in terms of teacher-pupil interaction, there is a danger that dogmatic assertions will be accepted, and observed teachers judged as good, bad or C+. It is improbable that any such prescription could be shown to be 'good', i.e. most effective for most pupils under any circumstances, so that no credence could be placed on such a claim. We would insist that good teaching must be defined in terms of its effects. Admittedly, teaching a class is sometimes described as one might describe playing a complicated piece of music on a difficult instrument. However, the instrument is expected to be the same at the end of a display of the musician's virtuosity; a class is not.

Nevertheless, patterns of interaction prescribed by a tutor (prescriptive), by the teacher himself (reflective), or indirectly by a curriculum development (matching), may be judged for goodness of fit.

Judgement in the case of process-product studies operates at another level. It requires answers to the questions, 'Is the description of the process of teacher-pupil interaction adequate?. Does it include variables likely to be causally related to pupil growth?'. Here, however, judgement is also involved at the level of statistical inferences when the two sets of data relating to process *and* product are available. Again, the design of the studies, the adequacy of the sampling procedures and so on are subject to judgements of another kind.

*Steps towards a more efficient classification*

It seems to be a fairly straightforward procedure to classify interaction analysis studies according to the purpose for which they were designed, but the result is not as informative as might be the case if a cross-classification could be devised to relate purpose to other features of these studies. Given such a cross-classification it would be possible to discern trends among classified researches. To achieve this classification we might use such properties of the interaction analysis instruments used in these studies as the use of sign or category systems, the use of high or low inference measures, or the range of events to which the observer is asked to attend. Such a classification would demonstrate any exclusive properties of studies carried out for a particular purpose. The comparative success or failure of systems in achieving their purpose might indicate profitable and unprofitable lines of investigation. An effective cross-classification which achieved an effective mapping of systems might contribute to more effective practice and might yield some theoretical insights into the study of interaction. The difficulty is that of deciding which features of interaction analysis studies to use to get the best pay-off. Taxonomists of the animal kingdom have frequently faced an identical problem when easily recognizable characteristics have been used as sorting-criteria to yield an apparently simple and efficient separation of animal species into groups, only to discover later better alternatives which led to a more comprehensive and comprehensible array. Often the more obvious criteria, simple to observe and efficient in use, turned out to be arbitrary and not to lead to the most systematic arrangement. Thus it may be that in devising a cross-classification of interaction analysis studies, obvious properties such as whether a sign or category system is used in the observation instrument may be arbitrary whereas other criteria, though less easy to apply, might yield more order. One such criterion which we have used, and which seems to give a useful if rather untidy mapping of interaction studies, is that of the origin of the observation instrument developed during the study, especially its relationship to a theoretical base.

We may use one arm of our proposed classification to divide inter-action studies according to purpose, as follows:

> Process studies. (Now that we intend to group studies on two dimensions, the name 'process studies' will be given to this class. As we will see not all process studies are inductively derived.)

> Comparative studies
>     Prescriptive
>     Matching
>     Reflective
>     Inter-subject comparison.

> Process-product studies.

We may now examine any one class, e.g. process studies, and by comparing them according to their relationship to an explicit theoretical base explore the possibility of a cross-classification on this basis.

### Case studies—Process

The well known studies of Smith and Meux (1970) from 1967 onwards furnish good examples of process studies which aimed at a 'theory free' position. In these studies there are restrictions on what is observed, but selection from the larger data-base, while it represents a view of what teaching is, does not relate explicitly to a theory.

(1) *The logic of teaching and the strategies of teaching and its modifications*
    Smith and his colleagues have developed two systems for the
analysis of classroom interaction, the first was concerned with the
'Logic of Teaching' and the second with the 'Strategies of Teaching'.
These were both inductive studies; their intent was to observe,
describe and classify the phenomena of teaching. The authors
believed that a knowledge of the process of teaching is needed before
theories of teaching based on philosophy and psychology can be
put into practice. Only then can the materials and procedures
designed for the latter be related to both the theory and the
phenomena of teaching.
    Both studies were limited to considering those characteristic acts
which the teacher performs in the classroom to induce learning.
Routine and procedural teacher behaviours such as giving examinations, grading papers or keeping order were excluded. The authors
explain, in detail, their idea of the phenomena of teaching as

> 'a system of social action involving an agent, an end-in-view,
> a situation and two sets of factors in the situation – one set over
> which the agent has no control (e.g. size of classroom and
> physical characteristics of pupils) and one set which the agent
> can modify with respect to the end-in-view (e.g. assignments
> and ways of asking questions). The latter set of factors constitute
> the *means* by which *ends-in-view* are reached. The means, in
> turn, consists of two types of factors: subject matter and
> instructional paraphernalia, and the ways of manipulating
> and manoeuvring the subject matter and paraphernalia. The
> first of these we call *material means* and the second *procedural
> means*. The procedural means have two aspects: large-scale
> manoeuvres which we call *strategies*, and smaller movements,
> constituting tactical elements of strategies, which we call
> *logical operations*.'

This has been expressed diagrammatically in Figure 1. The logical
operations are the focus of attention in the first study and the
strategies are the concern of the second study.

    (a) *The Study of the Logic of Teaching.* This study adopted an
'ecological approach' to describe the tactical behaviours of teachers
as they manipulate the subject matter. Since the authors believed

that teaching consists of mainly verbal behaviours, lessons were tape-recorded and then transcribed. Repeated study of these transcripts led to a system of analysis whereby the discourse was divided into episodes or monologues. An episode consists of verbal exchanges between at least two individuals, while a monologue is a single speaker unit. These units of classroom discourse were designed so that they could be identified at a low inference level with a fair amount of reliability, were independent of the subject matter and were capable of subsequent logical analysis.

**Figure 1: An outline of the logical components of teaching.** Based on descriptions given by B. O. Smith, M. O. Meux *et al.* in *A Study of the Logic of Teaching*, University of Illinois Press, 1970.

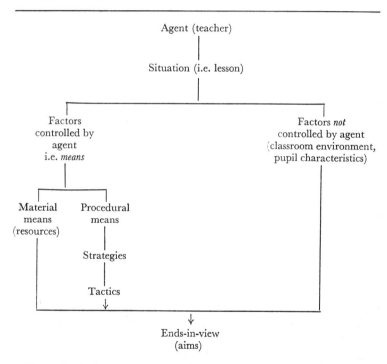

The episode is an attempt to define a 'natural' unit of classroom discourse. Smith conceives each episode as having three parts, an initiating phase containing a statement, question, invitation or direction; a continuing phase, or the verbal interplay resulting from the first phase; and a terminal phase. These episodes could be

classified according to any of these properties, such as length of all
or part of the episode, or by the nature of the continuing phase. In
practice Smith decided to classify episodes according to the cognitive demand made on pupils by the opening teacher statement,
question, etc. The following categories of *defining, describing, designating, stating, reporting, substituting, evaluating, conditional inferring,* and
*explaining,* were used. There was an additional category for procedural comments.

When teachers' initiating statements had been classified in terms
of inferred intent according to the list above, it was found that
a number of generalized descriptions could be made. For instance
describing, designating and explaining were the most frequently
occurring demands made on the pupils, while substituting, reporting
and classifying were the least used. Comparisons were made
between the teaching of different subjects. It was found, Table 1,
that in physics lessons there was more concern with defining and
conditional inferring, while biology and chemistry lessons dealt
more with designating, classifying and explaining. However, inter-
subject comparisons were incidental to the main purpose of this
study.

(b) *The Study of the Strategies of Teaching.* Smith and Meux then
turned their attention to another aspect of the procedural means
teachers use to achieve the 'ends-in-view'. In this study they were
concerned to identify and describe larger teaching patterns, called
strategies, by which the subject matter is controlled and manipulated to achieve certain objectives.

The original transcripts were again studied and this time were
divided into units called *ventures*. A venture consists of classroom
discussion (designed to achieve a specific objective) which is
concerned with an identifiable unit of subject matter. A venture
is usually longer than an episode, since it can contain a number of
verbal exchanges between the teacher and different pupils, while
the same subject is discussed. A typical lesson consists of six to ten
ventures. Ventures are units within which strategies can be identified
and described. Since a strategy is a way of achieving an objective,
ventures were classified on the basis of the lesson aims. Ventures were
further analysed in terms of the strategies employed. Eight categories
of ventures were finally identified according to their intended
objective. These were called, *causal, conceptual, evaluative, particular,*

*interpretative, procedural, reason* and *rule.* Each type of venture was distinguished by a particular type of objective, for example, conceptual ventures were characterized by the fact that they involved an analysis of a concept, while interpretative ventures put forward various meanings for an expression.

The authors then identified various kinds of verbal manipulations of the subject matter. A number of examples of a particular venture were examined and re-examined to identify and classify the smaller verbal units called *moves*. A move is a discussion or description of a particular item or unit of information and it is the patterning of these moves within a venture which constitute strategies.

Fifteen types of moves were identified within conceptual ventures. These conceptual moves were grouped into three main general categories: *descriptive moves* in which the content is explained by or through discussion of examples, *comparative moves* in which the content is explained by comparison of the primary concept with some other concept, and *instantial moves* in which a direct description of the characteristics or qualities of the concept is made. After classification of the moves, it was found that some generalizations could be made. A number of different types of conceptual venture were identified on the basis of the kind of moves it contained. The most frequently occurring conceptual ventures were those containing only descriptive moves or descriptive and comparative moves. When the pattern of moves within a venture was examined, one type of discussion was found to follow the rule that when a teacher starts with a characteristic move (one of the fifteen categories) he can proceed to another kind of move but returns to a characteristic move before proceeding to another kind of move again. Other patterns of moves exist which are much more complex. It is these patterns which constitute teaching strategies. Similar descriptions and generalizations have been made about the other seven types of venture. These results are not generalizable to other classrooms, since they are based on a small sample; only five consecutive lessons were recorded for seventeen different classes and these represented a number of different curriculum areas. However, this study which has led to the identification of patterns and rules is a good example of the application of an inductive process.

One obvious danger inherent in classifying interaction studies in terms of their relationship to an established theoretical base is that we may have to rely on statements by the researchers that their

c

methods of investigation were or were not related to particular theories. Smith and Meux use such terms as 'inductive' and the description 'ecological approach' to describe their work, but it could be argued that any selection of data is unlikely to be purely arbitrary and might therefore be informed by some kind of theory. However, this work was described by its authors as essentially a preliminary to the possible development of theories of teaching. So we may infer that decisions which these researchers took were consistent with their theory-free ideal. Such a view is supported by the rather complex terminology which they invented in order to describe and classify the components of verbal interaction. It may also be significant that permanent transcribed records were used as data and repeatedly scanned to yield descriptions in which the emphasis was qualitative. Quantification was only partial and introduced at a late stage.

The work of Aschner and Gallagher (1967), on the other hand, while still a process study was, according to Gallagher, strongly influenced by Guildford's model of the structure of the intellect, particularly that dimension most concerned with 'operations'.

(2) *Aschner-Gallagher Classification System*

This system was devised in an attempt to give a qualitative and quantitative description of productive thinking done by gifted children during a class discussion. It was part of an extended project which sought to '(a) identify productive thought processes in intellectually gifted children within the context of classroom verbal activity at the junior high school level, and (b) assess relationships between these thought processes and certain variables that may relate to their operation in the classroom'. (p. 13) The long term aim was to incorporate into teacher training programmes those teaching methods and procedures which had been found to be effective in developing high level thought processes.

The primary classification categories of cognitive memory: *convergent thinking, divergent thinking, evaluative thinking* and *routine* arose from consideration of the components of the operational dimension of Guildford's model. Secondary categories were derived in an inductive manner from transcripts of lessons. Behaviours taken to reflect different thinking operations were identified, labelled and classified under one of the primary categories. Thus the majority of the system was derived inductively, but this was within a framework related to a psychological model and also related to the type of variables measured.

The observation system contains five primary categories. One of these is *cognitive memory*, and this is used to record such thought processes as recognition, rote memory and selective recall. This primary category contains a subcategory of recapitulation into which such verbal behaviours as quoting, repeating, recounting and reviewing are classified. Verbal behaviours which appear to reflect thought processes which are both analytic and integrative and which also operate within a closely structured framework are classified into the primary category of *convergent thinking*. Thus questions or problems which are answered by reasoning based on given or remembered data are classified in this category. A third category is *evaluative thinking*. This has three secondary categories into which utterances of value-based judgements are classified. The primary category, *divergent thinking*, is used for the classification of verbal performances which indicate that an individual is freely forming his own ideas or taking a new direction or perspective on a given topic.

Each of ten classes on five consecutive occasions, having lessons in social studies, science and English were tape recorded and then transcribed. The transcript of both the teacher's and pupil's verbal behaviour was first of all analysed into 'thought units' for each speaker. A single utterance might consist of one or a series of these units, and these were then classified. Judges were able to achieve a percentage agreement of between 67 to 79 for units of the subcategories. Classification of the lesson transcripts gave the frequency of occurrence in rank order: (1) routine and cognitive memory, (2) cognitive thinking, and (3) evaluative thinking and divergent thinking. Compared to the other subjects, science lessons showed more convergent and divergent thinking, evaluative thinking and routine, but less cognitive memory behaviours. There was also a high association between thought processes asked for by the teacher and the kind of reply the students gave.

This system can be used to give descriptions or comparisons of lessons in terms of the thought processes involved. The categories were derived inductively. What finally emerged, however, was a set of behaviours with a restricted range, because of the need to accommodate the system within the framework of Guildford's factorial model of the intellect.

(3) *Gallagher Topic Classification System*

The earlier findings of the Aschner-Gallagher system strongly influenced Gallagher (1970) when he subsequently came to develop his Topic Classification System. It was hoped that the new system would provide a fuller account of classroom strategy and inter-action, particularly by taking account of the sequence of activities during the lesson. Although the manner of the development of the Topic Classification System is not recorded, it may be inferred that it was developed deductively, since a well-defined model was described as the basis of the system. The areas selected for attention were those which in the author's judgement was considered to be potentially most useful for observation. Another characteristic of this deductive approach was that studies were reported which were designed to test the limitations of the system, thus suggesting a classification system developed apart from the data.

Gallagher's system is based on a three dimensional model (see Figure 2). The three dimensions used for classification were *instructional intent, conceptualization* and *style*. The same transcripts as used in the previous study were first of all divided into units called topics, which were described as 'units where the focus of classroom discussion centres on a given action, concept or principle' (1970, p. 44). A topic is never less than fifteen lines of type-written script. If less than this, it is regarded as being under-developed. This larger unit was originally chosen since it was felt that the previous classification using the 'thought unit' sometimes detracted from the larger meaning of a whole sequence. Topics were classified on each of the three dimensions by a team of trained judges. The dimension *instructional intent* has two levels, one called 'content' which is used if the teaching goal is for the students to learn a given body of knowledge. The other is 'skills' used when the goal is for the students to learn some set of behaviours or skills. A second dimension is that of *conceptualization*. This dimension has three levels: 'data' if the discussion is concerned with specifics, 'concept' if the topic involves abstraction or application and 'generalization' for discussions relating concepts to one another. These levels of thought abstraction are described as being crude and providing a deliberately limited view of an infinitely complex abstractional ladder. The third dimension, that of *style* is made up of the five levels – description, expansion, evaluation-justification, evaluation-matching and activity, and is closely related to the earlier Aschner and Gallagher

**Figure 2: Topic Classification Dimensions** (From J. J. GALLAGHER, M. J. ASCHNER and W. GENNE, *Productive thinking of gifted children in classroom interaction*, CEC Research Monograph Series B., 55, 1967, p. 41.)

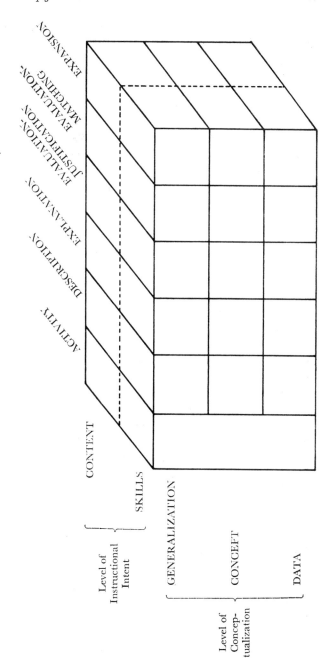

Level of Style

EXPANSION

EVALUATION-MATCHING

EVALUATION-JUSTIFICATION

EXPLANATION

DESCRIPTION

ACTIVITY

CONTENT

SKILLS

Level of Instructional Intent

GENERALIZATION

CONCEPT

DATA

Level of Conceptualization

system. The way in which classroom discussion is handled within a topic is classified as one of these five levels of style.

We could then, classify process studies into two groups, those like that of Meux and Smith which attempted to be 'theory-free' and those like that of Aschner and Gallagher which claim affinities with particular theories. There appears to be at least one group of studies which would not be appropriately placed in either of these classes. Such a study is that of E. M. J. Wright (1959). He made observational studies to obtain a direct record of verbal activities in the classroom where mathematics was being taught. This approach was chosen to provide both a record of the subject matter and to indicate the ways in which it was taught.

The categories of verbal behaviour selected for observation were based on statements of objectives. Statements of general educational objectives and specific objectives relating to mathematics teaching were collected from the literature and from personal experience. Each objective had to satisfy three criteria before it was incorporated into the classification system. Firstly, it had to be capable of careful definition, secondly, it had to be judged important both for general and mathematical education, and thirdly, its nature was such that a secondary school pupil might be expected to achieve it. Thus all the behaviours recorded were those that the teacher would expect to occur if the stated objectives were achieved. No attempt was made to monitor activities outside of this expected range even if there was evidence that these did occur.

The list of behaviours finally selected was found to group into the three mutually exclusive frames of reference – ability to think, appreciation of mathematics, and attitude of curiosity and initiative (see Figure 3). A neutral category was provided so that every behaviour observed could be recorded even if it could not be classified into one of the frames of reference. The system was designed for use in the classroom by an observer who classifies and records the verbal behaviour of the first speaker, teacher or pupil, which occurs in alternative fifteen-second time sampling units.

In all, twelve classes were observed. Each class was observed on four occasions. The two groups of classes following somewhat different courses were found to be very similar. Of the twenty-one categories, only two were significantly different for teacher, and one for pupil, behaviour. Descriptions and comparisons of the teachers were attempted by comparing the mean scores of an individual teacher with the mean score of the group. Thus it was possible to obtain a profile of a particular teacher which indicated the sub-set of behaviours present in their teaching.

If curriculum outcomes or objectives are described in terms of observable behaviour, observers might be asked to attend selectively to a list of such behaviours. This seems to be the case in Wright's study. It is possible that such a list may be related more or less explicity to some kind of theory, but it is not essential. It is therefore desirable to have a third category of process studies to accommodate cases where the selection of events to be observed is made in this way, i.e. where some concensus view of teaching objectives is translated into behavioural terms and this sub-set is the basis for an obervational study.

The tentative classification thus far developed, may be illustrated as follows:

| Origin – Relationship to Theory<br><br>Purpose | Inductive | Explicitly Theory-based | Bases on curriculum objectives |
|---|---|---|---|
| Process studies | e.g. Smith & Meux, 1967 2 | e.g. Aschner & Gallagher, 1967 16 | e.g. Wright, 1959, 19 |
| Comparative studies etc. | | | |

**Figure 3: An outline category system for observing Maths lessons** (Based on a description given by E. M. J. WRIGHT, 'Development of an instrument for studying verbal behaviours in secondary school mathematics classrooms,' *Journal of Experimental Education*, 28: 2, 1959).

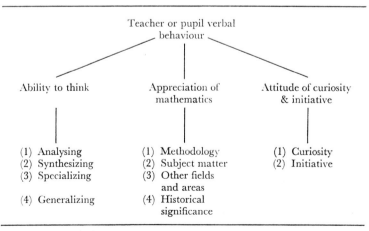

**Comparative studies**

Once a process study has yielded an operationally efficient system, it is commonplace for it to be used in comparative studies or in process-product studies.

Meux and Smith used their original data in order to compare teachers of Physics, Biology and Chemistry (see Table 1). They compared the distribution of 'episodes' among 'logical categories'. It would appear from their account that both teachers and subject matter were varied simultaneously, so presumably variance due to each of these sources could not be analysed. Later Nuthall and Lawrence (1965) adapted this system for their investigation in New Zealand schools.

These workers experienced difficulties with Smith's unit, the episode. They decided to classify only the initiating statement and ignore the continuant questions within each episode, but to classify all teachers' questions. As Nuthall and Lawrence state,

> '. . . it appeared it might be simpler, more reliable and equally valid to analyse *all* the questions used by teachers.'
> (p. 14).

This led them to identify a new unit of analysis, the *incident*, which they describe as

> 'basically a question (stimulus)–answer (response) unit adapted to incorporate the variety of forms of teacher-pupil interaction that may occur as the teacher directs and guides his pupils towards the correct or desired answer.'
> (p. 20).

In practice the distinction between Smith's episode and Nuthall's incident is not always easy to discern, and no examples are given where the alternative forms of coding are employed on the same transcript.

Nuthall and Lawrence analysed the transcripts of four lessons for each of two teachers, using the incident as the unit of analysis; those incidents classified as explaining, using Smith's criteria, were then examined in more detail. This study was exploratory and descriptive. The authors thought the analysis of transcripts using this method could be a useful training for teachers since it highlights the pattern of incidents and the type of questions commonly used. Thus the system derived inductively could be applied prescriptively.

**Table 1: Percentage distribution of logical categories**

|  | *Physics* | *Biology* | *Chemistry* | *All Subjects* |
|---|---|---|---|---|
| Defining | 7·8 | 3·3 | 3·8 | 4·1 |
| Describing | 37·9 | 33·5 | 32·7 | 25·3 |
| Designating | 6·0 | 19·8 | 11·1 | 14·8 |
| Stating | 7·2 | 1·5 | 3·8 | 6·8 |
| Reporting | 4·2 | 2·7 | 0 | 2·9 |
| Substitution | 2·4 | 0 | 0 | 0·3 |
| Evaluating | 2·4 | 0·3 | 7·2 | 4·6 |
| Opining | 0·6 | 0·9 | 2·7 | 5·3 |
| Classifying | 1·2 | 6·0 | 3·3 | 3·0 |
| Comparing and Contrasting | 4·8 | 7·0 | 2·7 | 3·3 |
| Conditional Inferring | 15·6 | 6·7 | 8·3 | 7·3 |
| Explaining | 6·0 | 14·3 | 14·4 | 12·9 |

## Process-product studies

Subsequently, Nuthall, again using the work of Smith and Meux, undertook an experimental process-product study. He sought to show the relationship in social studies between the type of strategy used in the teaching process and the resulting student learning. Programmed learning texts were devised employing four different teaching strategies which were selected on the basis of the earlier work of Smith *et al*. Three of the strategies used were those found to occur often. They were a sequence consisting of only descriptive moves, an alternating sequence of descriptive and instantial moves and an alternating sequence of descriptive and comparative moves. The fourth strategy did not commonly occur, and was an alternating sequence of comparative and instantial moves. Pre- and post-tests were administered; these were criterion tests designed to discriminate between groups of students on the basis of their knowledge of terms and related concepts in the pre-test, and of their knowledge of the meaning of the concept, and ability to use the concept in understanding and solving problems in the post-test. An analysis of variance showed that differences in teaching strategy could be related to differences in student performance.

More recently Tisher (1970) used Nuthall's earlier modification of Smith's system in a study of science teachers. Tisher's work had two main aims, the first to describe the nature, distribution and pattern of the verbal interaction in science lessons taught by nine teachers; the second to relate this ecological data to growth in pupil understanding. The initial process study enabled Tisher to describe grade 8 science teachers as exhibiting a high degree of similarity in their behaviour patterns. The questions they ask 'frequently require the pupils to recall names, terms and other factual material, and less frequently, to engage in higher-cognitive behaviours such as classification, explanation and inference' (p. 391) (see Table 2). In the second part, a process product study, the teachers were divided into three groups on the basis of the description of their teaching in terms of the Smith categories; these were teachers who engaged in the higher cognitive demand with high, medium and low demand frequency. The three groups of teachers contained small numbers, and differences between the groups were also small. However, no support was provided for the general hypothesis that 'the development of understanding will be greatest for the able and less able students when they are taught by teachers who frequently make higher-cognitive demands, and least when they are taught by teachers who less frequently make these demands'. (p. 400).

The two systems of interaction of Smith *et al.* were both derived inductively from transcripts of lessons. Only a limited selection of

**Table 2: Incident analysis for eight science teachers**

| Operation | Average Percentage occurrence |
|---|---|
| Describing | 29·7 |
| Designating | 32·5 |
| Stating | 10·7 |
| Defining | 2·1 |
| Substitution | 0·3 |
| Evaluation | 0·4 |
| Opining | 0·7 |
| Classifying | 0·8 |
| Comparing and contrasting | 2·4 |
| Inferring | 7·2 |
| Explaining | 8·6 |
| Management | 4·6 |

behaviours were analysed; these were the procedural means by which teachers manipulated and manoeuvred the subject matter.

Both systems have provided descriptions of a variety of lessons, and comparisons between lessons have been made on this basis. Other researchers have used their system or its modification to provide descriptions of teaching and relate this to the measured outcomes in process-product studies. Thus the use of these two systems of analysis has evolved from being purely descriptive to being process-product studies. It has also been suggested that they could be used in prescriptive or reflective studies.

These latter studies might therefore be classified as follows:

| **Origin – Relationship to Theory** | **Inductive** |
| --- | --- |
| **Purpose** | |
| Process studies | Smith and Meux 1967 Modified (presumably on the basis of an earlier publication) by Nuthall and Lawrence 1965 |
| Comparative studies Prescriptive Reflective Matching | Prescriptive or reflective use proposed by Nuthall and Lawrence |
| Inter-subject | Smith and Meux 1967 |
| Process-product | Nuthall 1968 Tisher 1970 |

### Systems derived from a theoretical base

In a similar way, systems derived explicitly from a theoretical base may be seen to have served a variety of purposes. Thus the studies of Aschner and Gallagher, later incorporated into the Topic Classification of Gallagher, were used in two comparative researches undertaken by the latter author.

In the first of these studies, Topic Classification, was used to compare 8 lessons of social studies, 9 of English, 4 of Science and 9 of general elementary school instruction.

The instructional intent dimension of science lessons showed an emphasis on skill topics whereas the other three subjects had a high percentage of topics concerned with content. There were no major differences between subject groups in the use of the concept and generalization levels of the conceptualization category. The data level, however, was used more in social science lessons than in science lessons. Analysis of variance showed only negligible differences between the four groups in the use of the cognitive style dimension.

In the second study (Gallagher, 1967), lessons of six teachers using this BSCS Blue Version were recorded, transcribed and then analysed by means of the Topic Classification System. Possible variation in subject matter was controlled by recording all six teachers while they were introducing the same concept, that of photosynthesis, to the class. The results are given in Table 3.

Significant overall differences were obtained between the teachers on the dimensions of instructional intent and level of conceptualization. This finding led Gallagher to suggest there was no such thing as a BSCS curriculum presentation, only each teacher's individual interpretation. On the cognitive style dimension, however, the teachers had a common pattern: the emphasis was on description and explanation topics.

The achievement of the pupils in these classes was also measured using the BSCS examination which included items on photosynthesis together with additional items from other subject areas. As there were no pre-test scores it was not possible to measure pupil gains and so relate the process to the product. There were no significant differences between the achievement of the pupils in the six groups.

We will now consider the significant and well-known system devised by Flanders and his colleagues (Flanders 1965) for the study of classroom interaction. By historical precedence this study must first be entered as a process-product study because its first use in 1965 was in the course of such a study. There is some doubt about the relationship between the origin of Flanders' system and theories from which it might have been derived, but on balance this study fits best with those studies such as Gallagher's which claim to be explicity grounded in theory. At one point in his writings (1965), Flanders refers to the psychology of superior-subordinate relationships as a basis for his system. We are, however, not acquainted with any theory describing the relationships and cannot therefore

**Table 3: Percent of topics in each dimension of classification system.** (*BSCS Newsletter*, No. 3, 1967.)

| Class | Total Topics | LEVEL OF INSTRUCTIONAL INTENT | | LEVEL OF CONCEPTUALIZATION | | | | | LEVEL OF STYLE | | |
|---|---|---|---|---|---|---|---|---|---|---|---|
| | | Content | Skills | Data | Concept | General | Descr. | Explan. | Eval-J. | Eval-M. | Expans. |
| Uriah | 55 | 96 | 4 | 7 | 91 | 2 | 31 | 40 | 7 | 0 | 22 |
| Virgil | 45 | 71 | 29 | 27 | 68 | 6 | 33 | 48 | 9 | 0 | 9 |
| Willie | 61 | 70 | 30 | 32 | 64 | 4 | 48 | 38 | 4 | 0 | 11 |
| Xavier | 48 | 85 | 15 | 26 | 58 | 16 | 44 | 37 | 2 | 0 | 17 |
| Yancy | 60 | 100 | 0 | 3 | 95 | 2 | 39 | 46 | 7 | 0 | 8 |
| Zorba | 57 | 100 | 0 | 11 | 80 | 9 | 38 | 47 | 2 | 2 | 11 |
| | | $\chi^2 = 48\cdot84$ | | $\chi^2 = 34\cdot77$ | | | $\chi^2 = 14\cdot98$ | | | | |
| | | df = 5 | | df = 10 | | | df = 15 | | | | |
| | | p = <·01 | | p = <·01 | | | p = <·50 | | | | |

assess its status as an explanatory theory of behaviour. The absence of description of the kind of inductive processes such as those in the work of Meux and Smith, coupled with the priority given to quantification, suggests that least error will be made by classing Flanders' system with those which are theory based.

Flanders' Interaction Analysis system was produced as part of a process-product study in which the process, teacher influence, was related to the products, pupil attitude and achievement. The following hypotheses were tested:

1. Indirect teacher influence increases learning when a student's perception of the goal is confused or ambiguous.
2. Direct teacher influence increases learning when a student's perception of the goal is clear and acceptable.
3. Direct teacher influence decreases learning when a student's perception of the goal is ambiguous.

Thus in this study, teacher behaviour was an independent variable which needed to be quantified in some way. The Interaction Analysis system was devised for this purpose. Two preliminary studies were carried out in which versions of the Interaction Analysis scheme were tried and modified. Other measures such as an attitude inventory for dependence-proneness were also constructed.

The teacher behaviours selected for observation were closely related to those identified by earlier research on classroom climate Direct influence was defined as 'verbal statements of the teacher that restrict freedom of action, by focusing attention on a problem, interjecting teaching authority, or both. These statements include lecturing, giving directions, criticizing and justifying his own use of authority' (Flanders, 1965, p. 9). In contrast, indirect influence was described as 'verbal statements of the teacher that expand a student's freedom of action by encouraging his verbal participation and initiative. These include asking questions, accepting and clarifying the ideas and feelings of students, and praising or encouraging students' reponses.'

The Flanders system was devised as a means of coding verbal communications between teachers and pupils in the classroom. The assumption was made that the teacher's verbal behaviour is an adequate sample of his total behaviour. Categories for classification were chosen wich allowed the observer to distinguish between those acts which resulted in compliance and those which invited more creative and voluntary participation, without his being diverted by the subject matter. The system has ten categories. Of these, seven cover aspects of teacher talk and two record student talk, while the final category is reserved for 'silence or confusion.' The teacher talk categories consist of four which measure 'indirect teacher influence' and three which describe 'direct teacher influence'. Indirect influence is recorded if the teacher *accepts feelings, praises or encourages, accepts or uses pupil ideas,* or if he *asks questions.* Direct teacher influence occurs when the teacher is *lecturing, giving directions, criticizing* or *justifying authority.* The two categories for recording student talk, are *response* and *initiation.* These provide a measure of the student's freedom of action. The observer in a classroom records the predominant behaviour which occurs during a three second interval. This recorded data gives the sequence of behaviours. Calculation of the ratio of indirect to direct teacher activity gives a way of separating teachers into those with above or below average patterns of indirect teacher influence.

In the original study (Flanders, 1967), sixteen eighth grade maths teachers and sixteen seventh grade social science teachers were each observed. Achievement and attitude tests were administered to the pupils at the beginning and end of the study. The main conclusion of the research was that 'teachers who were able to provide flexible patterns of influence, by shifting from indirect to direct with the passage of time, created situations in which students learned more. The students of teachers unable to do this learned less.' (p. 234).

No direct evidence was obtained to support the three main hypotheses since no measure of the student's perception of the goal was attempted. Flanders argues that the evidence of more variability among indirect teachers, particularly in the initial stages of the two week unit, when goals would still remain unclear, lends strong support to these hypotheses, and that there are important implications for teaching in the results.

Flanders' system of Interaction Analysis has been used in process-product studies by many other researchers (Flanders, 1970). It has also been used in a prescriptive fashion in pre-service and in-service teacher training. Research on the effects of its use in teacher training has been reported. It can be assumed that the system is also used in reflective studies, since a manual (Amidon and Flanders, *The Role of the Teacher in the Classroom*, Pub. P. S. Amidon and Associates, Minneapolis) has been published especially for classroom teachers. It is described as introducing 'the notion of investigating verbal communication as an approach to the improvement of classroom instruction.'

A derivation of Flanders system is the *Verbal Interaction Category System* VICS, which was designed specifically 'to help teachers select their verbal behaviour so that their practice will be more in line with what they want it to be'. Thus it appears that this system was developed for use in reflective studies, since both teachers and prospective teachers could use it to increase their awareness of their own classroom verbal behaviour.

The system was designed to record both teacher and pupil verbal behaviour. It consists of twelve categories (see Figure 4) derived from Flanders' Interaction Analysis System. The *teacher asks questions* category is split into 'teacher asks narrow questions' and 'asks broad questions.' Pupil response and pupil initiation categories are subdivided to record whether the response or initiation was either to the teacher or to another pupil. The silence or confusion category is also divided. Recording is carried out by an observer who classifies the verbal behaviour into one of the twelve categories every three seconds. The results can be analysed by plotting them onto a matrix in the same way as is used for the Flanders' system.

In their book, *Improving Teaching*, Amidon and Hunter use this system of analysis to describe the teaching process. They see teaching as an interactive process in which the teacher engages with pupils. Activities which do not directly involve both teacher and pupil are not considered. The teaching function is broken down into the seven activities of motivating, planning, informing, leading discussion, disciplining, counselling and evaluating, and a chapter is devoted to each of these. Situations involving teachers and pupils in a particular activity are presented, followed by an analysis and discussion of the talk in terms of VICS. Practice situations are suggested in which the reader can try out verbal behaviour skills. It is inevitable that the authors' own prescription of good teaching is conveyed during these chapters either by accident or intent. If the course in this book is followed, then the VICS is being used in a prescriptive fashion since the student is endeavouring to achieve verbal skills which the authors regard as valuable.

**Figure 4: An outline of the categories in the verbal interaction category system** (Based on a description given by Maidoc and Hunter, *Improving Teaching – an analysis of classroom verbal interaction*. New York: Holt, Reinhart and Winston, 1967, p. 4.)

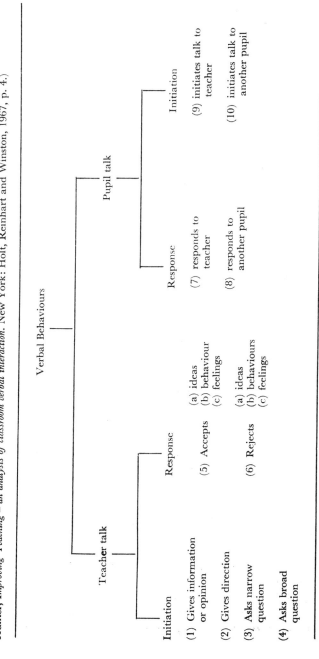

Verbal Behaviours

Teacher talk

Initiation

(1) Gives information or opinion

(2) Gives direction

(3) Asks narrow question

(4) Asks broad question

Response

(5) Accepts
  (a) ideas
  (b) behaviour
  (c) feelings

(6) Rejects
  (a) ideas
  (b) behaviours
  (c) feelings

Pupil talk

Response

(7) responds to teacher

(8) responds to another pupil

Initiation

(9) initiates talk to teacher

(10) initiates talk to another pupil

It is perhaps surprising that our search for examples of studies like those of Wright which gave rise to observation systems derived directly from statements of behavioural objective or outcomes was almost fruitless. Presumably the recent spate of curriculum development especially in science has involved excursions by curriculum developers into 'the field' when some attention must have been given to the interactions observed while their materials were being used. If this is so, such observations as have been made either used existing instruments or more frequently failed to yield published reports. One instrument, which was developed specifically to record teacher and student behaviour in relation to a new science curriculum, claimed by its authors to be the only one, is the Earth Science Curriculum Observation Instrument (Smith, 1970). It was developed as follows:

Articles about ESCP and the books produced by the project team were studied to provide a selection of statements as to the behaviour expected of teachers and pupils when using the package. These effectively constituted a retrospective statement of the course objectives. Categories of the instrument were then drawn up so that behaviours consonant with these objectives could be observed. A further source of categories were observations and audiotape recordings made with a teacher using the Earth Science Curriculum package. Categories from this source were therefore derived inductively. The categories finally included in the instrument were selected on the basis of ratings made by six judges. Each of the categories was rated using a three point scale consistent, neutral, or inconsistent with ESCP philosophy of inquiry, and the resulting categories of both teacher and student behaviours were divided into four major classroom situations: developing text material, pre-laboratory and laboratory activity, and post-laboratory discussion. All but three of the 92 categories relate to behaviours in the cognitive domain. Some of the categories, such as 'Teacher emphasizes historical development of knowledge in earth science' are specific to this subject but could be modified to fit other contexts. The majority of categories cover the type of teacher and student behaviours one would expect in any laboratory- or inquiry-based science lesson.

The ESCP Observation Schedule is a sign system without any fixed form of sampling unit. Each behaviour taking place in the classroom is recorded every time it is observed by the trained observer. Inter-observer reliabilities of 74 per cent were obtained when each of three teachers were visited by six observers working in pairs. This figure is based upon the overall percentage agreement between the three pairs of observers.

It has not been possible to trace the use of this system of observation but, given reliability and validity, there are a number of potential applications. Matching studies could be carried out to compare and contrast the way that teachers teach with ESCP materials as against the way apparently prescribed by the developers. Such matching studies could be incorporated into a curriculum evaluation programme either at the formative stage to recycle the material until the objectives of the package are met, or at the summative stage where the observed behaviour could be related to the learning.

**The conceptual map**

These *case studies* which we have described have been used to exemplify the main distinctions developed earlier, which enable interaction systems to be grouped and classified according to the purpose for which they were designed. However this criterion of classification is often inadequate and difficult to apply. For instance, authors may not make the purpose clear in their report, or a system may be taken by other workers to be used for a totally different purpose. Thus it is necessary to proceed a stage further and elaborate our classification into two dimensions, both based on factors closely related to purpose. The first is concerned with the way in which the system is developed and the second is that of uses to which the interaction system is put.

Three groups can be identified for the way in which the system was developed but they are not mutually exclusive. One group contains those studies which were developed inductively, e.g. Smith. Here the authors had no preconceived ideas of the categories of classroom behaviours they would eventually incorporate into a schedule. The categories of behaviour were evolved by repeated study of videotapes of transcripts of lessons. The second group consists of those whose categories of behaviour were more or less explicitly based on some theory, e.g. Gallagher. The third group consists of systems in which the categories of behaviour are defined in terms of behavioural objectives. This could be regraded as a sub-set of the second group since if the objectives selected for observation categories are also the objectives of a particular curriculum development, they may be curriculum developers' theoretical constructs (or simply beliefs) of the classroom process.

But the method used to develop the interaction system is not of itself sufficient to provide a comprehensive basis for classifying all systems. We therefore added a second dimension to our classification, that of uses to which the interaction system is put. These again fall into three groups, firstly process studies where the system of interaction analysis is used to provide a description; secondly comparative studies, where for example, the description of one class is compared with another, or one group of teachers with another; and thirdly process-product studies in which the description is related to some measurable change in the pupils.

These two dimensions can be used as the axes of a matrix, as in Table 4. The cells of the matrix relate the uses to which these systems have been put to the ways in which they were developed. It will be seen from the matrix that observation systems developed in a particular way tend to lend themselves to particular uses. Inductive studies by their nature lead to generalizations and to new information about patterns of behaviour. Systems based on theories (or beliefs) have a special application when they are used for comparison in teacher training either in a reflective or prescriptive fashion. In such cases, a teacher's behaviour is either compared with that which he desires to exhibit (reflective study) or with that his supervisor prescribes (prescriptive study). In both cases, the behaviours selected are believed to be effective or necessary in achieving certain outcomes without any empirical evidence to support this view. Process-product studies using these systems involve the testing of hypotheses. The behaviours observed are ones believed to be related to particular measurable outcomes, and the acceptance or rejection of the hypotheses is subject to statistical testing.

This group of studies in the third column of the matrix has a particular application in the area of curriculum development. They can be used comparatively when the behaviour of a teacher using an old curriculum is described in the same terms as one using a new curriculum. Yet another important use of matching studies is during *formative* evaluation when the actual teaching behaviour resulting from the use of a new curriculum can be compared with that hopefully prescribed by the curriculum developers. When this class of systems is used in a process-product study, curriculum evaluation

**Table 4: Classification of studies described in this paper**

| Purpose for which system was designed or used | Origin-Relationship to theory | | |
|---|---|---|---|
| | *Inductively derived systems* | *Explicit theory based systems* | *Systems based on behaviourally defined objectives/outcomes* |
| Process Studies | Smith & Meux 2, 11, 12, 13 Nuthall & Lawrence 20 | Aschner-Gallagher 14 | Wright 19 |
| Comparative Studies | | | |
| Prescriptive | | Amidon 34 | |
| Reflective | | Amidon 34 Flanders 32 | |
| Matching | | Gallagher 28 | Smith 35 |
| Inter-subject comparisons | Smith 13 | Gallagher 16 | |
| Process-product Studies | Nuthall 23 Tischer 23 | Flanders 9 | |

is carried out. The observation instrument can be used to ensure that the teaching conforms to the prescription defined by the developers, and the outcomes measured can then be related to a definite process. It can also be used to monitor the way in which teachers mediate between the curriculum package when an experimental comparison is made during *summative evaluation*.

In conclusion, we would refer the reader's attention to an article by Rosenshine and Furst on 'The Use of Direct Observation to Study Teaching' which became available in England after the development of our 'conceptual map.' As a prerequisite to assesing the use of observation instruments, they found it necessary to classify them on two separate systems, firstly, according to the source of the variables and secondly, according to the author's purpose in developing the instrument.

The classification on the basis of source of the variables had four sections:

(i)    instruments with explicit theoretical or empirical base
(ii)   instruments with implicit theoretical or empirical base
(iii)  modifications or syntheses of existing category systems
(iv)   Author-originated category (these contain variables the author believed important but did not specify their origin).

As they write, this classification separates 'the authors who apparently drew their variables out of the air from the authors who developed their variables from painstaking reading and thought' (Rosenshine, 1973, p. 146). Unfortunately, this classification is highly dependant on the extent to which authors describe the development process. Our classification on the basis of the development is also dependant on the fullness of the author's report but additional clues can be obtained from the purpose the system is used for and the nature of the categories.

Rosenshine and Furst divide the classification based on the purposes and uses of the observation systems into four groups. They are:

(i)    to describe current classroom practise
(ii)   to train teachers
(iii)  to monitor instructional systems
(iv)   to investigate relationships between classroom activities and student growth.

All these four groups can be found within our conceptual map, but a greater understanding is gained within this matrix by viewing them as particular examples of the purposes of the more generalized groups of uses.

It is interesting to note the similarities in our two approaches, for example the choice of criteria for the classifications. However, we feel that our two dimensional matrix with its broad generalized groups provides a more useful basis for understanding the observational systems already developed and gives a perspective framework for future authors. Nevertheless, there will always be difficulties of classification and the boundaries will sometimes be blurred. It may be that if Rosenshine and Furst's distinction between implicit an explicit theory can be sustained a useful fusion of the two systems might be possible.

## References

AMIDON, E. and HUNTER E. (1967). *Improving Teaching, the Analysis of Classroom Verbal Interaction.* New York: Holt, Rinehart & Winston, Inc.

BELLACK, A. A., KLIEBARD, H. M., HYMAN, R. T. and SMITH F. L. (1966). *The Language of the Classroom.* New York: Teachers' College Press.

BIDDLE, B. J. and ADAMS, R. S. (1967). *An Analysis of Classroom Activity.* Columbia: Center of Research in Social Behaviour, University of Missouri.

FLANDERS, N. A. (1965). *Teacher Influence, Pupil Attitudes and Achievement.* Co-operative Research Monograph No. 12, US Department of Health, Education and Welfare.

FLANDERS, N. A. (1967). 'Some relationships among teacher influence, pupil attitudes and achievement.' In: AMIDON, E. J. and HOUGH J. B. (Ed.) *Interaction Analyses: Theory, Research and Application.* Reading, Mass.: Addison-Wesley Publishing Co.

FLANDERS, N. A. (1970). *Analysing Teaching Behaviour.* New York: Addison-Wesley Publishing Co.

GALLAGHER, J. J. (1967). 'Teacher variation in concept presentation in BSCS curriculum program,' *BSCS Newsletter,* No. 30.

GALLAGHER, J. J. (1970). 'A "Topic classification system" for classroom observation.' In: GALLAGHER, J. J., NUTHALL, G. A. and ROSENSHINE. B. *Classroom Observation.* AFRA Monograph Series No. 6. Chicago: Rand, McNally & Co.

GALLAGHER, J. J., ASCHNER, M. J. and JENNE W. (1967). *Productive Thinking of Gifted Children in Classroom Interaction.* CEC Research Monograph Series B, No. B-5.

MEDLEY, D. and MITZEL H. E. (1963). 'Measuring classroom behaviour by systematic observation.' In GAGE, N. L. *Handbook of Research on Teaching.* A project of the American Educational Research Association. Chicago: Rand, McNally.

NUTHALL, G. A. and LAWRENCE P. J. (1965). *Thinking in the Classroom.* Wellington: New Zealand Council for Educational Research.

PARAKH, J. S. (1969). 'A study of teacher-pupil interaction in high school biology classes, Part 1. The development of a category system,' *J. Res. Science Teaching,* 6, 3.

ROSENSHINE, B. and FURST N. (1973). 'The use of direct observation to study teaching.' In: TRAVERS, R. M. W. (Ed.) *Second Handbook of Research on Teaching*. A project of the American Educational Research Association. Chicago: Rand, McNally.

RYANS, D. G. (1960). *Characteristics of Teachers*. Washington, DC: American Council on Education.

SIMON, A. and BOYER G. E. (1968). *Mirrors for Behaviour, an Anthology of Classroom Observation Instruments*. Philadelphia, Research for Better Schools, Inc.

SMITH, B. O., and MEUX, M. O. *et al.* (1967). *A Study of the Strategies of Teaching*. Urbana: Bureau of Educational Research, College of Education, University of Illinois.

SMITH, B. O., and MEUX, M. O. *et al.* (1970). *A Study of the Logic of Teaching*. Urbana: University of Illinois Press.

SMITH, J. P. (1970). 'The development of a classroom observation instrument relevant to the earth sciences curriculum project,' *J. Res. Science Teaching*, **8**, No. 3.

TISHER, R. P. (1970). 'The nature of verbal discourse in classrooms.' In: CAMPBELL, W. J. (Ed.) *Scholars in Context, the Effects of Environment on Learning*. Wiley & Sons Australasia Pty Ltd.

TISHER, R. P. (1970). 'Association between verbal discourse and pupils' understanding in Science.' In: CAMPBELL, W. J. (Ed.) *Scholars in Context, the Effects of Environments on Learning*. Wiley & Sons Australasia Pty Ltd.

WRIGHT, E. M. J. (1959). 'Development of an instrument for studying verbal behaviours in a secondary school mathematics classroom,' *J. Exp. Educ.*, **28**, 2.

# CHAPTER 5

# Teaching Styles: A Typological Approach

*S. N. Bennett, Department of Educational Research, University of Lancaster*

## Teaching styles

Research on teaching styles has been characterized by the use of inadequately defined terms. Wallen and Travers (1963) were critical of the fact that teaching methods were not unambiguously defined, and later, Travers (1971) again noted that the problem of operational definition was particularly acute. 'It is in this area' he contended 'that we have a long tradition of using very sloppy and hazy variables such as traditional *v.* progressive, pupil centred *v.* teacher centred, or authoritarian *v.* democratic. All these have been 'defined' in terms of general categories of behaviour, but since the limits of the categories are never specified the concepts remain obscure.' Stones (1973) argued similarly with reference to the term 'discovery'. 'The use of the word to refer to a vague and undifferentiated set of concepts in a general undifferentiated way causes severe problems. Spurious consensus is inevitable if the one word means all, and different, things to different people.' Kendler (1966) has even argued for the abolition of such nine letter dirty words.

What would seem necessary is a breakdown of such terms into their constituent elements, since there is a possibility that they may be composed of independent factors. Soar (1967) demonstrated this with the term 'permissive'. Recent research has indicated that this term could involve two dimensions – the emotional climate of the classroom, and the degree of closeness of control of pupils exercised by the teacher. Thus teachers could show warmth toward pupils, but also exercise a high degree of control. In addition there may be two sub-divisions of control – tightness of control exercised by the teacher in verbal interaction with the pupils, and control of physical movement. Emotional climate may also be subdivided, one facet being the expression of affect by the teacher, and the other being the expression of affect by the pupils. Similar analyses have been carried out on the terms used in experimental studies of teaching methods. Siegel and Siegel (1967), for example, commented that 'what has been named one mode of instruction ... in many instances can instead be considered as a quite heterogenous set of events.' It is perhaps not surprising therefore, that the global terms used by researchers have failed to relate to pupil outcomes in any consistent way.

The situation is further confused by the fact that the same terms are often used to refer to different aspects of the classroom, and different terms to refer to essentially the same aspects. In commenting on this confusion Herbert (1967) bemoaned the fact that 'descriptions of particular (teaching) methods are too vague or inconsistent to permit an observer to distinguish them in practice.' The current trend of using observational schedules to categorize teacher behaviours appears to have exacerbated this. There are now in excess of one hundred such schedules, many of which assess similar aspects of teacher behaviour, but which use different constructs to label that behaviour. Furthermore, since most schedules are used only by their creators, the extent of overlap of these schedules has yet to be established (Rosenshine and Furst, 1973).

An additional drawback of observation schedules is that they rarely provide an adequate description of the teaching situation, since they typically concentrate on a very narrow range of teacher and pupil behaviour. Nuthall and Snook (1973) recently stated that 'the current emphasis on observational studies has produced a proliferation of observational systems and frequency counts of the *minutiae* of teacher and student behaviours in their daily situation,' and Rosenshine and Furst (1973) added that, 'Current observation instruments disregard the materials being read, the assignments students write, the teacher's use of written and oral material, the physical features of the room, such as seating arrangements and lighting.'

Poor sampling of classroom events is paralleled by poor sampling of teachers. 'The inherent complexity of the classroom setting, and the consequent cost of researching it, have ensured that samples are small, that representativeness is rare, and that random selection is almost never achieved' (Adams, 1972).

It would therefore appear that investigators have commonly observed a narrow range of the behaviour of a small and unrepresentative sample of teachers, drawn from a population of unknown parameters, and have categorized them according to some global, ill-defined, dichotomy.

Although rarely used, questionnaire approaches have provided comprehensive information of a more general nature about classrooms. Adams (1970) developed a questionnaire to gain data on the perceived teaching practices of 12,293 teachers in the United Kingdom, Australia, New Zealand, and the United States. The questionnaire was composed of twenty-one items covering seven areas: content orientation, cognitive emphasis; interaction mode; organizational differentiation; control source; control mode; and motivational mode. However, since it was specifically developed for a comparative study, the analyses carried out are of little value in this context.

Of direct relevance is the study carried out by Simon (1972) on 189 primary school teachers in Leicestershire. The study set out to achieve two objectives: Firstly, to gain evidence about how innovations like modern teaching methods affect classroom organization, since 'very little is known in practice about how teachers organize either the classroom furniture, or the children's locations, movement and work.' Secondly, to collect data which could be used as the basis for some type of classification system which 'goes far beyond misleading simple terms like formal-informal, and progressive-traditional.'

To collect the information a three part questionnaire was developed to gain data on streaming and general school policy, aspects of classroom geography, and how teachers organized children's work and activities. The results indicated that widely held beliefs about modern educational practices were misconceived. The use of ability grouping was widespread, and many teachers appeared to be teaching traditionally, whereas it is commonly assumed that most primary school teaching is progressive in orientation.

A classification of teaching approaches was not in fact attempted, but the author concluded that classroom data of this type needs to be subjected to some form of multivariate analysis to permit a conceptualization of the observed variability which reaches far beyond the widely used labels progressive and traditional. Stake (1970) has expressed similar views, arguing that what is needed is 'some easy to administer, easy to understand, not very controversial, but valid, method of describing teaching.' Something is needed that 'appeals to the clinical experience of the teacher and that suits the technical sophistication of administrators and laymen. Common prose is not the answer. There is some general understanding when one says "lecture" or "authoritarian style", or "discovery method", but also misunderstanding.' He recommended multidimensional typologies of teaching styles, but noted that, 'Educators are offended by typploges that . . . might lead to some greater understanding of what is happening in their classroom. To call a Professor "Type III" or even "Type 3-16-4-0-9" is to invite being spat on. Yet the need for description, classification, and even over-simplification is apparent.'

As a first step to an understanding of the effects of teaching styles on pupil growth, an attempt has been made to provide a valid typology of teaching styles based on the self reported teaching practices of a representative sample of primary school teachers.

## The Questionnaire

In an attempt to overcome the problem of definition of terms, a review of relevant educational and psychological theory was

**Table 1: Characteristics of progressive and traditional teaching**

| *Progressive* | *Traditional* |
|---|---|
| 1. Integrated subject matter | 1. Separate subject matter |
| 2. Teacher as guide to educational experiences | 2. Teacher as distributor of knowledge |
| 3. Active pupil role | 3. Passive pupil role |
| 4. Pupils participate in curriculum planning | 4. Pupils have little or no say in curriculum planning |
| 5. Learning predominantly by discovery | 5. Accent on memory, practice and rote |
| 6. External rewards and punishments not necessary i.e. intrinsic motivation | 6. External rewards used e.g. stars, grades, i.e. extrinsic motivation |
| 7. Low teacher control on pupil movement and talk | 7. High teacher control on movement and talk |
| 8. Little testing | 8. Regular testing |
| 9. Accent on co-operative group work | 9. Accent on competition |
| 10. Teaching not confined to classroom base | 10. Teaching confined to classroom base |
| 11. Accent on creative expression | 11. Little emphasis on creative expression |

undertaken. This involved an examination of the philosophy underlying child centred or progressive education, the Progressive Education Movement, and its critics. It involved an examination of psychological theories of learning, and the controversy surrounding discovery learning, and an examination of relevant educational reports, particularly the Hadow Report (1931) and Plowden Report (1966). These sources were supplemented by information gained from interviews with primary school head and class teachers. These were undertaken to acquire the practitioners' perceptions of the elements constituting the different teaching approaches apparent in primary classrooms.

From these diverse sources it was possible to isolate the elements involved in the global terms progressive and traditional. Some of these elements are presented in table 1.

These elements were translated into classroom behaviours, and then into questionnaire items. The questionnaire finally contained six major areas:

　　Classroom management and organization
　　Teacher control and sanctions
　　Curriculum content and planning
　　Instructional strategies
　　Motivational techniques
　　Assessment procedures

Two pilot studies were carried out to enable the reduction and modification of ambiguous items. The final form contained twenty-eight items, although a number were in multiple form. Question 28 for example required a breakdown of the time spent on every aspect of the syllabus in the last full week prior to completing the questionnaire. The final form was included as a separate section within a larger questionnaire concerning details of school, teachers, and teacher attitudes.

Since the major aim was to create a typology of teaching styles it was necessary to gain a large and representative sample. An attempt was therefore made to carry out a census of all third and fourth year primary school teachers in the new administrative counties of Lancashire and Cumbria. This gave a total sampling frame of 871 schools situated in diverse geographical areas, from the centres of large industrial towns to isolated moorland villages.

The questionnaires were posted to each head teacher for distribution to the class teachers. In addition to a covering letter explaining the purposes of the study, and a stamped addressed envelope for the return of the completed questionnaire, each class teacher was provided with a separate envelope in which to seal his/her completed questionnaire. This was to ensure confidentiality. After two follow-up letters 88 per cent of schools responded, representing 1258 teachers. A further 3 per cent responded regretting their inability to take part due to various personal or organizational problems.

## General teaching pattern

The responses of third year, third and fourth year mixed, and fourth year teachers were analysed separately to ascertain whether differences in teaching style were apparent at different age levels. A striking similarity of response to most items was found, suggesting that overall, teaching styles are not influenced by age of pupil at the top end of the junior school. The three groups were therefore combined to gain the following general picture of primary school practice.

Most teachers sit their pupils separately or in pairs, rather than larger groups, and the pupils remain in the same seat for most activities. Teachers who seat their pupils by ability are in the minority, but this does not imply a high level of pupil choice in seating since less than half the teachers allow this.

Teacher control of the physical movement of pupils is generally high. More than two-thirds curb movement and talk, and a similar proportion expect their pupils to be quiet most of the time. Discipline does not appear to be a problem at this level. Less than one in ten teachers claim to have many children who create discipline problems, and 95 per cent find that verbal reproof is usually sufficient to deal with such problems. Nevertheless, for persistent disruptive behaviour a number of other measures are used. Most common are withdrawal of privileges, extra work, and smacking. Over half the teachers admit to smacking.

Teachers were asked how they organized work in the class, and to indicate the emphasis placed on teacher talk, individual *v.* group work, and teacher-given *v.* pupil-chosen work. The results, in terms of the percentage of time devoted to each type of activity, are as follows:

| | |
|---|---|
| Teacher talking to whole class | 19% |
| Pupils working in groups on teacher tasks | 21% |
| Pupils working in groups on pupil chosen tasks | 10% |
| Pupils working individually on teacher tasks | 37% |
| Pupils working individually on pupil chosen tasks | 13% |

It can be seen that, in general, individual work is more favoured than group work, and that the proportion of time set aside for work chosen by pupils is much less than that for teacher chosen tasks.

Teachers were also asked to indicate the number of hours devoted to each subject area in the last full week preceding the completion of the questionnaire. Three groupings were made of this data. 'Academic' subjects taught separately, including number work, English, Reading, History, Geography, French, Science and Scripture. 'Aesthetic' subjects, including PE, music, art and craft, music and movement and drama. 'Integrated' subjects, including environmental studies, social studies, project and topic work and free choice periods.

Of the estimated twenty-five hours a week devoted to teaching in primary schools, $15\frac{1}{4}$ hours are devoted to academic subjects, 5 hours to aesthetic subjects, and $4\frac{3}{4}$ hours to integrated subjects. These figures would indicate that a subject-centred curriculum predominates at this level. In organizing the curriculum it was found that 80 per cent of teachers use a timetable other than for specialist activities.

The findings on evaluation and assessment show that although relatively few teachers mark or grade work regularly, most of them correct spelling and grammatical errors. Sixty per cent administer tests of spelling and arithmetic every week, and over half give tests at the end of each term. Eighty per cent require their pupils to know their multiplication tables off by heart, and over one-third give homework regularly.

## A typology of teaching styles

Although this analysis is of interest it fails to isolate the wide variety of styles adopted by teachers. A cluster analysis was therefore computed, the statistical details of which are documented elsewhere (Bennett and Jordan, 1975). Basically the cluster analysis grouped teachers together who had given similar responses to all the questionnaire items. These groups are often denoted 'types' which

McQuitty (1967) defines as 'a category of persons wherein everyone in the category is more like every other person in the category then he is like any other person in any other category.' The analysis reported here is of the 468 fourth year teachers based on nineteen questionnaire items chosen by factor analysis. Twelve teacher 'types' were extracted from the cluster analysis, and the distribution of responses on the nineteen items for each type is shown in Table 2. Figures in heavy type indicate response levels that are considered significantly different from the total population distribution.

The twelve 'types' or styles are described as follows:

*Type 1* These teachers favour integration of subject matter, and, unlike most other groups, allow pupil choice of work, whether undertaken individually or in groups. Most allow pupils choice of seating. Less than half curb movement and talk. Assessment in all its forms, tests, grading, and homework appears to be discouraged. Intrinsic motivation is favoured.

*Type 2* These teachers also prefer integration of subject matter. Teacher control appears to be low, but offer less pupil choice of work. However, most allow pupils choice of seating, and only one-third curb movement and talk. Few test or grade work.

*Type 3* The main teaching mode of this group is class teaching and group work. Integration of subject matter is preferred, associated with taking pupils out of school. They appear to be strict, most curbing movement and talk, and offenders are smacked. The amount of testing is average, but the amount of grading and homework is below average.

*Type 4* These teachers prefer separate subject teaching but a high proportion allow pupil choice of work both in groups and individual work. None seat their pupils by ability. They test and grade more than average.

*Type 5* A mixture of separate subject and integrated subject teaching is characteristic of this group. The main teaching mode is pupils working in groups of their own choice on tasks set by the teacher. Teacher talk is lower than average. Control is high with regard to

**Table 2: Central profiles (percentage occurrence) at 12 cluster level**

| Item | 1 | 2 | 3 | 4 | 5 | 6 | 7 | 8 | 9 | 10 | 11 | 12 |
|---|---|---|---|---|---|---|---|---|---|---|---|---|
| | | | | | | *Type* | | | | | | |
| 1. Pupils have choice in where to sit | 63 | 66 | 17 | 46 | 50 | 18 | 7 | 17 | 3 | 7 | 77 | 00 |
| 2. Pupils allocated to seating by ability | 14 | 16 | 25 | 0 | 12 | 45 | 20 | 7 | 81 | 58 | 3 | 50 |
| 3. Pupils not allowed freedom of movement in the classroom | 49 | 38 | 83 | 76 | 100 | 84 | 87 | 100 | 86 | 97 | 97 | 100 |
| 4. Teacher expects pupils to be quiet | 31 | 34 | 92 | 61 | 23 | 55 | 56 | 90 | 81 | 74 | 90 | 100 |
| 5. Pupils taken out of school regularly as normal teaching activity | 51 | 50 | 83 | 49 | 81 | 45 | 17 | 47 | 31 | 19 | 26 | 42 |
| 6. Pupils given homework regularly | 9 | 22 | 8 | 27 | 65 | 3 | 13 | 43 | 36 | 29 | 21 | 56 |
| 7. *Teaching emphasis* (i) Above average teacher talks to whole class | 29 | 16 | 79 | 58 | 30 | 74 | 83 | 73 | 33 | 94 | 85 | 70 |
| 8. (ii) Above average pupils working in groups on teacher tasks | 46 | 13 | 83 | 12 | 77 | 92 | 3 | 3 | 22 | 68 | 10 | 8 |
| 9. (iii) Above average pupils working in groups on work of own choice | 89 | 3 | 29 | 94 | 19 | 32 | 13 | 3 | 0 | 23 | 0 | 0 |
| 10. (iv) Above average pupils working individually on teacher tasks | 9 | 97 | 0 | 3 | 42 | 0 | 73 | 83 | 100 | 0 | 72 | 92 |
| 11. (v) Above average pupils working individually on work of own choice | 94 | 9 | 42 | 85 | 42 | 18 | 57 | 57 | 8 | 3 | 8 | 28 |
| 12. Pupils' work marked and graded | 3 | 3 | 13 | 15 | 31 | 16 | 33 | 33 | 8 | 32 | 31 | 97 |
| 13. Stars given to pupils who produce best work | 9 | 31 | 38 | 55 | 8 | 18 | 17 | 73 | 17 | 87 | 69 | 75 |
| 14. Arithmetic tests given at least once a week | 9 | 9 | 71 | 88 | 100 | 8 | 10 | 70 | 50 | 94 | 56 | 81 |
| 15. Spelling tests given at least once a week | 23 | 19 | 67 | 94 | 92 | 18 | 7 | 73 | 92 | 94 | 87 | 92 |
| 16. Teacher smacks for persistent disruptive behaviour | 34 | 34 | 96 | 24 | 31 | 45 | 80 | 93 | 42 | 68 | 64 | 58 |
| 17. Teacher sends pupil out of room for persistent disruptive behaviour | 11 | 25 | 13 | 6 | 8 | 3 | 7 | 10 | 25 | 0 | 33 | 11 |
| 18. Allocation of teaching time (i) Above average separate subject teaching | 20 | 31 | 4 | 82 | 81 | 95 | 100 | 81 | 81 | 100 | 100 | 92 |
| 19. (ii) Above average integrated subject teaching | 97 | 91 | 100 | 24 | 65 | 8 | 10 | 93 | 14 | 7 | 0 | 0 |
| *N in cluster* | 35 | 32 | 24 | 33 | 26 | 38 | 30 | 30 | 36 | 31 | 39 | 36 |

movement but not to talk. Most give tests every week and many give homework regularly. Stars are rarely used, and pupils are taken out of school regularly.

*Type 6* These teachers prefer to teach subjects separately with emphasis on groups working on teacher-specified tasks. The amount of individual work is small. These teachers appear to be fairly low on control, and are below average on assessment and the use of extrinsic motivation.

*Type 7* This group is separate subject orientated, with a high level of class teaching together with individual work. Teacher control appears to be tight, few allow movement or choice of seating, and offenders are smacked. Assessment, however, is low.

*Type 8* This group of teachers has very similar characteristics to those in type 3, the differences being that these prefer to organize the work on an individual rather than a group basis. Freedom of movement is restricted, and most expect pupils to be quiet.

*Type 9* These teachers favour separate subject teaching, the predominant teaching mode being individuals working on tasks set by the teacher. Teacher control appears to be high; most curb movement and talk, and seat by ability. Pupils choice is minimal. Regular spelling tests are given, but few mark or grade work, or use stars.

*Type 10* All these teachers favour separate subject teaching. The teaching mode favoured is teacher talk to whole class, and pupils working in groups determined by the teacher, on tasks set by the teacher. Most curb movement and talk, and over two-thirds smack for disruptive behaviour. There is regular testing and most give stars for good work.

*Type 11* All members of this group stress separate subject teaching by way of class teaching and individual work. Pupil choice of work is minimal, although most teachers allow choice in seating. Movement and talk are curbed, and offenders smacked.

*Type 12* This is an extreme group in a number of respects. None favour an integrated approach. Subjects are taught separately by class teaching and individual work. None allow pupils' choice of seating, and every teacher curbs movement and talk. These teachers are above average on all assessment procedures, and extrinsic motivation predominates.

The types have been ordered, for descriptive purposes, in order of distance from the most progressive cluster (type 1). This suggests that they can be represented by points on an continuum of 'progressive-traditional,' but this would be an over-simplification. The extreme types could be adequately described in these terms, but the remaining types all contain elements of both progressive and traditional practices.

## Validation

The analysis provides an indication that the ubiquitous use of dichotomous descriptions of teaching styles fail to take into account the multiplicity of elements involved. When construed unidimensionally as progressive-traditional only a minority of styles are adequately described. The majority of teachers appear to adopt a mixed or intermediate style for which the progressive-traditional dimension provides inadequate description.

However, the claim that the typology provides a more adequate description of classroom reality is of little value unless it can be established that the classification is valid. Evidence of validity has therefore been sought from three sources: ratings by research staff, ratings by local authority advisers, and descriptions of the school day by the pupils.

Thirty-six teachers, whose responses most closely matched the central profiles of seven of the twelve clusters, have agreed to participate in the second stage of the project. It is from this group of teachers that evidence concerning validity has been derived. Research staff spent two days in each of the classrooms during the course of data collection, and on their return were asked to write a description of each classroom based on the items in the questionnaire and cluster analysis. Although they were unaware of the cluster membership of the teachers, their reports related closely to the cluster descriptions.

The second source of evidence was gained from the LEA advisers. All the primary school advisers from all of the participating authorities attended a meeting at which the questionnaire, analysis, and cluster descriptions were discussed. Although the thirty-six teachers were already known to them, the advisers agreed to visit each teacher in their authority again and report their observations in terms of the questionnaire items and cluster descriptions. Again, the cluster membership of each teacher was unknown to them. An analysis of these reports indicated an 80 per cent agreement between their ratings and the cluster description.

Of interest was the fact that the research staff and the advisers isolated the same two instances where the way in which the teacher said he taught did not correspond too closely with how he was actually teaching. Fortunately these were isolated cases, and other indications are that response bias did not operate widely. The fact that the analysis delineated so few progressive teachers when there appears to be pressure to teach in this manner, and that so many teachers admitted to smacking when this is discouraged both by the LEAs and the NUT, are indications of this.

The third, and perhaps most interesting, source of evidence is that gained from content analyses of an essay written by all the pupils in the thirty-six classes entitled 'What I did at school yesterday.' In this they were asked to record as accurately as possible all that had happened at school the previous day. Nine classrooms have been analysed so far. Initially, two assistants were given the essays from the same class and were asked to provide independent descriptions of the classroom. The two descriptions were virtually identical, indicating a very high inter-judge agreement. Each has since been working independently. Here are brief descriptions of two classrooms to indicate the type of data gained from this approach.

*Class A* (Class teacher – Mrs B.) Mrs B. allows her children freedom of choice and of movement before school officially begins and before she enters the room, and this freedom is mirrored elsewhere in the school day. Most of the children begin the day with verbal reasoning, though a few work in books titled *Objective English* and *Word Perfect*. When they have completed verbal reasoning, the first choice point in the day occurs. As Andrew E. explains it,

> 'we did verble resoning. After working a bit we could finish our paintings. But I did clay modeling with Paul C. And he made an awful mess . . .'

While some children were building models and painting, others were working on projects such as fossils and water, while still others worked on *Objective English* or *Word Perfect*. The choice which children have here seems a real choice, without teacher 'management'; most of the children have finished their work before assembly and have time for a second activity.

After assembly and playtime, children who have not already done so are expected to finish off the verbal reasoning. Then they may select an activity, again with no apparent management from Mrs B. The 39 pupils split into 10 activities including *Word Perfect*, *Objective English*, projects, modelling (apparently from oddments), a play (involving three girls), sewing soft toys, making collages for an exhibition, drawing, clay work, and maths. The children take an especially active interest in the work during this period; both evaluative and descriptive comments were prevalent:

> Then after maths I started to do a drawing about a war. The drawing had a main aircraft which had rockets on it. (Andrew G.)

> After playtime I started on the ship with David H. I made some brilliant steps for it. The ship was called the Graf Spee. (Christopher H.)

> Then Stephen and I did some clay modelling. I did a waterfall, but I didn't turn out right so I demolished it. (Jonathan S.).

> Then I did a play with Mary and Debbie. Debbie got Mandy and went away so Mary and I did it by ourself. We didn't do it all so we are going to finish it off tomorrow. (Louise B.).

Louise's comment indicates a firm expectation that tomorrow will once again include periods for pupil choice.

The choice period ends and the pupils move to one of three reading groups taken by Mr M., Mr K. and Mrs B. The children know which group to join, but it is not clear on what basis the groups are formed. This continues until lunch.

After lunch a short time is spent going over homework. A quiz follows, which had been requested by Stephen L. during the morning. This indicates that the pupils as well as the teacher are able to influence curriculum activity. The whole class are involved and it develops into a competition of boys versus girls.

During the last period most of the children are involved in a rehearsal for a Christmas play. The pupils who are not in the play can apparently choose what they would like to do in the classroom.

The degree of pupil choice in this classroom appears particularly high. All children had at least one choice period during the morning between playtime and reading. Most of the children had a second choice period just before morning assembly, and a few had a third choice time at the end of the day when the others were practising the Christmas play. Also all of the children had the opportunity for choice before school began when at least seven different activities were available without teacher supervision.

Class A was delineated as Type 1 by the cluster analysis, but this class was deliberately chosen to report for another reason: it highlights the effect of external factors or pressures on the teaching decisions taken. It may seem incongruous to some that a progressive teacher begins the day with verbal reasoning practice, and sets homework. However this is explained by the fact that the school is in an area which has retained the 11 + selection procedure. Separate analyses have been carried out relating factors such as the presence of selective examinations, size of school, church affiliation, and type of intake area, to teaching style adopted. The analyses demonstrate that each has a highly significant effect. Against this must be set the fact that these external variables are, to some extent, inter-related. Nevertheless, they indicate that these are real influences on the teaching styles adopted.

*Class B* (Class teacher – Mr M.) Before school a few of the boys play football in the playground, while one child goes into the building to open windows. After assembly their teacher, Mr M., 'gave us some of our marks from the test we had just took' (Pauline F.) until Mrs P. arrived to teach the class English.

After playtime, the class has French with Mrs H. 'who is the school only french teacher' (Ian C.). According to Andrew F. they 'learnt how to wright the numbers in French'.

After French, Mr M. returned to take part of the class swimming while 'the rest stay behind with Mrs P. doing Topic work' (Beverley H.). The topics were apparently determined by the individual students; Suzanne Ms topic book 'is on Ballet.' She later comments: 'When playtime finished I left school because I went to take my Ballet Exam at 3.00. Most of my friends hoped that I would do well.'

After dinnertime Mr M. 'gave out the names of the people who came in the Top Ten' (Suzanne M.). Several of the children reported positioning, and the exam results took up two periods in the day. Andrew F. reports: 'then at 2.10 we went down to the hall and had PE. We played a game called dogge ball. . . . Red's won every game, and I am in the Reds.'

After PE and playtime, the class wrote the composition 'Invisible for a Day' (this was for the project).

> When we came in Mr M. told us to get just our pencils out and I thought oh here we go another test. It was not a test it was a composition we had to write just like this one. (Nicola W.).

> We went in and wrote a composition about an Invisible day I made my story as funny as I could snipping strings of ballons making bottle of washing up liquid dance and frightening people I had fun both writing it and pretending to be Sylvia (Julie T.).

In contrast to class A no choice period is offered to pupils in this class. Choice within a session is only offered once i.e. topic work, but this almost seemed to be a 'filler' whilst the remainder of the class went swimming. Except for this period the class was taught as a whole throughout the day. There is an obvious stress on testing, extrinsic motivation and competition. It was delineated type 12 by the cluster analysis.

The content and sequence of the school day in classes A and B is presented in summary form in Table 3.

These brief outlines fail to do justice to the richness of the original descriptions. Nevertheless enough has been reported to demonstrate the type of information gained, and to indicate the usefulness of the technique as a complement to other approaches. For example, Hargreaves (1972) has argued that interaction analysis fails to explore the assumptions and perspectives of teachers and pupils. 'We discover little of the overall teacher-pupil relationship as it is experienced by the teacher or by individual pupils. Yet it is

**Table 3: Content and sequence of the school day for class A and B**

Class A: 39 pupils (Mrs B)

| Before school | Morning 1 | ASSEMBLY PLAY TIME | Morning 2 | Reading: | DINNER TIME | Afternoon 1 | Afternoon 2 |
|---|---|---|---|---|---|---|---|
| Badminton | Verbal Reasoning / Objective English | | Completing V. Reasoning | Mr M. | | Go Over Homework | Quiz: Boys v. Girls / Christmas Play Rehearsal |
| Reading | Models | | Word Perfect | Mr K. | | | |
| Drawing | Projects | | Object. English | Mrs B. | | | |
| Models | Word Perfect | | Projects | | | | |
| Word Perfect | Painting | | Models | | | | |
| Objective English | Objective English | | a play | | | | Soft toys |
| Chatting | Word Perfect | | soft toys | | | | project |
| | | | collage | | | | |
| | | | drawing | | | | |
| | | | clay | | | | |
| | | | maths | | | | |

Class B: 37 pupils (Mr M.)

| Before school | | Morning 1 | | Morning 2 | | Afternoon 1 | | Afternoon 2 |
|---|---|---|---|---|---|---|---|---|
| Football | A S S E M B L Y | Mr M. discussed their exam results | P L A Y  T I M E | Mrs H. French | D I N N E R  T I M E | Mr M. More exam results | P L A Y  T I M E | Composition: 'Invisible for a Day' |
| Opening Windows 'duty' | | Mrs P. English | | Mr M. Swimming | | PE | | |
| | | | | Mrs P. Topics | | | | |

Key: ——— School Organizational Framework

     – – – Class Activity changes

this relationship which may not only influence the meaning assigned to particular verbal statements or acts, but also exercise a pervasive influence which is not immediately obvious or directly open to measurement by traditional methods.' Content analysis of relevant pupil output could provide this sort of information. According to Kerlinger (1973), content analysis is a method of observation. 'Instead of observing people's behaviour directly, or asking them to respond to scales, or interviewing them, the investigator takes the communications that people have produced, and asks questions of the communicator.' In this instance classroom action has been observed through the eyes of the pupils, and would appear to have certain advantages. It can, for example, be considered a low inference procedure – an activity occurs, the children involved report it, the investigator tallies it, and incorporates it in the description. Since some thirty children are often describing the same event the resultant description would seem to have high reliability and validity.

## Postcript to Plowden

The cluster analysis of teaching styles makes possible a comparison between current practice and current conceptions of that practice. The Plowden Report described a pattern of teaching which it maintained, represented a general and quickening trend. It was stated that the primary school 'sets out deliberately to devise the right environment for children, to allow them to be themselves, and to develop in a way, and at a pace appropriate to them. . . . It lays special stress on individual opportunities for creative work. It insists that knowledge does not fall into neatly separate compartments and that work and play are not opposite but complementary.' The report prescribed self-chosen activity at the expense of class teaching so that the teacher could adopt a consultative, guiding, and stimulating role rather than a purely didactic one. Project work, centres of interest, and integration of subject matter were suggested together with visits outside the school to allow children to experience their immediate environment.

Extrinsic rewards such as marks and stars were deprecated in favour of strengthening children's intrinsic interest in learning. Punishment was severely forwned upon, being linked with 'psychological perversion.' Group work, communication between children in class, and non-streaming were all to be encouraged.

Later writers have attempted to quantify this 'general trend.' Blackie (1967) maintained that a third of primary schools were working along these lines, and Silberman (1970), drawing upon the work of Rogers (1970), felt safe in saying that 25 per cent of English primary schools fitted the Plowden model, and that another third were moving towards it. Simon's study did not substantiate this trend however, and neither do the findings reported here. Only Type 1 corresponds closely to the Plowden definition, containing just 9 per cent of the population studied. A separate analysis of third year teachers isolated similar types, and the corresponding group at this level contained only 8 per cent of the population. It could of course be argued that the sample studied is not representative of primary teachers as a whole. This may be true, but the HMI study of teaching practices, contained in the Plowden Report, found little regional variation. These findings together with those provided by Simon indicate that progressive teaching is less prevalent than has hitherto been supposed.

**Conclusion**

It was argued earlier that research on teaching styles has suffered from inadequate definition of terms, and a tendency to concentrate on narrow ranges of behaviours of unrepresentative samples of teachers. The typology appears to overcome these problems. The 'types' are defined in terms of a wide range of classroom behaviour, and are based on a large group of teachers who are representative of their region if not the country as a whole.

The major purpose of the typology was to provide an indication of the diversity of teaching styles so that a representative sample of these styles could be chosen for the second stage of the study. In this, thirty-six teachers and their 1250 pupils are being studied over a period of one school year. Pre- and post-tests have been administered which included a wide range of cognitive and affective measures. From these data it will be possible not only to relate teaching styles to pupil growth, but also to assess the effect of differing teaching styles on different types of pupil. Most studies in this area have been designed to answer the question, 'Is teaching style A better than teaching style B?' But answers to simple questions such as this throw little light on the complex interacting factors which are involved in determining levels of pupil growth. The study has therefore been designed to answer the question, 'Do teaching styles interact with the personality or cognitive characteristics of pupils to produce differential achievement?' Answers to questions of this sort will, it is hoped, provide a better understanding of the effects of classroom processes on pupil products.

## References

ADAMS, R. S. (1970). 'Perceived teaching styles', *Comp. Educ. Rev.*, Feb., 50–59.

ADAMS, R. S. (1972). 'Observational studies of teacher role', *Int. Rev. Educ.*, **18**, 440–459.

BENNETT, S. N. and JORDAN J. (1975). 'A typology of teaching styles', *Brit. J. Educ. Psychol.*, Feb.

BLACKIE, J. (1967). *Inside the Primary School*. London: HMSO.

CENTRAL ADVISORY COUNCIL FOR EDUCATION (1966). *Children and their Primary Schools*. London: HMSO.

HARGREAVES, D. H. (1972). *Interpersonal Relations and Education*. London: Routledge and Kegan Paul.

HERBERT, J. (1967). *A System of Analysing Lessons*. New York: Teachers College Press.

KENDLER, H. H. (1966). In: SHULMAN, L. S. and KEISLER E. R. (Eds.) *Learning By Discovery: A Critical Appraisal*. Chicago: Rand McNally.

KERLINGER, F. N. (1973). *Foundations of Behavioural Research*. New York: Holt, Rinehart & Winston (2nd Edition).

MCQUITTY, L. L. (1967). 'A mutual development of some typological theories and pattern analysis methods', *Educ. Psychol. Meas.*, **26**, 253–265.

NUTHALL, G. and SNOOK J. (1973). 'Contemporary models of teaching.' Ch. II in TRAVERS, R. M. W. (Ed.) *The Second Handbook of Research on Teaching*. Chicago: Rand McNally.

Report of the Consultative Committee on the Primary School (Hadow) (1931). HMSO. London: Reprinted 1959.

ROGERS, V. R. (1970). *Teaching in the British Primary Schools*. New York: Macmillan.

ROSENSHINE, B. and FURST N. (1973). 'The use of direct observation to study teaching.' In: TRAVERS, R. M. W. (Ed.) *The Second Handbook of Research on Teaching*. Chicago: Rand McNally.

SIEGAL, L. and SIEGAL, L. C. (1967). 'The instructional gestalt'. Ch. IX. In: SIEGAL, L. (Ed.) *Instruction: Some Contemporary Viewpoints*. San Francisco: Chandler.

SILBERMAN, C. E. (1970). *Crisis in the Classroom*. New York: Random House.

SIMON, B. (1972). 'The nature of classroom learning in primary schools.' Final Report to SSRC. HR 291.

SOAR, R. S. (1967). 'Whither research on teacher behaviour?,' *Classroom Int. News*, **3**, 9–11.

STAKE, R. E. (1970). 'The decision: does classroom observation belong in an evaluative plan?' In: GALLAGHER, J. J., NUTHALL, G. A. and ROSENSHINE B. (Eds.) *Classroom Observation*, AERA Series on Evaluation 6. Chicago: Rand McNally.

STONES, E. (1973). 'Voyage of discovery', *Education*, 3–13, 1, 18–22.

TRAVERS, R. M. W. (1971). 'Some further reflections on the nature of a theory of instruction.' In: WESTBURY, I. and BELLACK A. A. (Eds.) *Research into Classroom Processes*. New York: Teachers' College Press.

WALLEN, N. E. and TRAVERS R. M. W. (1962). 'Analysis and investigation of teaching method.' In: GAGE, N. L. (Ed.) *Handbook of Research on Teaching*. Chicago: Rand McNally.

CHAPTER 6

# Teacher-centred Strategies in Interaction Research

*A. Morrison, University of Dundee*

Classroom interaction research is now well established in Britain. The contending theoretical lobbies have moved in, each offering ways of representing the persons, processes and events of teaching and learning, and it has become a mark of respectability in research to carry out direct observation and intensive interviewing of teachers and pupils as they go about their everyday activities. Undoubtedly, these developments are having a refreshing influence upon educational research as a whole; opening up new ways of analysing educational practice and producing descriptive and explanatory findings of great theoretical and applied interest. At the same time, teachers and research workers are having to consider carefully what kinds of working relationships they are to foster if interaction research is to fulfil some of its promise to bring theory and practice about classrooms more closely together.

In this paper my concern is less with the actual topics of interaction research than with the strategies for carrying them out. This emphasis is deliberate for two reasons. In the first place, I think that the actual topics of research and, of course, the effectiveness of their treatment, are to a considerable degree contingent upon the nature of the relationship between teachers and researchers; and, secondly, I suspect that we shall have to look beyond our conventional ways of initiating and conducting research if we are going to pay more than lip service to the views that many of us hold that research ought to be inherent in educational practice rather than some occasional event in the lives of teachers and their pupils, often distant from immediate, practical and localized concerns, and typically controlled by researchers.

Studies of teachers' attitudes towards educational research, and the reported impressions of researchers themselves, suggest a situation in which teachers are generally sympathetic towards investigations and very helpful in providing facilities, but at the same time critical of aspects of current policies. Their research priorities are not always well matched by the kinds of studies being done; on matters of great practical interest to them, such as subject-integrations, the grouping of pupils, open-design schools and imported innovations in curriculum and methods, they either feel that insufficient study is done or its value is reduced because it comes after the event rather than as an accompaniment to it; and too often they are left with the impression that research is conducted for the purposes of letting researchers indulge their taste for writing to one another in technical journals or fostering ideological debates which seem more concerned with the shortcomings of teachers and schools than with illuminating the diversities of thought and behaviour in classrooms.

Some of the criticisms can and are being met through improved communication with teachers, either in the sense of trying to reflect teachers' research interests in the choice of topics or through more effective means of explanation of the purpose of research and the wider dissemination of findings in respectable but non-technical forms. For some kinds of educational research, for example, large-scale descriptive surveys or studies of prime interest to various groups of educational specialists – administrators, teacher-educators, and the like – improved communication with teachers to help them to appreciate the purposes of studies and to explain the general implications of findings is the major means of developing closer relationships and better understanding. However, better public relations can only be a palliative; for the most part, many criticisms will only be met by encouraging those forms of research which, through the intrinsic interest of their content, their relevance and applicability to the defined situations of particular groups of teachers, their techniques of study, and their collaborative demands on all concerned in them, make teachers a part of the process of research rather than simply facilitators or – more in hope than realization – consumers of reports.

It is in just these respects that research on classroom interaction offers exciting possibilities for different relationships between teachers and investigators and for integrating research and practice. By its very nature it is located in the situations which have most significance for teachers and pupils; it demands face-to-face relationships between all the parties; and it opens up the means to a more informed dialogue between them on various practical but complex concerns on which both teachers and researchers are experts necessary to one another.

However, the opportunities presented do not in themselves guarantee that classroom interaction research will lead to the kinds of situations I have envisaged. On the one hand, it is difficult to predict the extent to which teachers will be willing or feel able to involve themselves in a conception of research which will make great demands upon them. Nothing is easier than for teachers to complain about current inadequacies of research and then reject different expectations of themselves on the grounds that they are too busy getting on with the job of teaching to get more heavily involved. Yet the assumption of such willingness is worth making and putting to the test; otherwise we shall never know. On the other hand, only by adopting some research strategies instead of others is it likely that interaction research will differ in real substance from those kinds of educational research criticized for their remoteness, abstruseness and minor practical relevance. The importance of appropriate strategies can be illustrated from our past experience with classroom interaction research. The term, of course, has been used as an umbrella for many different kinds of investigations and it is difficult to generalize; however, some characteristics of 'first generation' studies – reviewed elsewhere in this book – are disquieting. Teachers, or for that matter, pupils, have not played a significant part in formulating and developing investigations; there has been considerable borrowing or adaptation of techniques for studying classrooms from outside sources, for example, from the USA, without adequate consideration of their general or particular appropriateness to our classrooms; and, with some notable exceptions, studies have tended to deal with generalizable descriptions and explanations of the behaviours of 'teachers' or 'students' or 'pupils' rather than with individuals or groups of individuals working in defined situations which give distinctive flavour to their intentions, sequences of interaction and interpretations of persons and events. These comments are not intended to decry the value of the work that has been done, but rather to point out that despite the apparent focus upon the classroom and upon interaction much of it has been researcher-oriented, has only marginally involved teachers and probably has little more to say about the practical concerns of teachers than have those large-scale surveys of schools and pupils that are popular with some educational sociologists. Thus, whilst 'first generation' studies have made an essential contribution to our descriptive knowledge of classrooms, have provided valuable ideas and content for the professional education of teachers, and have given additional information to educational policy-makers, they have probably done little either to strengthen links between teachers and researchers or to provide teachers with information closely relevant to themselves and their pupils, and translatable into ongoing practice in particular situations.

No one is going to argue that such research should be discontinued because it follows different strategies from those being advocated here. Rather, the need is to complement it with studies of classrooms which have different objectives, either in respect of content or the collaborative involvement of teachers. Nor am I suggesting that researchers are unaware of, or indifferent to, the development of teacher-oriented strategies; rather, they are conscious of the problems involved, recognizing that the practice will entail very much more than an extended process of negotiation with teachers, longer spells sitting at the back of classrooms or greater efforts on cyclostyling non-technical reports. It seems to me that ways will have to be found for dealing with three major issues: how to so change the status of the teacher in research so that he genuinely feels that studies, even where they are relatively theoretical and abstract, are about him and his pupils, and require his involvement at all stages; how the current organization of research is to be modified to create conditions in which sustained collaborative research can be realistically attempted; and how teachers and pupils are to be represented as interactors. This third issue is perhaps the most important, at least in the short term, for if teachers feel that they are being portrayed in unduly simplistic, narrow or prejudicial ways, then research findings will carry little conviction, attempts at closely collaborative procedures will be frustrated, and any changes which might be made in ways of organizing and financing research will be irrelevant.

How, then, are we to deal with this major issue of representing the teacher as an interactor? Firstly, there is the problem of finding some kind of common ground between teachers and researchers such that the practical activities and commonsense reasoning of the first are seen to be related to the abstract models and procedures for analysis and interpretation used by the others. Because they do have distinctive modes of access to matters of common concern – say the language of pupil control techniques, assessment procedures, or the teacher's perceptions of pupils in mixed-ability classes – there is a basic tension in their communication. Both forms of access are equally legitimate, but if the researcher imposes his in such a way as to make it seem at odds with that of the teacher, if he fails to do some testing of his preconceptions against the events and interpretations he encounters in the classroom, or if he fails to recognize the legitimacy of the teacher's accounts of persons and events then his work may be dismissed as another piece of research fiction. On the other hand, research which goes no further than the collection of teachers' accounts may end up as little more than a number of trivial and unsystematized anecdotes. Bringing the two together then in productive ways is extremely important. In part, as I shall suggest later, it is question of how we handle the general method of studies and the importance we attach to the negotiation of research, especially in the preliminary stages. But also, it means developing ways of categorizing data which reflect in related ways the categories of teacher and researcher. I have mentioned this particular but central matter because it is a characteristic of some of the research we have done, that ways of categorizing have been predetermined by investigators without any reference to the teachers or the classrooms in which they are employed. The prime example, perhaps, has been the use of Flander's Interaction Analysis. Most of us are now well aware of the limitations of the blanket importation of category systems, but we still need to take more account of what teachers say and do in the development of category systems for use in particular contexts.

However, there is a further problem concerning ways of representing classroom interaction which comes not from differences between teachers and researchers, but from divisions between researchers themselves. Two schools of thought have been particularly influential. One is markedly behaviourist and psychometric, emphasizing objectively-recorded descriptions of the manifest behaviours of teachers based upon predetermined categories for data. It has made important contributions in the description and comparison of the verbal behaviours of teachers and pupils, and in turn has begun the careful examination of possible associations between teaching behaviours and pupils' achievements and attitudes. Through the development of skills analysis, it has already had important practical effects upon techniques of teacher education, notably in the field of microteaching. The other school has been more concerned with the use of the subjective reports of individuals in classrooms and with observation as means to the analysis of the different perspectives of individuals in interaction, to the rules which presumably underpin particular behaviours of teachers and their pupils, and to an understanding of the ways in which particular social structures are developed and sustained.

A current danger is that these two schools may take up entrenched positions – in which case both researchers and teachers are likely to be the losers. The case for establishing working integrations of the two points of view is strong. For example, it presumably matters to a teacher that he is both a professional in some general sense, and therefore, concerned about the effectiveness of teaching methods and interested in sound systematic description of his own classroom and that of others; and an individual, teaching particular pupils in particular schools, and therefore involved in specific relationships and encouraged or constrained by distinctive features of the place in which he works. Neither research that seeks widely generalizable findings, say on teaching skills, but fails to relate these to the teacher's particular circumstances, nor research which gets so bedded down in subjective minutiae that the teacher can't recognize himself under the weight of the researcher's interpretations is likely to carry much conviction. On the one hand, there is the danger of tepid generalizations and on the other that of a mass of pretentious anecdote.

A greater measure of compromise may not be very attractive to some researchers but I think that it would be appreciated by teachers. Certainly, it is possible, both at a theoretical level and in the progressive design and carrying out of investigations. Given the variety of research, no single set of injunctions is possible, but we could perhaps agree among ourselves and with teachers about the kinds of assumptions worth making before we begin research. The ones I am going to suggest are not original, but taken together they seem to me to form a useful test of the adequacy of interaction research. At this point I am only concerned with how the teacher and his pupils are to be represented; however, this clearly bears upon the design and conduct of research and upon forms of support and financing of studies.

What, then, are the assumptions we might usefully start from?

1. The interaction of teachers and pupils is a constructive process in which selective attention, categorizing of information and interpretive plans underlie their behaviours. In this process teachers acquire and modify their perceptions of persons and events in the classroom, creating their personal views of its social and intellectual structure.

2. Teachers behave in rule-based ways. Although teaching is immediate, practical, and for the most part realistically conceived, it must be assumed that it rests upon general conceptions about tasks and relationships which are derived, among other things, from the teacher's subject discipline, his professional education and the school in which he works.

3. Interaction is symbolized in various ways, but primarily through the use of language. Teachers and pupils are speakers and hearers and the main access to the rules which guide the course of their encounters is through what they say to one another and what they say about themselves.

I have suggested these particular assumptions since they seem to me to be important both to the credibility of research and to the way it is carried out. Thus, the observation and recording of behaviour of teachers may in itself provide little more than descriptive lumber unless it is viewed either as the means of access to generalizable or particular rules for interaction or is carefully anchored to variables in the ways of thinking of teachers or the contexts in which they work. Secondly, studies which are concerned primarily or exclusively with teachers and leave out the pupils provide very limited analyses of interaction – although they may, of course, form necessary preliminary knowledge for more complex investigations. Thirdly, the recognition of the teacher as the practical expert, who can offer his reasoning about what he and his pupils do, and the constructive nature of interaction stress the case for extensive negotiation over the content and methods of research, for studies which take careful account of context variables, and for long-term investigation rather than the short-term cross-sectional ones we often find ourselves doing for one reason or another.

Several other points might be made about the importance of our assumptions about the teacher as an interactor. This is a central issue if research is to reflect a realistic model of the teacher and his work. However, I want now to consider some features of research methods as they bear upon the involvement of teachers. Again I shall have to generalize about current practices, recognizing at the same time that individuals differ in the extent to which they try to involve teachers.

Research method covers a number of sequenced and related activities: decisions about the topic for research and the kinds of information to be collected; the design and application of measures; the analysis of data; and the reporting of findings. Each of these calls for some degree of specialized knowledge. In general, teachers are not well informed on technical aspects of research, nor is it easy for them to appreciate the amount of work that has to go on behind the scenes when a large-scale study is being carried out. What commonly happens then is that all stages of design, data collection, and so forth, are almost exclusively in the hands of the researcher. The first thing a teacher may hear about a study is when he is approached for the use of his classroom – well after the initial design has been laid down, the sample been determined and the pre-liminaries of measurement work been done. He can accept the situation or not; but if he agrees to participate then he generally has to accept the decisions that have been taken and the techniques that have been developed. The next thing he may hear, if he is fortunate, comes a year or two later when a report reaches the school.

For some kinds of educational research, for example, large-scale surveys taking in schools over a wide area or studies which use schools because they provide ready access to children, there is basically little alternative to the situation described; there is either no need or it would be quite impractical. In interaction research, however, a failure to accord higher status to the teacher is both unnecessary and patronizing. After all, in this kind of work he is an expert. He is the one who makes important decisions in the classroom; he is the essential speaker/hearer and interpreter of persons and events. It is through what he does and says that the researcher develops his descriptions, explanations or interpretations. Yet how often do we involve him in the design of measurement instruments, or modify aspects of our procedures on his advice, or let him see and comment upon the report we are writing? As those of us who do research know, much of its excitement and stimulus to try this or that comes from being involved in it with our colleagues. It means little if one is on the fringes; an occasional contributor to an overall plan that one has neither been given nor helped to develop.

I do not think that it is possible to lay down a single policy for bringing research and practice closer together. However, I think we must start to change the status of the teacher by spending far more time on the initial stages of projects, developing a dialogue over our various concerns, assumptions and views about extended collaboration. Perhaps more can be done to actually involve teachers in the design of measurement techniques, in ways of analysing data and in the preparation of reports. Perhaps too we should see the benefits of research not predominantly in terms of some end product incarcerated in a report but more in the process of doing. Of course, we are after conclusions to our efforts, but for teachers a close involvement may have significance for him at a whole number of places in the total sequence.

Changed status for the teacher may depend in some measure upon altering the common research plan. At present most research in classrooms consists of one-off, cross-sectional studies, such as I mentioned earlier. Investigators flit from school to school, project to project; the whole thing jerking along almost at random. In such circumstances it is difficult both for the teacher and the researcher to establish and maintain close relationships. There would be considerable advantages in developing longitudinal programmes, of a cumulative or hierarchical type, based upon manageable school, community or subject contexts, and with sufficient built-in flexibility to allow for modifications along the way. In this way teachers would be involved to differing degrees in various parts of an extended endeavour which would incorporate not only the research programme but also that much neglected aspect of research, the translation of findings, as appropriate, into practice, and the monitoring of the changes.

Collaborative work is well established already in the field of curriculum development where, through panels of teachers aided by technical consultants, materials and methods are developed, tried out by teachers, and compiled for wider use. It is unfortunate in some ways that some form of distinction has grown up between research and development because it has led to the idea that the one is rather esoteric and peripheral while the other is practical and valuable – although it is an interesting reflection on the side that if curriculum development had taken more account of classroom interaction then it might not have had so many failures or pale imitations of innovation.

I can see the kinds of objections that would be raised against some of my suggestions: some of our cherished controls in research might be lost; some research topics would be impossible to undertake if teachers knew all about what was going on; teachers would be unwilling or unable to devote the time and effort required by closely collaborative work over long periods; the finance is lacking – and so on. There is no simple answer to such charges. To begin with, if some researchers wish to keep their research and its objectives to themselves for reasons which seem important, and they can persuade teachers to provide facilities then let them get on with it. But if we are concerned to make it a living rather than an academic exercise; if we wish to take away some of the mystique; and if we wish to give the teacher a real investment in it so that he can develop a wider understanding of himself and his pupils and can perhaps exert a greater influence upon local practice and wider educational policy-making, then its worth trying to solve the difficulties.

So far I have suggested that the representation of the teacher and his status in research are two essential elements in teacher-centred strategies. However, if we are going to lay more stress on some of the things I have proposed then changes are needed in the organization of research. In some respects the established structures for the initiation, staffing and funding of investigations are inadequate and inappropriate. Researchers tend to be physically isolated from schools and classrooms, living in a world of other researchers from which they make more or less frequent forays upon schools to collect data and then return to their processing and secretarial facilities. The funding of research is heavily influenced by central bodies and the procedures for getting funds can be slow; but more seriously, dependence upon central research bodies encourages initiative from researchers rather than from schools acting in concert with investigators, and the presentation of fairly cut and dried sets of proposals couched in ways that are suitable for researchers who want funds to persuade other researchers who disburse them. This professional structure is essential, providing powerful facilities, money, and the means to training research workers. It is perfectly suited to some kinds of research and has, through funding others or through doing its own projects, made invaluable contributions to educational research. Its major alternative at present is the individual, small-scale research done by someone in an academic or professional institution. Neither, it seems to me, provides the kinds of incentives, ongoing face-to-face support and modest funding over long periods which are the basis for what I would like to see being done.

There are several possibilities, yet one, the unit of local government, stands out both because of the minor role it has played and because it seems to offer what is needed. It is the recognizable unit for teachers; the one in which they work and meet. It formulates the general educational policies which have an immediate bearing upon those who work in the schools, and its administrative and advisory structure controls or influences such matters as staffing and promotion, curriculum development, in-service training provisions and allocations of funds. In general, education authorities are most helpful towards local research workers who wish to use their schools; their support for external projects is excellent; and they are active in curriculum work. But few have a sustained policy of classroom research worked out with their teachers and researchers. Financial support on even a short-term basis is typically small. And only in a small number of cases is there a permanent group of people trained in research who are employed specifically to liaise with schools over the initiation of local investigations, provide expertise for investigations, and promote a local policy.

Given the sympathetic attitudes perhaps what is needed is for teachers and researchers to press the advantages of interaction and other kinds of research for the processes of aiding policy-making, for informing the individual teacher about the practical implications of changes in curriculum and methods, and for widening the basis of locally-relevant content in staff-training programmes. Equally professional and advisory staff could build up initiatives from the schools, partly through encouragement but also in more tangible ways such as part-time release of teachers and promotion incentives. Under these conditions some of the developments I am arguing for could readily be realized. I am impressed through my contacts with schools and individual teachers by the kinds of questions that are raised about teaching and learning for which the information is lacking on a local basis but might be provided, if only in part, by collaborative and sustained research on interaction. Questions about what children do in nursery schools and how if at

all they are being affected; about the reactions of teachers to changes
in the staffing structures of local schools; about the use of open-
design schools and their implications for teaching methods and
working relationships with children; or about the grouping of
children in various ways. These and many other topics interest
the researcher as much as they concern the teacher. Yet so often
the two do not get together at the right time and in the most
effective ways.

On present form, classroom interaction research is likely to increase
greatly in the next few years, not only because of its theoretical
interest but also because of its practical importance for the understanding of processes of teaching and learning. As it increases, so
more and more demands will be placed upon schools to provide
facilities, and, inevitably the questions will be raised about what is
being done, why it is being done and what relevance it has to the
working lives of teachers and pupils. It seems to me to be important
therefore that we should be thinking about research strategies,
particularly as they might bear upon the teacher. I am sure that
improving    existing    communications    between    teachers    and
researchers has only a minor contribution to make and that we must
move on three fronts – a credible representation of the teacher,
greater collaboration in the process of research, and more effective
use of local research facilities. I have tried to qualify my generalizations since there are already various exceptions to some of the
criticisms I have made; nevertheless I do not think a concerted
effort on all three fronts has really got under way. Of course, the
difficulties are great. Some researchers, administrators and teachers
will be unwilling or unable to foster or practise forms of research
which make very heavy demands on time and effort, may mean the
surrender of cherished views about methods and objectives of research
or demand protracted negotiation. But if the effort is not made then
I suspect that we shall not only deny ourselves valuable forms of
practical knowledge, but also make little impression on some of the
attitudinal barriers within the educational professions.

I have tried to argue that classroom interaction research has
characteristics which, if developed, can lead to a more effective
dialogue between teachers and researchers. My views are not
intended as a cosmetic to make research appear more attractive,
but rather, some basis for sound research to offer its particular
contributions – an attitude of critical inquiry, a sensitive view upon

what we often take for granted about the arts of teaching and learning, and a breadth of information for our innovations in school and classroom. Research can be an informing and critical exercise for all of us and not just a luxury tacked onto the fringes of educational practice. This may seem a rather grand expectation, but, nonetheless one worth trying to realize.

CHAPTER 7

# 'Showing them up' in Secondary School

*Peter Woods, The Open University*

There are two punishment structures in schools, one formal, official and overt; the other informal, unofficial and concealed. Managerial discussions of school discipline concentrate, not unexpectedly, on the former to the almost total exclusion of the latter. Thus the 1970 ILEA document *Discipline in Schools* contains an 'exhaustive' list of punishments used in their schools, as presented by the head teachers. This includes corporal punishment, detentions, loss of conduct or house marks, report systems, reprimands from the head teacher, and loss of privileges and status. They are all conceived with the 'ideal official pupil' in mind, and from him should yield the required effects. They are standardized responses to deviance from institutional norms, intended to be executed without fear of or favour to any individual. Even 'loss of status' refers to loss of 'official' status, such as the withdrawal of badges of office. The big problem is of course that many of the teacher's clients diverge a long way from his professional conception of the ideal, and thus elicit 'unofficial' methods.[1]

We might therefore expect 'unofficial' discussions of school discipline to concern themselves with those methods; but in the heat of the current debate over corporal punishment, in which child-centred ideologies[2] clash with traditional ideologies,[3] other forms of punishment are forgotten or left unexplored. It is assumed that corporal punishment is by a very long way that form of punishment which inflicts most pain on most pupils. In support of this assumption two points are usually offered: (a) in most schools where

[1]H. S. Becker made this point in 'Social class variations in the teacher-pupil relationship', *Journal of Educational Sociology*, (1952), 25(4).
[2]See e.g. National Council for Civil Liberties, *Children's Rights in School*, NCCL, 1970.
[3]As enunciated, for example, in Cox, C. B. and Dyson, A. E., (eds.), *The Fight for Education: A Black paper*, The Critical Quarterly Society, London, 1968.

it is used, it is put out by the staff as the ultimate deterrent; and (b) pupils' feelings are held to reflect the views of the abolitionists. Since it is the consumer who discriminates among the effects, the second would appear to be the more important point. But a glance through the literature reveals that many of the methods used to seek pupils' views restricted them to the area of 'official' punishments.[1] I am not here doubting the validity of their claims, nor contesting their overall position. What I am suggesting is that the smoke generated by the fire and brimstone of the attack on corporal punishment has occluded the more general picture, in which other forms of, perhaps unofficial, punishment may impinge on the pupil to a great extent.

Nor have these been tackled in the few sociological accounts of school discipline that we have. These seem to suffer from the same imputational bias.[2] This appears at times as a confident, but rather bland claim to insight into the pupil's interpretation of various techniques. There seems to be a strong normative element in these accounts, suggesting a 'teacher-training' ideology, which in turn involves in part an acceptance of basic structural conditions and a depersonification of the pupil.[3]

I want to focus on one particular technique in the informal punishment structure which seems to me to have received less attention than it deserves. It is, in the pupils' terms, 'showing us up'. It is well known of course that this happens, but I think its scale and intensity have been underestimated. Its own nature may have contributed to this, for the essence of it as a punishment lies in the force with which an individual's deviation from the norm can be emphasized in the eyes of his peers – and nobody likes publicizing his shame. Also, sometimes it is concealed in the official programme and not intended as a punishment. Or it may otherwise be done unconsciously or unintentionally. The pupil may find the outcomes hard to define or to place within his scheme of things, so that it

[1] See for example the researches reported in Newell, P., (ed.), *A Last Report? Corporal Punishment in Schools*, Penguin Books, Harmondsworth, 1972.

[2] Here, for example, Lacey imputes to a boy the consequences for that boy of a teacher's outburst against him: 'The tension this incident generated was such that the boy had obviously stopped thinking about the task long before the final stages. He was so worked up that he was incapable of concentrating.' Lacey, C., *Hightown Grammar*, Manchester University Press, Manchester, 1970, p. 178.

[3] There seems to be quite a strong strain of this teacher-training ideology running through the account of school discipline in Hargreaves, D. H. *Interpersonal Relations and Education*, Routledge and Kegan Paul, London, 1972, pp. 228–266.

becomes too commonplace to talk about. For all these reasons, it is hard to pinpoint, unlike the uses of the cane, or indeed other forms of physical punishment.

The importance of 'showing them up' as a punishment was revealed to me in the course of a field study in one co-educational secondary modern school. During the two terms that I spent there, I observed many lessons and other school functions, talked with staff continually and interviewed over 200 pupils in the 3rd, 4th and 5th years. I was interested primarily in interpersonal relationships, and pupils' experience of school. Now and again pupils would talk about 'being shown up' with an intensity that caused me to think this was more than just a petty grumble or a mere 'con'. I reviewed my field notes, reflected on my own career and experiences in other schools and restructured my observations with a view to finding empirical illustrations of the technique. This, as it happened, was not difficult.

Reviewing these illustrations, there seem to me to be three basic types: (1) those which result from pure accident; (2) those which result from official policy as part of the official programme (not perpetrated as a punishment, though that is how they are received); (3) those deliberately executed as punishments.

The first type we can hardly cater for. Wherever people interact, some will cause embarrassment to others unintentionally, e.g. by seeing or hearing them in a disadvantaged situation, by interpreting them in a way different from that intended, by a slip of the tongue, and so forth.

Regarding the second category, many of these officially sponsored embarrassments are a by-product of institutional requirements. Among the best examples are those which stem from a pseudo-olympian creed which extols the taking part in an event as opposed to the winning of it. It is perhaps most clearly manifested on the sports field and is closely associated with the House system, which itself is believed to be functional for the school. Slogans such as 'taking part', 'having a go', 'he does at least *try*', are used in the mystic folklore of inter-House competition as *a priori* justification for putting pressure on pupils to engage in activities in which the public manifestation of enormous differences in skill, ability and physique is positively degrading for the non-athletic.

At my study school, each of the four houses was required to enter teams for Sports Day. Each event demanded two competitors and one reserve from each House. The value placed on mere entry was emphasized by the award of a point (though the point was not awarded unless the event was begun). A morning was set aside to select these teams by trial, i.e. the House teachers undertook to find the best at each event by observation. I accompanied one male teacher concerned with the selection of the girl's team for one of the Houses. I was impressed by the difficulty he had in persuading them – particularly the senior girls – to take part in the events he wanted them to. Before he began he was approached by two members of his own form:

SHIRLEY:   Can we be excused games please to go and help Mr Gough?
MR TOWN:   (frowning, hesitant). Whose house are you in? Go and see your housemistress, I can't give you permission.

(They approached Mrs Bell. Mrs Bell was very busy organizing some other girls. She reasoned with Shirley, then finally dismissed the matter with 'Well . . . try a jump or something!' Shirley looked aghast. I never saw her do it.)

When he came to selecting his team, he began in a friendly, democratic way by asking for volunteers for events, with a slight touch of cajolery ('This is not the time to be modest Susan, you are the best at the hundred aren't you?') Before long, however, he was forced by the administrative necessity[1] of finding a team in limited time into subterfuge (asking all of them 'Who's the best at this?') and later authoritarianism. The following extract from my field notes is typical of these negotiations:

Mr Town is trying to persuade Kim to do the high jump, Lee to do the 100 yard hurdles and long jump, and Sandra to do the shot. Kim and Lee bombard him with excuses 'I ain't any good at it', 'I've hurt me ankle', 'My mum said I ain't got to jump', 'I can't do it'.

MR TOWN:   It doesn't matter, we get a point. (He turns to Sandra) You're a shot putter aren't you, Sandy?
SANDRA:    No!

[1]All those who work in institutions are inhibited by this constraint, but because the education of children is veiled in idealism, rarely is sufficient allowance made for the extent to which this acts as a bar or break on a teacher's good intentions.

MR TOWN:   Yes you are (writes her name in). Who are discus throwers?

GIRLS:     Tracey! Claire!

MR TOWN:   Right, you can both do it (writes names in).

CLAIRE:    Javelin she's (Tracey) good at.

TRACEY:    No I'm not, Claire does Javelin.

SANDRA:    (aside) It makes you sick, this.

MR TOWN:   So you're in high jump and discus, Barbara (writes).

BARBARA:   No I'm not. Honestly, I haven't done high jump for three years.

MR TOWN:   I'll put you down for shot then.

BARBARA:   I can't do shot, I hurt my arm skiing.

MR TOWN:   (to Tracey) I'll put you down for shot as well (goes).

BARBARA:   What I want to do is discus and long jump and he won't let me do either of the bleeders.

There was much evasion, by silence, by denying any sort of ability at the event in question, or by deliberately under-performing the trial event. But the teacher was not to be taken in. After an apology of a long jump from one senior girl, he simply said in weary, authoritarian tones: 'and again'. And after the next, slightly less of an apology: 'and again.' And after the next: 'You're in, Susan.'

In fact he was joking but Susan turned, and very heatedly shouted 'I'm not. Shut up!' and returned to her friends with a very high colour and many hostile glances at the teacher. When I asked her later what she felt so upset about she said, 'Well they make you look such a fool in front of everybody . . . I wouldn't mind if I was some good at it.'

By tradition apparently, all took part in the 100 yards senior girls' trial. But Tracey, a large girl, was reluctant.

MR TOWN:   Come on Tracey.

TRACEY:    No! Show me up!

MR TOWN:   (cajoling) Come on, come on.

TRACEY:    No, I show myself up. I always come last.

MR TOWN:   (laughing) Come on, get up, everybody else is doing it. (Tracey got up, ran, and came last.)

In interviews, I talked with pupils about the sports while they were still topical. Some enjoyed them of course, but the majority were not interested. 'It's all right for those who are good at them, but if you're not, you just look ridiculous.' I think it true to say that many did not want to take part simply because they did not want to, but I was satisfied that many perceived participation as a threat to their social identities. I marvelled at the teacher's administrative and organizational expertise in parrying and countering the oppositional thrusts from the girls, and in getting his lists complete. 'We're experienced campaigners', he said. In fact nearly all the encounters I witnessed had an air of ritual about them. Everybody seemed to know how everybody else would react. For example, the teacher would have been astonished if all had agreed first time; pupils likewise would have been astonished if the teacher had accepted their excuses. In this sense they seemed to be operating in clearly-defined roles, and with clear expectancies of others. This teacher incidentally was very popular among the pupils generally. It seems that if there is a strong element of ritual about the activity and, even more, if it is part of the sacred institutional order, the teacher can avoid personal hostility, as long as he keeps to the clearly defined teacher role. In turn, some pupils may be able to transcend the situation when it comes to running, jumping, throwing and so on, by performing as pupils rather than persons.[1] This, together with the lack of intent to punish considerably softens the embarrassment felt in this type of 'showing up'.

We now come to the third category, deliberate punishment. This is the type of showing up that causes most distress, and I will therefore consider it in more detail. I want to look at the properties and functions of deliberate showings-up.

*Properties*

Showings-up require certain properties. They need a public arena. They are much more likely to occur in formal settings where there is probably considerable distance between the rules governing the formal procedure and the rules governing the everyday inter-

[1]Bernstein *et al.* make a similar point in their discussion of 'consensual' and 'differentiating' rituals in schools, which function to 'maintain continuity, order, boundary, and the control of dual loyalties and ambivalence'. But they are thinking mainly of formalized ceremonials. There is a kind of second-order ritual, apparently informal but in fact quite stylized, which functions to the same end, and which paradoxically includes some ritualized opposition. Bernstein, B., Elvin, H. L., Peters, R. S., 'Ritual in Education'. *Philosophical Transactions of The Royal Society of London*, 1966, 251 (772), 429–36.

action – hence they frequently happen in meetings like assemblies
and co-active, formal teaching situations. They require an object
who is sensitive to such treatment. Obviously he needs to be able to
interpret the stimuli in the manner intended – it is no use using wit
or scorn that someone does not understand, or adopting a tactic
that he will interpret in other ways, for example as a joke. The
victim must also be someone who has the ability to stand over against
his 'self', take the role of the other and see himself as others see him.
In Mead's terms, the 'me' is perceived as the object of humiliation,
and the subject 'I' feels the humiliation (see also Blumer, H., 1962).
The perpetrator acts deliberately, though quite often impulsively,
with the intent of discrediting a person or persons in ways they
themselves value.

   Time and the progression of events are also relevant considera
tions (Bennett, 1970). The time can be very short or long and
drawn-out, depending on the sub-type. For example, the 'cata-
clysmic explosion' relies partly on the rapidity of execution for its
effect. Another sub-type, by contrast, depends on length rather than
brevity for its effect. This is the calculated, clinical, often sarcastic
exposure of an individual before his fellows. Consideration of the
'progression of events' reminds us that showings-up have careers
(Gross and Stone, 1964). They begin, typically, with the perception,
on the part of the perpetrator, of some sort of deviance. Often the
latter is embedded in interactions which to the pupils represent a
reasonable reflection of their expectations (for example it is not
unreasonable to them, though it may be against the rules, that
people talk in assembly). The perpetrator then interrupts these
expectations. The situation is fractured, and people must redefine it
and their expectations of others anew. The exposed person
experiences an assault on his 'identity' and feels confusion, since his
previous identity was the basis of others' expectations of him. There
are a number of possible outcomes. He may, for example, try to
invalidate the manoeuvre by parrying the assault, trying to turn the
tables and exposing the teacher; or by attempting to redefine it as
unserious, by, for instance, smiling, laughing or by some such indication to his fellows to the effect of gaining group support (Coser,
1959). At the other extreme, a showing-up can have such a poignant
impact that the basis of one's whole presentation of self are permanently damaged (Goffman, 1955). The degree of discredit is
dependent on its reception, i.e. if the victim shows no signs of con-

fusion, the discredit will be less.[1] Hence the attempts to cover signs of confusion, the compounding of confusion by the manifestation of it (by which he loses social poise) and the actual accumulation of credit to persons who can disport themselves through such incidents with aplomb.

Further characteristics of showings-up might be revealed by comparison with this definition of embarrassment:

> 'Embarrassment occurs whenever some central assumption in a transaction has been *unexpectedly* and unqualifiably discredited for at least one participant. The result is that he is incapacitated for continued role performance. Moreover embarrassment is infectious. It may spread out, incapacitating others not previously incapacitated. It is a destructive disease. In the wreckage left by embarrassment lie the broken foundations of social transactions.' (Gross and Stone, 1964.)

While we may accept the first part of the definition as being equally true of 'showings-up', it has certain other and different properties, arising mainly from its institutional situationing. Showings-up are not always unexpected. In fact in some ways, the expectations can have more severe repercussions in terms of punishment than the actual deed. Again, showings-up may or may not be infectious. Others present may in fact contribute to, rather than share in, the embarrassment, especially if the person is unpopular. Classrooms develop their own norms, and frequently those of society in general cannot be applied. Thus it is not uncommon for people in classrooms to shout at one another, hit one another or try to embarrass one another. Also, in some instances where perpetrated as an act of deliberate policy, showings-up may be intended to be constructive, inasmuch as they aim to restore social order.

*Functions*

Gross and Stone mention three functions of deliberate embarrassment: (1) socialization, (2) as a negative sanction, and (3) as a means of establishing and maintaining power. Showings-up might

[1]Goffman makes this point in his *Interaction Ritual*, Anchor Books, New York, 1967, p. 101–2. 'To appear flustered, in our society at least, is considered evidence of weakness, inferiority, low status, moral guilt, defeat, and other unenviable attributes.'

have these functions, but they could also have at least two others: (4) as a means of motivation, and (5) revenge. I will consider each in turn.

1. Particularly apt here is Mead's definition of socialization: '. . . not an internalization of norms and values, but a cultivated capacity to take the roles of others effectively'. What keener way could there be of encouraging the development of this capacity than by involving the individual in a process which depends on his perceptions of others and which focuses on himself? Thus teachers might be considered as having a legitimate role here. And since much learning requires emphasis and repetition, they might be excused what at times may appear to be unreasonable or exaggerated styles.

We might say pupils must learn how to behave in society. In a questionnaire sent to all parents of children in the third year at the school concerning another issue, this was rated as one of the two chief aims of the school. Attitude-training is an important part of the curriculum. A pupil must learn what to expect of others so that he can measure his own behaviour against that predicted of others. His peers are important here too (and they are quite good at showing-up also), but the teacher as a more fully socialized member of society has deeper and wider knowledge of those expectations.

2. Many of the incidents causing the showings-up are seen as a threat to order, in relation either directly to goals, for example where an individual submits a particularly bad piece of work, especially when it is common knowledge; or, and this is more frequent, to conduct deemed likely to jeopardize the normal running of the school, the most common instance of which is infraction of the learning situation. Thus to stop an outbreak of talking in assembly, a teacher might make use of an outburst directed against one person, relying on the shock waves to silence the rest. Or in class, by developing a reputation for showing people up, a teacher might rely on its deterrent effect to secure general order. Otherwise and more frequently, showings-up might be directed at one individual to stop him doing something, the teacher relying on the implicit or explicit support of others present. The philosophy seems to be that, just as people attempt to hide physical deformities, so they will hide behavioural deformities if they can be made sufficiently conscious of them.

3. The teacher is continually having to face challenges to his authority, and assaults on his power and status. The 'trying out' of new teachers by pupils, seeing 'how far they can go' is well attested in the literature.[1] In the formalized power structure of most of our secondary schools, teachers are regarded as fair game for this kind of sport. Pupils may play up through sheer devilment, to 'look big', to embarrass the teacher, or to provoke certain responses such as blushing or loss of temper. Throwing missiles around the room, directing reflected sunlight onto the teacher's face, ventriloquizing his nickname while his back is turned are commonly known items in the pupils' repertoire. Arriving late for lessons, walking out of the room, talking back to the teacher are all infractions of the rules governing the teacher-pupil relationship, and are explicit denials of his authority. If, in reply, the teacher miscues by, for example taking no action at all, or showing some signs of confusion, or by over-reacting i.e. by losing his temper and thus self-control, he loses status in the eyes of the class as a whole, while some gains in prestige might accrue among the students for the perpetrators. If he continues to miscue over a period, he will lose all power as teacher, and all prestige ('respect') in the pupils' eyes as a person.

In a very real sense the teacher is on a hiding to nothing in the traditional co-active teaching situation that obtains in most of our secondary schools. For he is set up as an individual against the group. He is the focus of attention, and he it is who is making demands on the group that may not accord with their wishes. For many a pupil he is the agent of an alien, authoritarian world who is continually challenging the pupil's conception of self. Pupils therefore seek to neutralize the situation by showing the *teacher* up. There are a number of countermoves a teacher can make, but none more appropriate perhaps than by turning the tables on the pupil or pupils concerned, making capital out of the situation and instead of losing status, *gaining* it at *their* expense. Teachers, like pupils, make representations to themselves. They need to maintain status in their own *eyes*. This may lie behind the rhetoric of toughness and pupil flagellation that prevails in many staffrooms, which lends such solid support to techniques like 'showing up'.

4. Teachers might attempt to 'shame' pupils into better work or

[1] e.g. Stenhouse, L., 'Discipline and the dynamics of the classroom', in Stenhouse, L., (ed.), *Discipline in Schools*, Pergamon, London, 1967.

an attitude more conducive to it. Most frequently this is done on a one-to-one basis, and there is no public humiliation. But sometimes it is done in front of others, to inspire them also.[1] The belittling may be by reference to age – 'a child of five could have done this' – or perhaps insinuations will be made about one's personal standards or conduct such as to discredit one's cultural milieu – 'You're too busy knocking about with that boy friend of yours!' Sometimes a direct assault is made on one's attributes or capacities – 'You're thick, lad, you're thick.' Or the same may be implied by 'long-suffering' oaths ('Oh my God!') and facial contortions, indicating in vivid style to all present that the student in question falls ludicrously short of requirements. Groups can be shown up in attempts to influence other groups. Even in the absence of the victims, word can get back to them and they can feel publicly outraged. For example, teachers often talk about year groups as entities having characters of their own. Thus there are good and bad years for pupils just as there are for wines. Sometimes a particular vintage may get publicly lampooned, as if to say to another year, 'look how ridiculous and stupid they are, don't you get like that!' A fifth-year girl told me 'the thirds were told we were a rotten year, always mucking about, wouldn't get many passes and that. I didn't think that was very nice.' This neatly illustrates the ethical clash involved.

A common ploy with pupils of supposedly high status is to emphasize their deficiencies in front of their 'inferiors'. Thus prefects, or senior pupils who are not conforming in the required manner, may get shown up in front of junior pupils. Again the thrust of the manoeuvre is double edged, for by displaying the conduct of the senior pupils as discreditable the teachers are informing the juniors, who otherwise might seek to emulate them, either that it is unworthy in itself, or that it earns this sort of punishment. And they are informing the senior pupils that if they wish to earn and maintain status they must conform, otherwise teachers might make inroads into their positions in the informal structure of the school.[2]

[1]Lacey, C., *op. cit.* Also see Moody, Eileen, 'Right in front of everybody', *New Society*, 26th December, 1968.

[2]This is a good example of one of the vicious spirals that teachers and pupils can get caught up in. Among the senior pupils I spoke to, the biggest plea was for a status more appropriate to their age. One teacher told me 'they want to be treated as adults, but they don't *act* like adults, they behave like children'. A senior girl told me 'they treat us like little kids, so we act like little kids.' The self-fufilling prophecy is well-known (see e.g. Rosenthal, R., and Jacobson, L., *Pygmalion in the Classroom*, Holt, Rinehart and Winston, New York, 1968). But who starts it?

5. A showing-up may have the functions 1 to 4 in varying degrees; but at the time the object may simply be to give as much hurt as possible. In his 'teacher-training' chapter on discipline Hargreaves (1972) suggests many experienced teachers have a limited repertoire of techniques, and these are nearly all *'punishments'*, because they see disorder as a threat to their control and mastery and therefore as a personal affront. 'Almost instinctively therefore, counter-attack seems the best form of defence.' Hargreaves introduces Schutz's (1967) distinction between motives and intentions. Taking into account only the latter the teacher frequently acts out of a spirit of 'angry revenge.'[1] In estimating what will convey most hurt, some might resort to blows; others will choose a form of words designed to inflict psychological harm. In a cultural sense, the latter might seem more appropriate, that is it might seem more of an 'intellectual' response. Some teachers become extremely skilled at delivering this kind of riposte even though under pressure in the heat of the moment.

**Some examples**

Perhaps the most sophisticated, appropriate and least unpleasant way of showing somebody up is by the use of wit. But this is a scarce resource, and more commonly sarcasm is employed. This is strongly disliked:

> 'I could not stand that subject. The teacher kept being nasty and sarcastic. He called us louts and said we all had lice, that was the sort of thing, in front of all the class . . . because we had long hair, we were dirty . . . just because he had not got none' (third year boy).

'Sarcasm' was frequently mentioned. But it was difficult to get illustrative data sufficient for a satisfactory definition. It frequently seems to contain a sneering, deprecatory quality, it reflects on a pupil's person (as opposed to his role as pupil), and carries hurtful intent at least as perceived by the pupil.

[1]The teacher's dilemma is illustrated by this anecdote taken from Kounin. When teaching a course he noticed a student reading a newspaper that he was holding completely unfolded in front of himself. 'Contrary to what I advocated in the course, I angrily reprimanded him without diagnosis or understanding (I failed to administer psychological tests, to invite him for a counselling session, to interview his parents, or to study his community).' Thus he took into account only the student's intentions.

The following extracts from a talk with four fifth year boys illustrates some of these points, and also compares the 'mock' showing-up, which is pleasurable rather than hurtful, with the real thing:

INTERVIEWER: What are they like, these teachers that you don't like?
ANDREW: Sarcastic.
ROY: One especially. Say you do something, then next day, say you don't do your homework or something, he will completely change round.
INTERVIEWER: Is that sarcasm?
ANDREW: Well I don't mind sarcasm in a friendly way but when he means it I can't stick 'im.
INTERVIEWER: What do you mean?
ANDREW: Well, another teacher, he's sarcastic but in a friendly way again you know. We can all have a laugh with him, but can't with this other one.
ERIC: He shows you up in front of the class.
IAN: You don't feel free with him do you?
ANDREW: He's not easy to get on with.

It is when an individual is singled out for 'shock' treatment that maximum feeling is aroused:

CHRISTINE: I don't like that subject because I can't stand the teacher. I've never really liked him since I got caught skiving, and he made that right fool of me, and I sat next to Kevin . . . don't you remember? . . . When I was at the back of the class . . . do you remember . . . I've never been so bright red in all my life.
INTERVIEWER: What did he say?
CHRISTINE: Oh nothing. I'm not telling you.
INTERVIEWER: Come on, tell us what he said.
CHRISTINE: I was sitting next to Kevin, and he'd got this cartridge in his pen and he was going like that (she indicates an obscene gesture), and I just pushed him away, and the teacher was writing on the board and he must have eyes in the back of his head . . . and he says . . . he turns round with a fuming face and he says 'will you two stop fiddling with each other!' I never went so bright red in all my life, and he pushed me over

one side and him on the other . . . and everybody
turned round, didn't they . . . in front of all my
friends! You know . . . he made such a . . . mockery
. . . can't stand him! Everybody was scared stiff in
that class, everyone just sits there, all quiet.'

This vividly portrays the consumer's experience and a common
teacher problem. So acutely had she felt the embarrassment that
she found it very difficult to relate, but having started almost by
accident, she responded to her three friends present, and addressed
most of her remarks to them.[1] There was no doubting the intensity
of the hostility felt towards the teacher in question, chiefly based on
that one incident. According to Christine's account, she was the
victim of both Kevin and teacher. With Kevin however, it was
privatized. The teacher made the matter public, implied illicit
sexual activity, very plausibly to others perhaps because the pair
were sitting at the back unseen, and everyone discontinued activity
to turn around and gaze. This sudden transformation of position
*vis-a-vis* others, from being at the back one moment, to being at
the front the next is a necessary feature of the 'Shock' show-up.
That her closest friends were present made things worse, and that
it was a 'mockery' of what had actually been happening compounded
her sense of injustice.

The following extract from a discussion with four 3rd year girls
suggests that 'showing-up' is a commonly used technique in this
school, and not a rare event; and how the embarrassment can be
compounded by inter-sex rivalry.

INTERVIEWER: Are there any bad things about school?
ALISON:       Being put on report . . . getting into trouble.
INTERVIEWER: Do you get into trouble a lot?
ALISON:       Yeah, mostly from Mr Black, like today. I came in late.
INTERVIEWER: What's so bad about getting into trouble?
ALISON:       I go red.
INTERVIEWER: It embarrasses you does it?
ALISON:       Yeah.
KAY:          Yeah, all the teachers embarrass you. All the boys
              *look* . . . horrible it is . . . horrible.

[1]This is an example of the pay off that can come from talking to people in
friendship groups. Often I felt I was favoured with privileged access to information
which I certainly would not have got from individuals or randomly selected groups.

INTERVIEWER: Give us an example.

KAY:                 One of my friends . . . a teacher belted her ever so
                        hard and she started crying and all the boys started
                        picking on her . . . calling her a baby.

INTERVIEWER: Do you think teachers show you up on purpose?

KAY:                 They probably think if they show us up we won't
                        do it again because we're so embarrassed.

Implicit in all these showings up is the 'display', even though the
people concerned may not alter position. Some techniques used in
schools make the display explicit, and economize perhaps on words
and gestures. 'Standing out at the front' or 'on chairs' for example is
designed to preserve order amongst the mass by fear of embarrassment. This is a frequent occurrence in ritualised ceremonials, such
as assemblies. In these formal, and closely regulated public meetings
nothing succeeds in restoring order better than the explosion directed
at one individual and its accompanying shockwave. Quite often,
because of the depersonification of the occasion and the associated
nature of the showing up (which is likely to be a very sudden, sharp
and loud command, full of sinister implications such as 'Wilson! Go
and stand outside my room'), embarrassment is minimal. The individual is more likely to feel his emotions rising when reflecting on the
*justice* of the matter. This is not to say that humiliations do not
occur in these meetings. As a matter of policy, the headteacher in
his address might seek to discredit an individual in the eyes of the
multitude. One example that came my way concerned a third-year
boy, widely recognized as a deviant and leader of a group. The
head had summoned him to talk about an offence, then the next
day in assembly represented him as 'a boy who had gone to the
Head and "complained" about certain matters.' Thus the leader of
a deviant group was made to appear something of a 'creep', one
of the most despicable types according to the group sub-culture. The
boy concerned recounted this to me with great feeling. It is a good
example of how to show up a 'deviant' – it is no use abusing him in
more customary ways.

## Who does, and who doesn't get shown up

Not all pupils are treated the same. There is a tendency among
teachers – very human and therefore difficult to detect and counter-
act – to reward (in the fullest sense of the term i.e. in continual

day-to-day interactions) those who conform most closely to the ideal pupil role as they perceive it, and to punish those who deviate a long way from it. This of course is quite well-known. Lacey for example presents incidents to illustrate that 'teacher behaviour, conditioned by the reputation of the pupil, is one of the central factors producing differentiation.' Hargreaves (1967) also discusses the categorization of pupils, a process which 'provides the plan for all future interaction between the two parties.'

In relation to the phenomenon under discussion, there are two contrasting groups which predominate in pupils' perceptions of teacher-pupil relations. There are firstly 'pets' and 'creeps' and secondly those who get 'picked on.' In any group, whether streamed or not, there are likely to be some of each. The number of them, and who they are, might vary from teacher to teacher, but usually there is a hard core of each. It is the latter who are far more likely to get shown up of course, as indeed to receive any kind of punishment. In fact, in a sense, the two terms are synonomous. To be 'picked on' is to be singled out, unjustly, for unfavourable treatment, perhaps because of teacher dislike or perhaps simply because he needs a scapegoat.

You can become a 'pet' by 'creeping', for example, 'by always being in there dinnertime and breaktime, offering to do jobs, *volunteering* to do things.' Not all teachers have pets of course. Why do some?

JUNE:              I dunno. He just has pets. And if they do something
                   they don't get told off: if we do something, we get
                   blinking killed!
INTERVIEWER: Why don't they get told off?
JUNE:              They do jobs for them. They go around always doing
                   little jobs.

'Picked ons' are usually 'known' deviants. Somehow or other, rightly or wrongly, they have acquired reputations. Their behaviour is 'predictable.' Teachers have a great deal of police work to do, and in the work of detection they have not always the time, nor would it necessarily always be best policy, to conduct discreet inquiries. Moreover they need to maintain their own 'success' image. 'Good' teachers are those who can keep order, and this involves knowing always everything that is going on, and spotting the miscreants – or at least appearing to do so. The rise or fall of many a deputy headmaster hangs on whether he can carry off a successful 'police' image. Pressures of status, self-esteem, and good order demand that he find solutions. 'Picked-ons' in a sense, offer themselves up for the slaughter.

Apart from the attribution of blame for deviant acts, teachers might also interpret similar behaviour from 'pets' and 'picked ons' in very different ways. This of course is well attested in the literature.[1] The teacher's problem in dispensing pure justice is compounded by unscrupulous pupils, as the following extract from a talk with three 5th-years boys shows:

ROBERT:        In the classroom they'd tell us to get out and we'd ignore them. Or they'd tell you to do a detention and we wouldn't go. We swore at them – I got sent to the Head for that – and we just said they were picking on us and we got fed up and swore at them. He just told us off.

INTERVIEWER: Were they picking on you?

ROBERT         No, we were just mucking about, they weren't really picking on us.

## Results of showings-up

If effectively performed, showings-up might seem extraordinarily functional as far as immediate appearances are concerned. The sudden and complete transformation from general disorder to complete silence; the blushing and confusion of an individual who has threatened the teacher's authority; the ridicule of his peers; the self-satisfaction experienced; the deference shown by pupils who never challenge the teacher or misbehave in any way – all these would appear to testify to their effectiveness. But there have been hints throughout this report that this is more apparent than real.

Certainly what work we have on such matters breeds scepticism. Hargreaves (1972), for instance, talks of a 'punishment illusion'. A pupil might be stunned or humiliated into silence, but may smoulder in such resentment that he awaits the next opportunity for his revenge. Redl (1966) also distinguished between 'surface' and 'deeper' behaviour. Are the pressures on teachers such as to

[1]Lacey, C., *op. cit.* Also see **Moody, Eileen, 'Right** in Front of Everybody', *New Society,* 26th December, **1968.**

direct their attention almost exclusively to the first to the neglect of the latter? Interestingly, Kounin (1970) in his experimental study found that the only correlation in his sample for both high and low motivated students concerning a desist that contained anger, was with some felt 'emotional discomfort', but not 'attention' or 'conformity'.

My study also suggests that the more short-term the aims, the better the chance of success. For example, I witnessed many instances of the 'shockwave' effect following an explosive showing-up designed to restore order at that particular moment. Individuals have ostensibly been changed from troublesome deviants to silent conformists. What is not so clear is how the pupils actually interpret these interactions, and whether the outcomes accord with the aims, or whether the long-term effects invalidate the short-term. Certainly those narrated to me were experienced with much bitterness.

There are two points I would like to make concerning these results. First, taking them at their face value, they are a good illustration of those perennial teacher problems of resolving instrumental and expressive, and particular and universal aims. The teacher might value expressive relationships, and individuals, but above all, the school must be run, order maintained, and his subject must be taught. In these interests, the individual might occasionally be sacrificed. What then are the effects for the individual? Showings-up can lead to a devaluation of the self. As Rose (1962) has suggested, employing Mead and Cooley's conception of the self, 'a depreciated or mutilated self is a major factor in the development of a neurosis . . . because an individual's ability to accept strongly held views of any kind and to act effectively to achieve those values is a function of his conception of himself – a conception that he is an adequate, worth-while, effective and appreciated person'. I am not suggesting that most showings-up are so serious as to produce neuroses. They might do so, if kept up over a period of time, and especially if reinforced by the subject's peers. Most pupils seem able to draw strength from the group in their definition of self and of the situation, and instead of internalizing the humiliation, project it back on to the teacher in a feeling of intense dislike. It is for teachers to decide whether the restoration of order, the reinforcement of status, the quashing of the obnoxious individual and so on, is fair exchange.

The second point is this: If we accept a conflict model of teaching, such manifestations of tension and hostility may be a necessary feature of teacher-pupil interactions. They may be functional in that they provide relief mechanisms for the outlet of such tensions. Thus the 'showing-up' may be one of a number of ways in which the teacher externalizes and defuses the conflict, just as the relating of it, together with all the other ways he tries to get at the teacher, does the same for the pupil. There is conflict, certainly, in most teaching situations. There is an air of ritual about many interactions, as already noted, which suggests heavily structured situations. But it does not account for those teachers and classrooms where conflict does not occur; nor does it account for those conflicts which supersede the ritualized norm and which could not, by any stretch of the imagination, be considered as contributing to the stability of the institution. We need to look more closely at those teachers who habitually use the technique.

## Who does the showing-up?

Not all teachers employ this technique. Perhaps there are schools that are entirely free of it. This is because, I suggest, 'showing-up' like corporal punishment, is associated with certain conditions, attitudes and ideologies, which in turn support certain systems of rule. I will outline some of their main features.

## Traditionalism

Recently, Esland (1971) has considered the bases of two broad pedagogical styles in British schools. The one which concerns us here is the traditional or 'psychometric' style, which he claims is underwritten by psychological models and occasionally a touch of social Darwinism. It rests on the following assumptions:

1. Knowledge is objective, bounded and 'out there'.[1]
2. The child has a finite amount of intelligence or 'capacity'. Likewise he has other attributes which can be clearly labelled.
3. Teaching therefore consists of fitting (1) into (2), and pedagogy is designed and school organized to facilitate this.
4. The teacher is fully acquainted with (1), and has the expertise for (3).

[1]As opposed to 'Socially constructed knowledge', as described by BERGER, P. and LUCKMAN, T. in *The Social Construction of Reality*, Penguin, Harmondsworth, 1967.

5. The child has a moral responsibility to seek to fill his capacity, and the teacher has a moral responsibility to provide the means for him to do it.
6. However (if social Darwinism is added) the child is innately socially irresponsible, and therefore needs to be motivated to learn and to conform.[1]

The emphasis on matters of control and discipline, the periodic expressions of conflict, the explicitness of the authority structure of the school, follow from these premises. So do certain systems of rule, such as paternalism.

**Paternalism**

The two key elements in 'pater's' position are (a) infallibly knowing what is good for those he governs, and (b) dispensing it in ways he chooses on the grounds of superior expertise. For the governed it follows logically from (a) that they are bound to benefit as long as they are loyal and obedient. Infractions of the latter invalidate the contract (in which the government, of course, has acted for both sides). Thus in the case of infractions, the benevolence disappears and the deviants are punished in ways designed to remind them – and others – of the superiority of their mentors. 'Showing-up' is a way of cutting down to size more in keeping with the spirit of this system of rule than detentions, reports, and even corporal punishment. If the victim accepts the humiliation, the contract will be restored and the benevolence return. Often a kindly remark or deed will follow a hurtful one, as long as the pupil is duly penitent.

Thus the showing-up technique is the product of a system of beliefs which dictates how a teacher regards his pupils. This system has been around for a long time, but during the last 30 or 40 years there have been profound changes in the teacher's raw material, and it is this which helps make features of school like 'showing-up' such big issues for pupils today. A generation or two ago, pupils may have been more conditioned to accept the consequences. Since

[1]Several similar dichotomies and typologies have appeared recently. See, for example, Barnes, D. and Shemilt, D. 'Transmission and Interpretation', *Educational Review*, vol. 26, No. 3, June 1974; Partlett, M. and Hamilton, D., *Evaluation as Illumination: A New Approach to the Study of Innovatory Programs*, Centre for Research in the Educational Sciences, University of Edinburgh, Occasional Paper 9, 1972; Lister, I. *The Whole Curriculum and the Hidden Curriculum*, in Lister, I. (ed.), *Deschooling*, Cambridge University Press, London, 1974, pp. 92–93.

then we have gone through a period of 'child liberation' promoted
by two concurrent factors. One is quite enormous changes in child-
rearing practice, focused on greater liberty, fewer rules, punishments
and jobs;[1] the other is the consigning of a new status to teenagers
by the business section of society in recognition of that greater
liberty, and of a new economic independence (Abrams, 1963). All
this provides a conception of self very much different from that of
the pupil of 30 or 40 years ago. It is one not inured to adult dominance and ridicule; on the contrary, it is hypersensitive to such
assaults. The nascent conflict between teacher and pupil becomes
then a clash of cultures to which there is no solution.[2] It has many
manifestations: Pupils must not smoke; but mum hands the cigar-
ettes round after tea. Pupils should conform to school regulations
on dress and appearance which usually condemn all marks of
individuality and require uniformity in accordance with the 'good
pupil' image; the external pressures on the pupil stress individuality
and for the teenager a sophistication quite out of character with the
humble pupil role. Pupils are expected to be obedient, respectful
and to accept the teacher's authority without question; elsewhere,
they are encouraged to reason and to speak their minds. Thus
pupils exposed to this pedagogical paradigm find powerful pressures being exerted on them to perform two quite distinct, and
frequently contradictory, roles.

## Alienation

Until fairly recently there was a widespread belief that the
education system and schools were 'neutral', and that teaching was
a vocation. However, contributors to the burgeoning deschooling
debate have strongly suggested the education system's dependence
and subservience to the political and economic systems. Whether
regarded as training future citizens for consumption or production,[3]

[1]Some of my own research points to the magnitude of these changes during
the adolescent years. See Woods, P.E.

[2]Though I am using 'culture' in a wider sense here, the 'cultural deprivation'
thesis is part of the syndrome connected with traditional paternalism. Most
children's experiences and ways of life are seen as inadequate and of limited value
and are frequently deprecated. This often provides substance for the showing-up,
as in the example on p. 19. See Keddie, N., *Tinker, tailor . . . The Myth of Cultural
Deprivation*, Penguin, Harmondsworth, 1973.

[3]See Illich, I., *Deschooling Society*, Harper and Row, New York, 1971 and
Gintis, H., 'Towards a political economy: a radical critique of Ivan Illich's deschooling society', *Harvard Educational Review*, vol. 42, No. 1 (February, 1972).

the education system might itself be regarded as an industry serving the capitalist system, and its teachers as industrial workers. The alienating effects of current education have been widely discussed,[1] but what of the alienators? How many teachers, I wonder, would feel a sense of identification with this:

'The work is external to the worker, that it is not part of his nature, and that consequently he does not fulfil himself in his work but denies himself, has a feeling of misery rather than well-being, does not develop freely his mental and physical energies but is physically exhausted and mentally debased. The worker therefore feels himself at home only during his leisure time, whereas at work he feels homeless. His work is not voluntary but imposed, forced labour. It is not the satisfaction of a need, but only a means for satisfying other needs. Its alien character is clearly shown by the fact that as soon as there is no physical or other compulsion it is avoided like the plague . . . Alienated labour alienates (man) from the species . . . (and) from other men' (Marx, 1961).

I am suggesting therefore, that for many teachers their work far from being vocational has become alienated. It does not fulfil the needs of the individuals it affects. The product of their labour has become reified and the development of their own human potential blocked. Other professionals might identify with this, and they might seem too, pillars of the establishment. This, for example, is a 34 year-old advertising man, a resident of an upper class Chicago suburb:

'Do I like my job? No. I deplore it. I hate it. I come home sick at night about it. . . . Maybe I'm ready to try to make it on my own in freelance writing. But at this point it's irrelevant. I now have a family, two children, and I've got to weigh that balance against the other balances. . . . The trap of course, is my past. I've been very successful writing for advertising agencies and I have a mortgage and a standard of life.'[2]

[1]See for example, Holly, D., *Beyond Curriculum*, Hart-Davis, MacGibbon, London, 1973.

[2]Terkel, S., *Division Street, America*, Pantheon Books, New York, 1967, pp. 218-19; quoted in Glaser, B. G., and Strauss, A. L., *Status Passage*, Aldine-Atherton, New York, 1971.

Teachers have laid down similar side-bets (Becker, 1964) and suffered similar disenchantment.[1] The result is the development of what Hargreaves calls the 'mediocrity norm' and 'the norm of cynicism' (Hargreaves, 1972). He notes that 'perhaps the most favourite topic for staffroom discussion is the pupils. They provide an endless course of amusement and outrage'. But while he notices the effects of such chatter, he totally ignores its origins – though it must be said that the reinforcement provided by colleagues can generate an impetus of its own over the years, so effect can indeed become cause, as in the initiation of young inexperienced teachers into what teaching is 'really' all about. These origins, I suggest, lie in the thought systems and assumptions about pupils and the teaching process connected with psychometric pedagogical styles and paternalism; and in the repercussions for the pupil consequent to alienation.

The latter can explain a great deal of teacher attitudes and behaviour. The point I wish to make here is that to some degree, pupils are held responsible for the 'chore' of working. It has often been said, apparently in jest, by practitioners, that 'teaching would be all right if it were not for the pupils'. The jest, I believe harbours the truth for many teachers. Unlike the raw material of many other alienated workers, the teacher's raw material will not do what it ought to do. Pupils (similarly alienated) fail to do work properly, misbehave, cause trouble, make a noise, break rules, threaten one's self-respect. In ordinary life, we would avoid such people. But the teacher cannot avoid his pupils, though he might do his best to engineer the timetable so that he misses the worst of them. He must face them and deal with them. Moreover he must do something with them, otherwise the 'capitalist' employer will exact retribution. Many teachers are caught in this three-way fix between 'real life', pupils and headteacher, and the pupils, being in the middle, and with least power, receive the brunt of any sour feeling arising from the teacher's alienation.

If alienation envelopes psychometric pedagogical styles and paternalist systems of rule, we have a powerful combination of factors for engendering that type of attitude and feeling of which 'showing them up' is but one symptom.

[1] G. M. Coverdale has considered this problem in relation to teachers in Australia in 'Some determinants of teacher morale', *Educational Review*, vol. 26, No. 3, June 1974. But he calls it 'low morale' and seeks explanations for it *within* the system.

## Acknowledgement

This paper is part of a wider research project into pupils' experience of school. It is not, of course, 'about' any one school and the people in it, though the basic ideas and illustrations come from one school. My thanks are due to the pupils and teachers concerned for their unfailing help, generosity and good humour. In any descriptive account of the school these elements would require emphasis in order to do it justice.

## References

ABRAMS, M. (1963). 'How and why we spend money', *Twentieth Century*, Autumn.

BECKER, H. S. (1964). 'Personal change in adult life', *Sociometry*, 27(1), 40–53.

BENNETT, D. J. and BENNETT, J. D. (1970). 'Making the scene.' In: STONE, G. and FARBERMAN, H. (eds.) *Social Psychology through Symbolic Interaction*. Waltham, Mass.: Ginn-Blaisdale.

BLUMER, H. (1962). 'Society as symbolic interaction.' In: ROSE, A. M. (ed.) *Human Behaviour and Social Processes*. Boston: Houghton Mifflin.

COSER, R. L. (1959). 'Some social functions of laughter: a study of humour in a hospital setting', *Human Relations*, 12 (May) 1959.

GOFFMAN, E. (1955). 'On face-work', *Psychiatry*, 18 (August).

GROSS, E. and STONE, G. P. (1964). 'Embarrassment and the analysis of role requirements.' *American Journal of Sociology*, vol. 70, pp. 1–15.

HARGREAVES, D. H. (1967). *Social Relations in a Secondary School*. London: Routledge and Kegan Paul.

HARGREAVES, D. H. (1972). *Interpersonal Relations and Education*. London: Routledge and Kegan Paul.

INNER LONDON EDUCATION AUTHORITY (1970). *Discipline in Schools*. London: ILEA.

KOUNIN, J. S. (1970). *Discipline and Group Management in Classrooms*. New York: Holt, Rinehart and Winston.

MARX, K. (1844). 'Economic and philosphical manuscripts, 1844', reprinted in FROMM, E. (ed.) *Marx's Concept of Man* (translated by T. B. Bottomore). New York: Frederick Ungar.

MEAD, G. M. (1935). *Mind, Self and Society*. University of Chicago Press.

REDL, F. (1966). *When we deal with Children*. New York: Free Press.

ROSE, A. M. (ed.) (1962). *Human Behaviour and Social Processes*. Boston: Houghton Mifflin.

SCHUTZ, A. (1967). *The Phenomenology of the Social World*, translated by G. Walsh and F. Lehnert. New York: Northwestern University Press.

WOODS, P. E. (1971). *Adults' Perceptions of Intergenerational Changes in Socialisation Environment*. Unpublished MSc. Thesis, University of Bradford.

CHAPTER 8

# The Problem of the 'Unmotivated' in an Open School: A Participant Observation Study

*Andrew Hannan, University of Leicester School of Education*

Classroom research has developed in several directions, as illustrated by other articles in this collection. One of the factors influencing this divergence of styles has been the type of classroom observed. Flanders (1970) type techniques are best applied to the 'chalk and talk' traditional classrooms centred around teacher instruction. On the other hand, Adelman and Walker (1974) have developed techniques to observe the very different world of the 'open classroom' where such innovations as team-teaching, resource-based and discovery-centred learning have radically changed the rôle of teacher. Such a divergence has important consequences for the study of learning and teaching contexts that have not been fully developed in recent research.

The classroom has often been studied as if it were a discrete unit, almost a closed world. Such an assumption has allowed research to narrow its focus onto the interactions involved in classroom situations. The existence and nature of the classroom have been taken as given, and the wider context of the school has been neglected. Case studies in the tradition of Hargreaves (1967) and Lacey (1970) have attempted to provide a fuller account by basing classroom observations in a model of the school as a social system. Little research has been done which examines in a similar fashion the predicament of the 'open classroom' in the 'open school'. The open classroom has highlighted the dependence of the learning and teaching context on the policies of the school as a whole. The teacher may be part of a team teaching 'integrated' subject matter crossing the boundaries of traditional disciplines. As a member of a team he is dependent on a sharing of aims and ideals in the negotiation of policy. In implementing a curriculum innovation, for instance a

Schools Council project, he is part of a wider attempt to carry out a specific programme. To understand the behaviour of the teacher in the classroom under such conditions it is necessary to understand something of the wider context of the course and its aims in relation to planned innovations or the policy of the school as a whole.

The new developments in education require a re-working of research technique. The modern comprehensive schools are arenas of negotiation[1] where different educational philosophies, new aims and structures, are fought for and opposed. This process is not one which ends with the setting up of the schools; it is likely to be continuous. The commitments of staff to various ways of teaching, types of course, forms of administration, of pastoral care and so on, will then be expressed in the discussion of the problems which face the school in its everyday experience as well as its plans for the future. The school chosen for study in this research was particularly rich in the depth and scope of its 'negotiating process' and its commitment to educational innovations. This paper examines the official aims and structure of the school studied and shows how the problems faced by the teacher in the classroom can be interpreted in terms of a model derived from Bernstein and Durkheim. One of these problems is taken as an illustration for analysis.

The research upon which this paper is based was begun in October 1973. The original concern was to study the consequences of innovations in curriculum in an individual school. The model used to direct the project was derived from Bernstein's *Open Schools, Open Society?* (1967) and *On the Classification and Framing of Educational Knowledge* (1971). The 'open school'/'closed school' and 'integrated code'/'collection code' oppositions seemed to offer the basis of a model which could be applied to a case study of an innovative school. The school studied is an Upper School and Community College (recently redesignated 'College') in the Leicestershire system. It is co-educational, with 1500 full-time students aged, mainly,[2] 14 to 18. Transfer from High School (11 to 14) to Upper was

[1]The term negotiation is meant here in its political sense, but the meetings held by staff might also be seen as negotiations in the 'social construction of reality' (Berger and Luckman, 1967).

[2]Apart from the adult community college with its attendant crèche facilities, the school boasts some returned students over the age of 18 and some part-time adult sixth formers. Numbers are in single figures, as yet.

voluntary until 1972-3, when the raising of the school leaving age
meant the total transfer of all students from the High Schools.[1]
The Upper School opened as a new comprehensive in 1969, having
been formed from an old grammar school of 400 students. The
present complex includes provision for adult education and recrea-
tion as well as a popular youth centre. The choice of the school
studied was based on its publicly presented image as innovative
in methods used and subjects taught.

Once access to the school had been gained, the problem became
one of selecting contexts and techniques to study the consequences
of innovation. An approach based on attaching the observer to a
group of pupils throughout their in-school programme was not
possible where every student was engaged in a 'self-chosen, individual timetable'. Any one group of students did not remain
together across subjects or periods in a school day. In a school of
1500 students and 100 staff it seemed more feasible to observe the
body of staff rather than any section of the student population. The
'innovations' attempted by the school, such as individual time-
tabling, mixed-age tutor groups and integrated curricula had
certain consequences for the classroom, but these could not be
understood purely by classroom observation. Their meaning was
contained in aims expressed in the structure of the course and
of the school itself. Their consequences, in the form of problems perceived by staff, were discussed by the decision-making
bodies of the school. The culture of the open classroom, the
aims and structure of the school as a whole, could not be understood by direct observation or by introspection on the basis of
shared experience. The perceptions of the observer had to be
placed in the context of teachers' perceptions of the school and
its problems.[2]

I based myself as a participant observer among the teaching
staff, who accepted me very readily into their company. My interaction with the students[3] was not really extensive; those contacts

[1]The school's catchment area is largely rural but covers the outskirts of Leicester
on one side and several suburban and industrialized villages; the intake thus
includes many urban students.

[2]The place of the school in the wider educational, economic, social and political
systems might be the focus of other studies. The students' and parents' perceptions
of the school would also be of interest in examining the ongoing world of the
school.

[3]The school always refers to its pupils as students.

I did maintain were with the members of a tutor group[1] I attended and with the school council,[2] and with some of the more notorious 'trouble-makers'. I was conscious of the dangers of observer effect in my research, and attempted to minimize this by refraining from giving opinions on matters concerning the school. The participants varied in their curiosity about their observer: some students were convinced I was an overgrown fifth-former; some staff were concerned to discover how far my research related to their own interest in sociological problems in education. There were even questions from a sociologically trained member of staff on the possibilities of applying Bernstein's model of the 'integrated code' to some of the school's curriculum activities. Such self-conscious and sociologically well-informed staff made my attempt to minimize observer effect somewhat hazardous.[3] My original research strategy was based on asking the participants what they thought I should be studying. If pressed I would say I was interested to see how the school worked.[4]

The best opportunity to observe innovations in practice was provided by the new humanities course which, in its second year, was now moving into a new block of open-plan classrooms. The humanities course included the English taught up to 'O' level and CSE as well as elements of other traditional subjects such as geography, history, economics, sociology and religious studies. The course was structured around units focused on particular issues or topics. Each team of 3 to 4 teachers was responsible for about 80 students, grouped, at least in the 4th year, on a mixed-ability basis. In order to understand the open classroom situation it was felt necessary to attend the team teaching meetings that mapped out teachers' strategies for a section of the course. The direct observation of teaching led to an investigation of the structuring of the lesson or

[1]The tutor group is composed of 'sociometric bunches' of friends who chose each other in questionnaires given at the High School. The tutor is responsible, in a pastoral sense, for about 24 students of both sexes who may include 4th, 5th, 6th and 7th years. The group meets every morning.

[2]The school council is composed of 20 elected students and 2 teachers along with the Principal's representative and the senior administrative officer (formerly the Registrar). The council is supposed to serve as an avenue for student involvement in the school's decision making.

[3]Such conversations are recorded in my field notes.

[4]My approach was a honest one in as much as my research strategy was constantly changing and was concerned to elicit the teachers' views of the problems in the school.

unit and of the course itself. The course and the difficulties it faced could only be understood in the wider context of the school's structure as manifested in its decision-making hierarchy of representative bodies. The 'decision-making' meetings of staff directed to the consideration and attempted solution of staff-defined problems were seen as arenas of negotiation where the official structure and aims were discussed and amended or retained.

In terms of the original theoretical model the school under study offered several difficulties in comparison with the ideal types of Bernstein's Open School/Closed School opposition (see Figure 1). Firstly, Bernstein provided no operational definitions of his descriptive terms[1] such as 'heterogeneous – homogeneous' 'achieved – assigned' 'sharp – blurred' and 'fixed – fluid'. Allocation to one or other type could be almost arbitrary. Secondly, it appeared that Bernstein had some notion of an absolute structure which could be extracted from the ongoing world of the school to be measured against his ideal type. His system does not allow for the existence of alternative definitions of what the school was. The headmaster might see ample 'opportunities for self government' for the students, the students might see none or at least none in areas that interested them. Thirdly, the model was a static one. The development from closed to open, or open to closed, was not examined to any great extent – at least in terms of a single school. The presentation of opposing ideal types does little to explain the process of development from one to the other. This paper will attempt to provide an analysis of some of the problems of the transitional state in terms of a Durkheimian model. Similar limitations to the above are present in attempting to apply the 'integrated code'/'collection code' of curriculum ideal types. In the light of these difficulties it was decided to examine the teachers' perceptions of the school and its structure; to investigate the coexistence and interaction of alternative definitions of the school; and to study the school as an ongoing system.

The open school model of Bernstein, and more generally the 'organic solidarity' model of Durkheim,[2] were found to correspond

[1]Bernstein provided his diagram (Figure 1 here) in the belief that it 'sets out the basic analysis . . . and also provides a scale for the degree of openness or closure'. It is the difficulties of operationalizing this scale which I wish to identify.

[2]According to Durkheim in *The Division of Labour* (1933), the form of social solidarity present in an advanced society with a highly specialized division of labour is organic in that each individual is an integral and unique part of the whole, and his

very closely with the officially stated aims of the school and its formal structure as presented in official statements made by the school. If the school could be seen as an attempt to implement a structure similar to Bernstein's open school type, it was of interest to study how this model was confronted by the reality of the school and its problems. The series of problems defined by the staff related to the formal structure of the school in ways which illuminate the bases of the model. Some of Durkheim's reflections on the difficulties of achieving organic solidarity can be shown to relate to these problems. Such insights will be illustrated by reference to a particular staff-defined problem later in this paper.

In order to obtain some indication of the teachers' perspectives on problems and the school, I took field notes in various staff meetings, attempting to record utterances as near verbatim as possible. Tape recordings were unacceptable in the situations researched, and may well have yielded too complex and bulky an array of information. The participants I observed in meetings were discussing questions I could, and did, ask them about in interviews. The context of the meeting was less artificial than that of the interview. The meetings had a pre-ordained purpose in terms of agendas. Their discussions in some cases led to decisions, and the decisions to new official policy to be implemented in the school. It is not suggested that the opinions or arguments given in a meeting are somehow nearer to the participants' 'true' or 'real' opinions or arguments. Neither is it assumed that such formal arenas are the only means by which the school is administered. It *is* assumed, however, and this assumption is supported by observation, that most if not all the important[1] issues, problems and decisions were reflected in the debates of these bodies. The data are not interpreted in terms of individuals' underlying ideologies, as Esland (1971) has proposed. It is, however, argued that the official account of the aims

---

removal would damage the functioning of the system. Each individual is specialized in his occupation to a degree that makes him socially and economically dependent on others in complementary specialisms. The 'conscience collective' no longer dominates and represses but celebrates choice and individuality in the 'cult of the individual'. The sacred barriers of the segmental society have now been broken down, the forced division of labour is ended. Such is Durkheim's 'organic solidarity' a model which serves as a basis for Bernstein's open school type. Since certain arguments are made on the basis of Durkheim rather than Bernstein, the model developed in this research is called the 'organic solidarity – open school' type.

[1]Important in the eyes of staff, as determined by observation, conversations, interviews and questionnaires.

**Figure 1: Bernstein's open school/closed school opposition.** From Bernstein (197–) – see references. Permission to reproduce is gratefully acknowledged.

|  | Mixing of categories (TYPE – OPEN) | Formal Controls ORDERS INSTRUMENTAL | Purity of categories (TYPE – CLOSED) |
|---|---|---|---|
| Teaching groups: | Heterogeneous – size and composition varied | | Homogeneous – sizes and composition fixed |
| Pedagogy: | Problem setting or creating; Emphasizes *ways of knowing* | | Solution giving; Emphasizes *contents* or states of *knowledge* |
| Teachers: | Teaching roles cooperative/interdependent; Duties *achieved*; Fluid points of reference and relation | | Teaching roles insulated from each other; Duties *assigned*; Fixed points of reference and relation |
| Curriculum: | Subject boundaries blurred (interrelated); Progression: deep to surface structure of knowledge; Common curriculum | | Subject boundaries sharp (less interrelation or integration); Progression: surface to deep structure of knowledge; Curriculum graded for different ability groups |
| Pupils: | Varied social groups reducing *group* similarity and difference – increased area of choice; Aspiration of the *many* raised; Fluid points of reference and relation | | Fixed and stable social groups emphasizing *group* similarity and difference – reduced area of choice; Aspirations of the *few* developed; Fixed points of reference and relation |

TYPE – OPEN
(1) Ritual order celebrates participation/cooperation
(2) Boundary relationships with outside blurred
(3) Internal organization:
  wide range of integrative sub-groups with active membership and success roles across ability ranges
  *If* prefect system – wide area of independence from staff, but limited exercise of power
  Range of opportunities for pupils to influence staff decisions, e.g. opportunities for self-government
(4) Teacher–pupil authority relationships:
  Reward and punishment less public and ritualized
  Teacher–pupil relationships of control – inter-personal
Mixing of categories

TYPE – CLOSED
(1) Ritual order celebrates hierarchy/dominance
(2) Boundary relationships with outside sharply drawn
(3) Internal organization:
  narrower range of integrative sub-groups with active membership and success roles confined to high ability range
  *If* prefect system – under staff control and influence, but extensive exercise of power
  Limited opportunities for pupils to influence staff decisions, e.g. limited opportunities for self-government
(4) Teacher–pupil authority relationships:
  Reward and punishment public and ritualized
  Teacher–pupil relationships of control – positional
Purity of categories

EXPRESSIVE

and structure can be compared to the 'organic solidarity – open school' type. It is not argued that the similarity is a conscious one, but that the underlying philosophy or logic is very similar. The operational definition of 'official' is taken to be those statements made on behalf of the whole school. These may be either more or less public. 'Notes for members of teaching staff', for example, are internal; *School for the Community* is a published book about the planning of the new school available to all. Those in the school may have other aims, they may construct alternative structures of an unofficial nature[1] but they share a common concept of what constitutes the official aims and structure. It is hoped to demonstrate this by the use of data from interviews and questionnaires in the thesis proper.

An account of the aims of the school is offered by the headmaster (now called the Principal) in a piece entitled 'Looking to the future' included in the book published about the planning of the new school (Rogers, 1971). This extract, like others to follow, is given in rather fuller terms than is usual in such works of interpretation so that the reader may have the opportunity to put the later specific quotations in context and receive a description of the school in the participants' own words.

'It is easy to fall in with those who say that schools should prepare students for the world as it is. As it is now? As it seems likely to be tomorrow? In that case, God help the students, God help the world. A third century Persian poet wrote of children:

> You can give them your love, but not your thoughts,
> For they have their own thoughts.
> You can house their bodies, but not their souls,
> For their souls dwell in the house of tomorrow.
> You can strive to be like them,
> But seek not to make them like you
> for life goes not backward, nor tarries with yesterday.

.   .   .   .   .   .   .   .   .   .   .   .   .   .   .   .   .   .   .

'It follows that our first aim educationally is not in terms of class subjects – though always they should provide a means – but in

---

[1]Examples of this would be the construction of walls in an open classroom area, thus challenging the official integrated policy, or the conspiring of those of like-mind to by-pass the official decision-making structure.

terms of each student's self-discovery. This was expressed by the eighty-year-old pianist Artur Rubinstein, who when asked recently by a television interviewer what he taught his pupils, replied: 'I try to discover who they are for them.' We think that this discovery can be made most profitably within the framework of a curriculum largely chosen by the student. But we know too, that we must move much further than we have so far ventured in breaking down those artificial barriers which divide subjects. The Design Centre, both by its architecture and by the design team's response to it, is pointing the way here, and very exciting it is to see the results of this. Our scientists are currently discussing a scheme for a foundatiom course on similar principles to that in design. But these are beginnings only. We have far to go before we can claim that each of the self-chosen, individual fourth-year courses is, in a true sense, integrated.

Subject barriers are only one expression of man's preoccupation with fencing himself in. We have hoped in our social organization to break down barriers caused by class, money, neighbourhood, intelligence, sex – and to point the need – and provide the means – for a caring community. We have rejected one method of supplying a sort of intellectual motivation – one which is still used in schools, and sometimes upheld by parents as an ideal of our society: competition between people. The sort of competition we encourage is that which impels the athlete to beat his own record (in metres or seconds) not that which impels him to beat someone else. In physical terms the contest between people may be healthy and this is indeed the basis of games-playing. In intellectual terms it can be both artificial and destructive. One of the less successful of the school's teachers, Dr. Samuel Johnson, had the good sense to remark: 'By exciting emulation and comparisons of superiority, you lay the foundations of lasting mischief; you make brothers and sisters hate each other.' Even if our academic standards (insofar as they can be measured objectively by external examinations) had suffered as a result of our policy, I should have thought it justified for the reasons I have suggested. But the evidence so far is that they have not suffered: rather the reverse. . . .

'If an open university, why not an 'open school'? Its aim, first and last, is to serve the community. I see it as an educational resource centre to which all may come (and from which all may go) as needs and interests dictate. Our services will, in part, depend on what priority the country sees fit to set on them. . . . Perhaps the pressures of the environment will bring us to new discoveries. Religion was defined by a great Christian as 'the total response of man to his environment'. I should like to think that . . . we could encourage that response.'

It is possible to find several elements in this official declaration of aims that relate to the 'organic solidarity – open school' model. For example 'our first aim educationally is not in terms of class subjects – though always they should provide a means – but in terms of each student's self-discovery' and 'this discovery can be made most profitably within the framework of a curriculum largely chosen by the student'. These quotations are evidence of the commitment to the sort of pedagogy where 'Problem setting or creating . . . *ways* of knowing' (see Figure 1) would be appropriate.

The 'declaration of aims' here cited was written in 1970, a year after the school's opening and three years before my study commenced. The school had changed by 1973, and began to produce a series of follow-up papers 'to bring the book up to date and to cover new developments' (Rogers, 1973). The first of the papers, *Postscript 1973* by the Principal, intended to 'outline some of the general areas of change . . . and to record present thinking about the future'. Of the framework established in the original planning of the school it is said that 'there have been modifications, refinements and elaborations . . . but there have been few if any basic changes'. Thus 'we were, and remain, much concerned that every student in the school should be treated as an adult member of a community for which he or she felt responsible. Writing now in our fourth year (1972-3), we are encouraged by the sense of personal responsibility shown by the great majority of our students. By their developing self-discipline – a far more valuable quality this than submission to any external 'discipline' – they are learning to stand on their own feet in a difficult and changing world. This they will have to do if they, and the world, are to survive' (Rogers, 1973). The official aims of the enterprise and the form of solidarity envisaged (see Figure 1, the expressive axis) have changed little.

Given that the aims as officially and publicly offered by the Principal resemble the ideal type, what of the official structure of the school? It is not possible to separate aims and structure completely, for in the terms of the people who constructed and who operate the systems each element has its function or purpose. To identify any component of the official structure it is necessary to recognize its declared aim. The school's 'official structure' is always presented in terms of the guiding philosophy of the school.

Here is an extract from the 'Notes for members of teaching staff' 1973, circulated to all teachers at the beginning of the school year which serves as an account of some aspects of the 'official structure'.

'1. *Organization*

There are two interrelated structures in the school's organization: they may be broadly distinguished as 'social' and 'academic'.

a. *Social*

The social unit is the tutor group (Tutor and 20+ students), each within one of six divisions (Division Head and Deputy of opposite sex). The tutors within a division meet with their Division Head after school on alternate Tuesdays. On the Thursdays of the same week the Division Heads meet together with the Principal, the two Vice-Principals, the Senior Master, the Director of Studies and two School Counsellors as the Pastoral Committee. By this means there can be two-way communication between the Division and Division Heads' meetings, and every member of staff can be informed on all 'social' matters and involved in the machinery of decision making.

b. *Academic*

The academic unit is the subject set with its teacher, under the overall responsibility of the Head of Department. Coordinating the work of the Departments is the responsibility of the appropriate Faculty Head, together with the Director of Studies.

There are Faculty and Department meetings for staff after school on alternate Tuesdays, in the following four groups: Humanities, Design, Science, and the non-Faculty departments.

On the Thursday of the same week the Faculty Heads together with the Principal, the two Vice-Principals, the Senior Master, the Director of Studies, the Senior Academic Tutor and a representative of the Division Heads meet as the Curricular Committee. This arrangement provides similarly for the two-way communication and information and involvement in decision making.

Clearly these two structures are related both in staffing and functions and there must be the closest coordination between them. The need for coordination can be illustrated by the Careers Staff who in the very nature of their work provide an obvious link. Again, the Principal and his two Vice-Principals, with the overall responsibility, combine both functions

.   .   .   .   .   .   .   .   .   .   .   .   .   .   .   .   .   .   .

'5. *Staff Meetings*
As outlined in (1) above, there is a regular provision for members of staff to meet. A working party on decision-making (1972-3) recommended a six-weekly meeting for all staff in place of a division meeting. This recommendation will be put to the test in the autumn term. The meeting will make recommendations to the Principal who will consult with a Joint Meeting of the Pastoral and Curricular Committees held on Thursday of the same week.

.   .   .   .   .   .   .   .   .   .   .   .   .   .   .   .   .   .   .

'10. *Punishments*
We believe these to be unnecessary. We do demand that students have a high standard of personal and social behaviour (note guidance given in Student's Guide). The ultimate sanction is exclusion from the community.
It is essential that all members of staff should at all times help students to keep within the guidelines of behaviour, and talk out with them difficulties in interpretation (whether deliberate or un-knowing) and any breaches of the guidelines. The Principal, Vice-Principals, Senior Master or Division Heads should be consulted if there is doubt, or where clarification is needed.
It is particularly important that staff and students should have a common understanding in this area if a just, caring and well ordered community is to continue to grow in mutual strength and confidence.'

The above extract outlines an intricate and complex bureaucratic system based on principles of representative democracy. The Principal makes decisions 'in committee', reserves the right to refuse to allow changes which he opposes strongly and retains the responsibility for decisions made in the school. Vetoes are rarely used; the only occasion during the year was the refusal to alter the constitution of the school council against a vote of the majority student members of that body. In this school the teachers are to treat their students as 'young adults', students are to be accorded the right to choose whenever possible and are to be guided by 'self-discipline' rather than external rules. The principal tries to apply the same expectations to his staff as he expects his staff to apply to the students. Evidence for this is given in an extract from a Staff Bulletin by the Principal dated 10th December 1973 under the title 'Meetings and decision-making':

> '. . . I shall hope to resist any pressure upon me to dictate. Do we not resist that same pressure from our own students? When we are rightly concerned that they should be helped to grow through their own decision-making and a sense of student responsibility, it would be unfortunate and inconsistent to say the least if we denied a similar opportunity to ourselves.'

A school for 'the young adult' which believes punishments to be unnecessary rests on an 'organic solidarity – open school' type model. It remains to be seen how such a model is confronted by the school's problems. The deviant in such a community is the person who refuses to choose or who chooses an alternative outside the acceptable range offered by the school. In a major debate that consumed much staff time in official and unofficial meetings, the staff confronted the problem of 'the motivation of the unmotivated'. The presence in the school of those who refused to accept or were incapable of employing the prevailing official philosophy aroused great concern.

The problem had arisen in several ways before, but had never confronted the machinery of decision-making in such a demonstrative way. Among the subsequent events in the school the following can be seen as related to this problem and its discussion; the remedial or 'supplementary education' department went through a period of flux and review; the staff re-worked their lunch-time supervision system; moves were made to integrate the pastoral and curricular functions of the teacher to give the academic unit a pastoral identity. Thus the full analysis would proceed on the following lines: (1) how the 'problem' arose in terms of its source in various teachers' definitions of the situation; (2) how the problem was handled by the official decision-making procedure; (3) how the official aims and structure were invoked in discussion of the problem; (4) how the problem continued to be discussed; (5) how the official aims and structure changed if at all. A preliminary approach to steps (1), (2) and (3) is attempted in this paper.

Here is an extract from a leaflet circulated before the second general staff meeting, which is evidence from stage (1) above:

'Item 4. Agenda of the GSM Tuesday November 27th.

Division 1 proposes that action should be taken to motivate the unmotivated. The proposal originates from a lengthy and involved discussion which took place during our last division meeting. Many of us felt that the presence of 'unmotivated' students in a class made such demands on our energies that we were not doing justice to them or to the 'motivated'.

We wish to share our concern with the rest of the staff and therefore formulated this proposal.'

The General Staff Meeting was able to devote only a small proportion of its time to this motion. A series of meetings lasting two weeks was devoted to the discussion of this problem.[1] The last meeting of the series on Thursday 13th December combined Pastoral and Curricular Committees with 17 senior members of staff present. I was also present at this meeting and was asked to take the minutes, as the secretary was expected to be late. The discussion that took place surveyed the debates of the previous weeks and attempted to establish the major aspects of the problem. The collection of notes I took at this and other meetings is seen as evidence from stages (2) and (3) above. Extracts from the field notes illustrate the applicability of the Durkheimian theory of social change in a school whose official aims and structure are based on the 'organic solidarity – open school' model. The problems arising in the classroom, for instance, are defined in similar terms to Durkheim's (1952) 'anomie' and 'egoism' experienced in the transition towards a

[1] At the general staff meeting it was proposed that the motion be discussed in division and faculty meetings and placed first on the next general staff meeting agenda. The following meeting of the joint pastoral-curriculum committee composed of senior staff voted (by 9 to 5 with one abstention) to ask the staff whether they would like to devote two weeks of normal meetings (4 in all) exclusively to this motion. The staff in a morning meeting carried this narrowly by 33 to 30 (among a staff of 100). The normal 'democratic' consultative procedure was suspended, leaving the Principal, much to his annoyance, to make 'executive decisions' in other matters concerning the school.

fully integrated society. The causes of the 'problems' defined in this way may also be seen in terms of this model.

The key elements in the participants' arguments in the above respect centre around four issues: the lack of regulation; the lack of attachment; the existence of alternative group identities; and proposals for improving the integrative function of sub-groups. Thus 'lack of regulation' is given as a contributory cause to 'unmotivation'. For example; the Head of Division F: 'Some of the problems arose more from out of classroom situation – when not being supervised'; and C's document submitted to the meeting: 'There is a great need for staff vigilance. Discipline in the classroom is not an out-moded idea. It does depend on a degree of firmness without which no subject can be taught. And students prefer it this way'.

'Lack of attachment' to the school is another explanation. For example; the Head of Division H: 'If only some students would do something, sense of identity with the school, the division or themselves as body of people'. And the Head of Division L: 'Basis for discipline through Pastoral system. Division identity. Tutor contact with tutees before come to school – week's camping in summer for all tutor groups. Identity with them before rest of school'. The deviant peer group is seen as a threat to the school structure and aims, which were based on the full individuality of each student. The Head of Division I expresses this quite eloquently: 'Response to peer group far more than to us – unmotivated will say 'can't work because it is not thing to do'. Felt that we were perhaps realising that the perspectives of these kids very different from ours – go round to homes, ideals and motives for remaining alive for 24 hours very different.'

Teachers in the school are concerned to find some group which would act as an integrative force, offering both regulation and attachment. Some propose the strengthening of the tutor group (for example Division L, quoted above). Some propose the development of a pastoral identity for academic units, for example the previous general staff meeting received a proposal 'that we discuss possible ways of co-ordinating academic and pastoral roles of teachers, particularly with regard to helping unmotivated students'.

Thus the official aims and structure of the school correspond to the organic solidarity – open school type, the problems are interpreted by the teachers in terms that correspond to the problems of the transitional state between the societies of mechanical and organic solidarity as identified by Durkheim. In Durkheim's studies in the transitional state, 'anomie' (lack of regulation) and 'egoism' (lack of attachment) manifest themselves in anti-social behaviour such as suicide or crime. Lack of integration persists in a society with a forced, unequal division of labour. The 'religion' of organic solidarity, 'the cult of the individual' is insufficiently present in the individual consciences of the members of society. The situation is similar in a school where the official aims and structure represent an attempt to create a form of solidarity around the 'cult of the individual' in an unintegrated, unequal world. The student as a young adult would ideally be able and willing to choose his own education, to discipline himself and to identify himself with the school. The impact of the second year of compulsory intake, and the retention of those who would otherwise have left school at 15, highlighted the problem of some of those who were seen to fall outside that definition, the 'unmotivated'.[1]

The organic solidarity – open school model has thus provided us with a means by which the problems facing the teacher in the classroom can be better understood. The problems themselves are associated with the implementation of certain policies which must be seen in the context of the aims of the teachers and the structure of the school as a whole. The observer's account of the classroom and its problems must include an analysis of the teacher's perception of his world. If this is not done the sociologist presents a one-sided account where he appears to be the only reflective or critical participant, much in the fashion of imperialistic culture-centred schools of anthropology.

**Acknowledgements**

Thanks firstly to the staff and students of the school studied for putting up with my sometimes bewildering presence and for aiding my studies so generously. I am grateful for permission to quote from *School for the Community* and various other school documents and meetings.

Thanks are due to Messrs Routledge and Kegan Paul for permission to quote from *School for the Community* and to the Open

[1]Further research will examine the importance of the official aims and structure among the school's staff by the use of interview and questionnaire data as well as other less formal observations. The account given here will be offered to the staff of the school and any comments or criticisms obtained will be included in later work.

University and Professor Basil Bernstein for the extract from
Bernstein's 'Postscript'.

I am greatly indebted to Dr Sara Delamont, Professor Gerry
Bernbaum, Mr Tom Whiteside and Miss Kate Taylor for reading
this paper and offering so many helpful criticisms. The faults that
remain are mine alone.

Finally I wish to acknowledge the financial support received from
the SSRC for my PhD research.

## References

ADELMAN, C. and WALKER, R. (1974). 'Strawberries.' In: STUBBS, M. W. and DELA-
   MONT, S. *Explorations in Classroom Observation*. London: Wiley (forthcoming).
BERGER, P. L. and LUCKMAN, T. (1967). *The Social Construction of Reality*. London:
   Allen Lane.
BERNSTEIN, B. (1967). 'Open schools: open society?' *New Society*, 14 September.
BERNSTEIN, B. (1971). 'On the classification and framing of educational know-
   ledge.' In: YOUNG, M. (ed.) *Knowledge and Control*. London: Collier-Macmillan.
BERNSTEIN, B. (1974). *Class Codes and Control*, volume 1. 2nd edition. London:
   Routledge and Kegan Paul. (This first appeared in an educational studies
   course of The Open University in 1973.)
DURKHEIM, E. (1933). *The Division of Labour in Society*. London: Collier-Macmillan.
DURKHEIM, E. (1952). *Suicide*. London: Routledge and Kegan Paul.
ESLAND, G. (1971). 'Teaching and learning as the organization of knowledge.'
   In: YOUNG, M. (ed.) *Knowledge and Control*. London: Collier-Macmillan.
FLANDERS, N. A. (1970). *Analysing Teaching Behaviour*. London: Addison-Wesley.
HARGREAVES, D. H. (1967). *Social Relations in a Secondary School*. London: Routledge
   and Kegan Paul.
LACEY, C. (1970). *Hightown Grammar*. Manchester University Press.
ROGERS, T. (ed.) (1971). *School for the Community*. London: Routledge and Kegan
   Paul.
ROGERS, T. (1973). *Postscript: 1973*. Published by the school.

# CHAPTER 9

# In Cold Blood: Bedside Teaching in a Medical School

*Paul Atkinson, University College, Cardiff.*

Unlike the majority of research presented in this collection, the following paper is not concerned with classroom processes in schools. It is about a branch of higher education – medical education. Rue Bucher has pointed out that:

'I frequently have the impression that students of medicine are second only to freshman psychology students in being objects of study by social scientists' (Bucher, 1970).

I share Bucher's feeling – although one should certainly add school pupils to the list of over-researched captive populations. Medical students tend to be used as research-fodder by their own teachers in the medical school, and by such 'outsiders' as sociologists and psychologists. The extent of such research is partly indicated by the existence of specialist journals on medical education in Britain and the United States. In this country the greater involvement of behavioural scientists in medical schools as a result of the recommendations of the Royal Commission on Medical Education (1968) will no doubt reinforce this trend. But I offer no apology for adding to this research myself. My justification is that teaching processes that lie at the heart of medical education have been almost universally overlooked hitherto. One such lacuna is the topic of bedside teaching – the oldest and least explored method of medical instruction. This paper is an attempt to show one way in which this lack might be remedied.

My own research was done in the Edinburgh medical school. I spent the major part of the academic years 1971/72 and 1972/73 acting as a participant-observer with two cohorts of students in their fourth year of the undergraduate course. I donned a white coat and 'walked the wards' with groups of students and their teachers. The

medical course at Edinburgh follows the traditional pattern in that
it is divided into a preclinical period, followed by a phase of clinical
studies. It is in the fourth year of the course that formal teaching in
clinical subjects begins.[1] Students receive instruction in medicine
and surgery in a number of teaching hospitals each morning.
Students are attached to a clinical 'firm' for one term at a time. For
the first term of the year all students attend medical units; for the
second and third terms they spend one term on a second medical
unit, and one on a surgical unit.[2] My research was organized in such
a way that I spent the first year observing medical teaching, and in
the second year transferred my attention to surgical work. In
addition to observing the teaching, I also interviewed the students
I observed and distributed a questionnaire to the first cohort
(cf. Atkinson, 1973). The research was done by taking field-notes,
either while the action was going on, or as soon after the action as
possible. In addition, I had access to videotape recordings of bedside
teaching. These had been made for demonstration purposes, by the
Edinburgh University Audio Visual Services. I was able to use these
recordings as sensitizing devices before entering the field, and I have
also used transcripts of these recordings as illustrative materials.[3]

The time spent in the hospital units is divided between a number
of different activities. These include the following types of instructional situations that are recognized by students and staff alike.

*Bedside teaching*   This is the most distinctive aspect of medical
education in the hospital. A doctor takes a small group of students
into the ward and teaches at a patient's bedside. He may spend all
his time with one patient, or conduct a 'round' – teaching on a
number of patients in succession. This is an opportunity for a number
of topics to be worked on: students practise taking histories and
performing physical examinations; physicians and surgeons them-

[1]There is a two-stage entry to the Edinburgh medical school. Students who lack
adequate 'A' level passes in the basic sciences enter in the first year; those with the
necessary exemptions enter into the second year directly. Thus after one year of
basic science and two years of medical sciences, clinical work begins in the fourth
year, which is the third year of study for many of the students.

[2]For the second and third terms the class is divided into two and the halves
rotate – whilst one is doing medicine, the other is doing surgery.

[3]I am extremely grateful to the Edinburgh University Audio Visual Services
for the preparation of a tape of the sound-track. I am also indebted to the
consultants concerned for their permission to make use of this material; they must
of course remain anonymous.

selves demonstrate these skills to the students; the individual patient may also be used as a starting-point for more general discussion of pathology, treatment, clinical method and so on.

*Tutorials* Each clinical unit has a teaching room attached. Here doctors may conduct small group teaching sessions of a more 'theoretical' or 'didactic' nature, without recourse to patients in the wards. (The teaching room may also be used for the discussion of points that arise at the bedside, or to avoid discussing features of the case within earshot of the patient himself. These latter activities are usually seen as extensions of 'bedside teaching' sessions rather than 'tutorials'.)

*Waiting nights* The hospital wards receive emergency admissions on a rota basis. On their weekly 'receiving' or 'waiting' night, students attached to a given unit are expected to attend for the evening. They can thus see patients brought in in acute conditions.

Students in both medicine and surgery also attend out-patient clinics. In surgery they visit operating theatres and observe, either from a gallery or from the theatre floor. These, then, are the main forms of clinical instruction that students are engaged in during their fourth year medicine and surgery. In the following discussion I shall be concentrating on aspects of the bedside teaching encounter.

As I have already suggested, in observing bedside teaching, I found that I was venturing into relatively uncharted territory. The topic has received scant attention from most writers on medical education. As in many areas of educational research, concern has been first and foremost on methods of selection, assessment, attainment and failure, motivation, attitudes and career aspirations. In contrast, the *process* of face-to-face teaching has been poorly covered. (The relative stress on different research areas is well illustrated by reference to a recent survey of the relevant literature (Simpson, 1972) where the lack of research on clinical instruction is shown up quite strikingly.)

In the sociological sphere there are three major works on medical schools – all American. Firstly, there is the study of Cornell and Pennsylvania undertaken by Merton and his colleagues from Columbia (Merton *et al.*, 1957). This was followed by the ethnography of Kansas University medical school by Hughes and his

Chicago-based colleagues (Becker *et al.*, 1961). These have recently been supplemented by Bloom's account of the State University of New York Downstate Medical Center (Bloom, 1973). It is not necessary to review the differing approaches of these works in this context (see Atkinson, 1973, for a discussion of the relevance of these studies to the Edinburgh study). It is sufficient to point out that none of them contains any adequate description or analysis of the processes of clinical teaching. They all stop short at discussing students' attitudes to patients; their interaction with them is almost entirely by-passed. In Britain we do not as yet have any parallel studies of medical schools. The largest single piece of published research on medical students in this country derives from a survey undertaken jointly by the Association for the Study of Medical Education and the National Foundation for Educational Research. This was done in connection with the Royal Commission on Medical Education (1968) – The Todd Report – and some of the data are published in an appendix to the report. This was entirely conducted by means of a questionnaire, and thus presents no direct evidence on teaching interactions. The main text of the Royal Commission has little to say on the topic of clinical instruction; it deprecates the use of large ward rounds, and commends consideration for the patients, but adds little else.

If the main sociological sources have ignored the topic, it has to some extent been approached by those who are more closely aligned with the tradition of social psychology and so-called 'interaction analysis'. There have been a number of attempts to apply the techniques of pre-coded observation schedules to the observation of bedside teaching. I am aware of three methods that have been tried – all stemming from the United States. There is one summary rating-scale system and two varieties of category system.[1]

The rating scale system that I refer to is the Medical Instruction Observation Record – developed by Hilliard Jason at the University of Buffalo and subsequently used in a number of settings (e.g., Jason, 1962, 1964). The system consists of eight separate scales, each with twenty points. The scales are labelled: 'Attitude to difference'; 'Sensitivity to physical setting'; 'Attitude to students'; 'Use of instructional materials'; 'Attitude to patients'; 'Reaction to students' needs'; 'Use of teaching methods'; 'Use of challenge'.

---

[1] I have not attempted to summarize the *findings* of the studies mentioned; I am concerned solely with an evaluation of their adequacy from the point of view of method.

Jason (1964) claims that in the use of his scales, 'the observations were purely descriptive and were not concerned with the quality of the teaching'. Yet it is hard to see how such ratings can be seen as anything but frankly evaluative. Consider, for instance, the exemplars that are offered in the user's manual to illustrate the extreme poles of one scale – 'Attitude to patients'. On the one hand we find: 'Frank disregard for the patient is evident. The patient is not greeted, is given brusque instructions, and manipulations are undertaken without explanation.' On the other hand there is: 'Kindness and consideration characterize the contact. Permission is requested for all that is done; reassuring explanations are offered and protection of modesty is assured.' It is, it appears to me, difficult to maintain that the evaluative stance is even an implicit one here.

As will be apparent from the wording of the scale titles, Jason's system is concerned only with the evaluation of the medical teacher; students and patients enter into the picture only as incidentals to the clinician's performance. In common with other rating summaries, MIOR is extremely wasteful, insofar as it preserves none of the original interactions. The MIOR does preserve an underlying concern apparent in much of the American tradition of classroom interaction research, stemming from the work of Lewin, Lippitt and White (1939). This line of research is concerned with the theme of democracy and authoritarianism (or, as Jason labels it, traditionalism). Explicitly, underlying his scales, he sees a single bipolar dimension:

'. . . for the seven scales,[1] they *tended toward* the extremes of: rejecting student differences, disregarding the physical setting, showing an antagonistic attitude to students, using instructional materials ineffectively, disregarding student needs, employing teaching methods ineffectively and making no use of challenge. Henceforth, for summary purposes, teaching that tended in these directions is referred to as "traditional"' (Jason, 1962).

By the same token, instructors who tended towards the opposite extremes were described as 'democratic'. The use of such value-laden descriptions severely undermines Jason's claim to a non-evaluative position. Indeed, one is tempted to suggest that he comes

[1]The exact number of scales depends on the version of MIOR in use – they differ only slightly.

out into the open and describes the first type as downright un-American teaching activities.

At first sight more promising than the MIOR are the two inter-action schedules of the category type. The first that I shall consider is that used by Payson and Barchas (1965) in what they describe as 'a time study of medical teaching rounds'. The analysis proceeds by monitoring the allocation of time to a number of different activities, classified according to whether they take place with the patient present or absent. The categories for coding are as follows:

*Patient present*

Talk with patient  – (a)  physical factors
                       (b)  other factors
Examination [of the patient]
Talk about patient – (a)  physical factors
                       (b)  other factors
Theory

*Patient absent*

Talk about patient – (a)  physical factors
                       (b)  other factors
Theory
Walking and waiting
Miscellaneous

When one remembers that 'patient present'/'patient absent' represent two different social contexts in which the instrument is used, it will be seen that the schedule is based on five categories of talk and one of action, plus two residual categories. It is a very blunt instrument indeed. Additionally, the mixture of action and talk involves an inherent ambiguity in the recording. All the time devoted to the examination of the patient is allocated to that category; any talk – either with the patient or the students on the part of the doctor – is not recorded as such.

The system used by Payson and Barchas shares a basic problem with the MIOR in that it is used to record only the talk and activity of the teaching clinician:

'The same procedure was used in each hospital. The allocation of discussion and examination time of the senior

physician present was measured with a stopwatch and
recorded according to a pre-coded schema . . . All use of
time was considered to be under the direction of the
senior physician and was so recorded' (Payson and
Barchas, 1965).

Thus, quite apart from the failure to distinguish the talk and acts
of patients and students, the use of the scheme makes a very extreme
assumption about the nature of social order in the teaching situation
– that it is solely under the control and management of just one of
the interacting parties.

More sophisticated is the third coding scheme to be considered.
This bears closer resemblance to the most frequently used methods
of classroom observation. Anderson (1966) developed Flanders'
(1955) category system (FIAC) for use in clinical settings. The
scheme consists of ten major categories, of which several are
subdivided – producing twenty-one categories in all. Additionally,
there are three residual categories – 'Silence', 'Confusion' and
'Patient talk'. As with FIAC, the underlying logic of the system is the
four-way classification of talk into 'Instructor initiation', 'Instructor
response', 'Student initiation' and 'Student response'. Strikingly,
patient talk does not figure in the subsequent analysis. In fact,
Anderson's study appears to be addressed primarily to what my
Edinburgh students would have recognized as 'tutorials' in the
teaching room. Although he states that ward rounds were included
in the analysis, it seems that these were primarily classroom-based
sessions, with just occasional forays into the ward to the patient's
bedside.

Yet even Anderson's approach leaves much to be desired, and
my criticisms apply *a fortiori* to the other two systems I have referred
to. As I have already pointed out, students' and patients' contributions to the teaching session are not dealt with in the MIOR, nor by
Payson and Barchas. The Anderson system does include categories
for both, but the patient's talk is treated as a residual category,
and does not play a significant part in Anderson's description of
teaching practices. In other words, Anderson treats the process
of clinical teaching as essentially similar to that of school-based
classroom teaching. (Indeed, his description of his own work
explicitly describes it as classroom-based although it purports to
include ward-based bedside teaching.) Thus the design and use of

Anderson's system leave matters very close to the classic Flanders model of two-party games of 'linguistic ping-pong' (Hamilton and Delamont, 1974). In doing so, I argue, Anderson (and the other authors cited) have managed to distort the most distinctive feature of clinical teaching at the patient's bedside – that it is a *triadic* situation. The doctor, students and patient are all engaged in the creation and maintenance of the social situation. Further, they are all engaged in the exchange and control of medical information and knowledge. The patient can in no sense be treated as a lay figure, a passive 'resource' or 'topic' for teaching: he or she is also called upon to act as a participant – as a social actor. Any approach which failed to accommodate the part played by all parties to the interaction cannot cope adequately with the distinctive and recurrent features of bedside teaching in the medical school.

My solution does not lie in the development of yet another pre-coded observation system, however. Despite the pre-eminence of a few systems such as the FIAC, educational research has been inundated with a vast number of observation systems. But, apart from the establishment of a few norms – such as Flanders' 'two-thirds rule',[1] the development of adequate generalizations about teaching has eluded the interaction analysts. Interaction analysis may prove useful for a limited range of practical problems (cf. Hamilton and Delamont, 1974, for a discussion of pros and cons). It does not attempt to solve fundamental problems of social order. Rather, this style of research is primarily concerned with the enumeration of surface features of the interactions. Or, to put it more eruditely, the level of analysis is 'etic' rather than 'emic' – with the proviso that the 'etic' descriptions are generally very crudely drawn.[2] Essentially, the interaction analysts are involved in the production of classifications and building typologies (e.g. of 'teaching styles'). Yet the criteria which inform the selection of the descriptive categories remain largely implicit (cf. Hamilton and Delamont, 1974). The construction and use of such schemes is

---

[1] This 'rule' – that approximately two-thirds of time in classrooms is devoted to talk, and two-thirds of that is taken up with teacher talk (Flanders, 1970) – is not a 'rule' of discourse, but a statistical norm or trend. This is in contrast to, say, the rules of conversation derived by Sacks (forthcoming) – for instance, that 'at least, and not more than, one party speaks at a time in a single conversation' and 'speaker change recurs'.

[2] The contrast between 'emic' and 'etic' in this context is taken from Walker and Adelman (n.d.). The distinction was originally formulated by Pike (1954).

dependent upon knowledge and assumptions about the social realities of classroom life which remain unexamined. Interaction analysis is afflicted with 'quantiphrenia' – with the belief that classification and enumeration can replace the process of *generalization* in generating theory.[1] All too often, the failures of interaction analysis are couched in terms of pious hopes for the future: 'We are not yet in a position to . . .'; 'We hope that future research will clarify . . .'. The assumption appears to be that if you count enough things for long enough, then theory will somehow emerge.

Although the approach of interaction analysis relies on the quantification of phenomena, there appears to be no valid basis for the assumption that the repetition or duration of events provides the only ground of social order, or provides the only rationale of members' understandings of social interaction. Of course, the sense of repetition of typified acts may be a part of one member's typification of another: 'Oh, he's always . . .'; 'He's forever saying . . .' and so on. But such assemblages of 'similar' events are the products of members' interpretations on concrete situations. They are not once-for-all classifications which can be abstracted from the members' formulations. Additionally, members may recognize as the most important element in an interaction an act which is seen as atypical, unique, unforeseen, unrepeatable or whatever. What the students see as the most salient feature of a teaching period may well be fleeting – lasting perhaps a few seconds – yet prove a crucial event in the students' shared definitions and understandings. (For such an event and its subsequent significance, compare Walker and Adelman, forthcoming.) Let me also cite an example from my own research. The incident concerns a relatively young consultant in medicine. In the middle of teaching one day he suddenly groaned and 'collapsed'. Dumbfounded, the students stood about, wondering what to do – and in fact doing nothing. After a moment or two, the consultant leaped back to his feet and berated the students for standing around and taking no action. They were supposed to be training to be doctors – but what good would they have been if he had genuinely collapsed? This incident clearly had a considerable effect on the students, and was entered into their word-hoard of myths and folk-tales about their teachers. He was seen as a 'charac-

---

[1]This point is also made by Leach (1961), who castigates his fellow anthropologists for 'butterfly collecting' in the construction of their typologies rather than searching for general structural properties.

ter', who was often described to me as illustrating his teaching with such 'dramatic' antics. For myself and the students alike, the incident recounted above appeared to be a prime example of an extremely characteristic facet of this clinician's teaching. Yet it lasted a few moments only, and would probably have occupied about ten tallies of a Flanders/Anderson three-second sampling technique. (Presumably, in FIAC it would be represented by category 10 – 'silence or confusion' followed by 7 – 'criticizing or justifying authority'; similarly, Anderson would represent it as z followed by 6B.) Even stated in baldest outline, the doctor's action and the students' reaction suggest a number of comments on clinical teaching and professional values. I am not convinced that such comments are in any way retrievable from 'Silence or confusion followed by criticism'.

My own method derives rather from an ethnographic stance.[1] Rather than assuming an understanding of social order in clinical teaching, I take it as problematic to account for how such social encounters are successfuly accomplished by the members involved. (See Hamilton and Delamont, 1974, for a discussion of some of the main contrasts between this style of research and interaction analysis.) My analysis is influenced by Erving Goffman's accounts of everyday life (e.g., Goffman, 1961, 1967); in particular, I follow the game-theoretic approach advocated by Lyman and Scott (1970), and derived from some of the ideas of Goffman.

In criticizing the previous research I referred to, I pointed out that they failed to take account of the most distinctive aspect of clinical teaching – that it is a three-party game.[2] The usual teacher-student model must be broadened, as the most important 'teaching resource' is also a participant. Locating this weakness also suggests a possible approach to the study of clinical teaching. In the rest of this paper we shall concentrate on work done by the patient in the construction of the bedside teaching encounter.

One way of approaching the social construction of reality –

[1]Hamilton and Delamont (1974) and Parlett and Hamilton (1972) use the term 'anthropological'. I prefer 'ethnographic' insofar as it refers primarily to *method*, whereas 'anthropological' carries stronger connotations of subject matter which are inappropriate.

[2]This is of course an over-simplification. There is not a single student, but several round the bedside. Sometimes individual students are chosen to talk with the patient, while on other occasion, students ask questions and comment in rotation. The problems of how individual students' utterances are 'tied' to each other to produce a single history are beyond the scope of this paper.

though by no means the only way – is through an analysis of events which *disrupt* it. Such an approach has been used to good effect by Garfinkel (1967). Such disruptions of everyday life make visible the taken-for-granted background features of social life which may normally pass unnoticed. When things go wrong, we may get some leverage on the ways in which events are normally managed, and how actors routinely produce smooth, untroubled interactions. Disruptions may be deliberately contrived (as with Garfinkel's illustrative exercises) or may be naturally occurring episodes in ongoing encounters.

In adopting this starting point, I shall use a type of naturally occurring action which can disrupt, or spoil a bedside interaction between students and patients (with or without a clinician present). To begin with, I shall present a summary of the event which first drew my attention to this specific line of inquiry. I was standing with a small group of students who had been taking histories from patients, either individually or in pairs. As we hung about in the corridor, we were joined by one of the female students. When she came up, she immediately began to complain about 'her' patient: as she had begun to take the patient's history, the patient had immediately told her that she had mitral stenosis, as a complication of rheumatic fever contracted in adolescence. She had, the student complained, 'spoiled all the fun'. This episode, and its connotations of a spoiled encounter, gave me an entrée into the problem of social order at the bedside. The feature which emerges in this context is the diagnosed nature of the patient's illness. By the time that students see the majority of patients in the course of morning teaching rounds, their trouble has been at least differentially diagnosed, and the diagnosis may in fact be considered definitive by the hospital clinicians. At least management of some sort will have been initiated, tests ordered, procedures undertaken. Symptoms such as severe pain will have been controlled if possible, and physical signs may have abated or disappeared altogether (e.g., high fevers, blood loss, etc.). This aspect of the teaching round is recognized by students. They contrast it with cases that they see on waiting nights. In student jargon, the distinction was sometimes characterized as a difference between 'hot' and 'cold' medicine. On the one hand, 'hot' medicine was seen as exposing the students to 'real' medical situations: histories are being taken for the first time and are crucial to the patient's treatment; the illness must be managed and diagnosis must be attempted. There is a sense of the dramatic, the unpredictable, and the rough-and-tumble of acute hospital medicine. On the other hand, 'cold' medicine is seen and characterized as 'contrived' situations.

Although a history may have been elicited from the patient a number of times already, students may be asked to take a history from the same patient yet again. For example:

> 'Mr I said at one point, "Half the students here have seen me before, and my history is as big as that . . ." He held his hands apart to indicate a thick pile of notes.'

> 'The patient interjected that she had told her story so often that "I should have brought along a tape-recording".'

This feature of bedside teaching was also recognized by members of staff. For example, in the introductory talks at the beginning of the year I noted the following:

> 'Dr M. commented that they might experience a natural feeling of depression on seeing a patient who had already been thoroughly examined, and of thus being an imposition on the patient.'

It was sometimes stated by clinicians that it was always a possibility that new information might be thrown up in the course of bedside teaching, which might affect the management of the patient and his illness. But my observations suggest that this is in fact a very rare occurrence; such new observations as are made, or discrepancies which appear, are not usually of importance in the management of the case.

To summarize this point, then: *the patient's hospital career is already under way.* It follows from this that: *the patient may have become well-informed on the nature of his or her condition.* It is by no means the case that *all* hospital patients are well-informed. On the contrary, some are systematically denied accurate knowledge of it (cf. Glaser and Strauss, 1965; McIntosh, 1974). Nevertheless, insofar as clinical work, including diagnosis and investigations, has been done, patients may be in a favourable position to be aware of what has been said and done. Additionally, there may be patients who, by reason of long and/or unusual disorders, have come to occupy a position, vis-a-vis the doctors which approximates more to that of 'colleague' than 'client'. Such a relationship is described by Fox (1959) – in the context of experimental academic medicine, where the patients' cooperation and self-monitoring made them indispensable members of the research enterprise.

Additionally, the teaching rounds that I am describing were specially scheduled teaching occasions. The students were not simply taken on to the physicians' working rounds. They were specifically *teaching* rounds, with a single clinician and a group of students. (This is in contrast to the traditional stereotype of students straggling along behind a grand round, with consultant, junior dcotors, ward sister, nurse, senior students and so on – the sort of thing immortalized in *Doctor in the House*.) To put it another way, and to take up my earlier point: *the bedside teaching situation is not therapeutic in nature.*

These features that I have outlined begin to define the nature of 'cold' medicine. It is a 'mock up' situation (cf. Garfinkel and Sacks, 1970). Although differing from it in a number of respects, it is one purpose of the 'cold' encounter to produce something which, at least in part, simulates the supposed reality of 'hot' medicine. Hence, if it is to be brought off successfuly by the participants, the previously acquired knowledge – on the part of the patient and the doctors – may have to be supressed or at least managed with care, in the course of the teaching encounter. Thus, to echo the previous incident, if a patient, in reply to a student's initial question of 'What was it that brought you into hospital?', should reply 'Thyrotoxicosis', instead of offering a lay account of the symptoms, then the reality of the diagnostic exercise will be difficult to sustain. In other words, in negotiating the reality of the bedside teaching situation, both teacher and patient may well have control over an important resource. That is, they may both be well informed as to the nature of the patient's illness. Even if the patient is not accurately informed of the *diagnosis* as such, he or she may be aware of crucial events in the patient's career that could 'give everything away', that the students could pick up as clues which by-pass the diagnostic process. Most research has tended to emphasize patients' *lack* of understanding rather than their potential mastery over such resources. But my approach is not necessarily antithetical to such a view: it makes little difference whether my hypothetical patient understands the clinical import of 'thyrotoxicosis'; it is sufficient that the term be known and can be divulged.[1]

It is therefore a concern in the construction of these encounters that patients and doctors should engage in monitoring the flow of information. They need to attend the problem of what may be told and when. This can be illustrated in the following extracts from my field notes.

'The students had been told to examine the patient's precordium, one by one. As the first student began, the registrar came back and poked his head through the curtains to see if everything was O.K.

PATIENT:     Doctor, do I tell what's wrong?
DOCTOR:      Under no circumstances. If they ask you what's wrong, ask them their names and I'll come back and find out who they were.
PATIENT:     It's just that the other day I was told not to tell, but I slipped . . .'

'A girl student was exploring whether the patient (an elderly lady) had any signs of anaemia. As she was examining her eyes, the inside of her mouth, the creases in her palms etc., the old lady chipped in, "I've had a blood transfusion since I came in . . ."
The doctor interrupted, "Don't tell them too much. You're giving the whole show away – giving away the whole shooting match!"
The old lady clapped a hand over her mouth.'

These two extracts illustrate how, on occasion, patients and doctors may engage in metacommunication. That is, talk-about-talk; in this context talk about what may be divulged to the students. Such talk-about-talk serves to articulate the rules of the game. It provides a running commentary whereby the content of the talk is allocated to the speakers.

The shared knowledge at the disposal of the patient and the doctor

---

[1]It must be emphasized that by no means all patients are in the position of being 'well-informed'. But in stressing the accomplishment of bedside teaching sessions with such patients I do not wish to imply that work with 'uninformed' patients does not also require management. To cite one obvious example, patients may have been deliberately kept from knowledge about their condition and prognosis – e.g., where the illness is terminal (cf. Glaser and Strauss, 1965). Teaching encounters may need to be carefully managed by students and staff in order to preserve such a state of 'closed awareness'.

may therefore enable them to enter into a conspiracy of silence – to suppress information. On the other hand, their shared knowledge may also provide a base on which information may be artfully divulged – again, in a way which provides for the successful accomplishment of a diagnostic exercise. Let me exemplify this with some extracts from a transcript of one of the videotape recordings I mentioned.

One of the students had begun to take a history from the patient. After a few minutes of question-and-answer, the consultant broke in:

CONSULTANT: Okay, fair enough. Now I would like you, in turn, to ask relevant questions – one question each – trying to get further into his history. And I think it is only fair to say that so far you have not elicited all the main symptoms. What other questions are you going to ask? You know, this is not the diffuse interrogation of what we have now got.

We can see how the previously accomplished diagnostic work informs these comments. The consultant's advice that there is still a symptom to be drawn from the patient implies some already established list of symptoms. This is available as a topic by virtue of the fact that the physician himself has already taken a history, or has a history available in the patient's folder of case-notes.

Despite the fact that the consultant had offered this guide to the students' talk, the elusive further symptom was not forthcoming. The consultant turned to prompting the patient:

STUDENT: Is there anything else that you feel – symptoms that you get with this pain?

PATIENT: No, its just the pain I feel. That's all, nothing else.

CONSULTANT: Is that actually strictly true? You know, is there anything – I think the question really is – is there anything which is happening recently?

PATIENT: Well, apart from the pain I seem to have been drinking, likes of water, milk, things like that. Because of this, I seem to go to the toilet a lot more than I used to . . .

Here the consultant orients the patient to the possibility that there is additional information that they both know of – his further symptom. The consultant's metacommunicational work now indicates to the patient that this information may now be divulged legitimately. He reformulates the question, by re-phrasing it in terms of recent events, rather than additional symptoms, in such a way that it can be heard by the patient as an appropriate request to be answered, in terms of the patient's recent feelings of thirst.

In the first extract from this encounter, the consultant addresses the students; it becomes their responsibility to try to elicit the additional information for themselves. They continue the questioning but apparently fail. The consultant then takes a hand once more, and in the second extract the onus is shifted to the patient. In each case the consultant's teaching task involves formulating the pattern of information-seeking, and the uncovering of legitimate information about the patient.

Talk-about-talk is a constant feature of everyday discourse. Stubbs (forthcoming) argues that it is a particularly important feature of teachers' talk. It is therefore not particularly noteworthy that it should appear in this context at the bedside. What I want to draw attention to, however, is the specific work that is being done through the talk here: it is the management of knowledge between three parties. And it is this which is the peculiar attribute of bedside teaching.

The framework within such interactions take place can be described as an 'information game'. An information game is one of a number of analytic devices which can be applied to the study of everyday interactions and which derive from the work of Goffman. A number of such devices have been codified by Lyman and Scott (1970). They define these as: face games; relationship games; exploitation games; information games. Face games are those 'which involve preventing damage to one's own or another's identity or the salvaging of honour when it has been impugned' (cf. Goffman, 1955). In relationship games the interacting parties are concerned to manage their self-presentations in such a way as to increase or decrease their social distance. Exploitation games occur when parties seek to achieve the compliance of others. Lyman and Scott define information games in this way:

'Information games arise whenever one actor wishes to uncover information from another who wishes to conceal it.' (p. 58)

It must be emphasized that such descriptions are analytic abstractions; they are not intended to provide total characterizations of interactions. Such games may operate simultaneously, be overlapping and interdependent. For some purposes, however, they may be treated separately. The notion of an information game has been applied in a particularly telling way in Scott's ethnography of race track punters and their attempts to discover 'tips' and reliable information concerning the runners. Similarly, it can be brought into play when blacks pass for white, when homosexuals pass for straight and so on. They seek to ensure that information and aspects of their identities remain undisclosed. In the same way, in Scott's work on horse-racing, just as punters seek to uncover information, so owners, trainers and jockeys may be involved in covering up the information that the betting man seeks. In the case of the bedside teaching session, what is at stake is not so much that information should *remain* undisclosed, but rather that it should appear in the appropriate manner and at the appropriate time. It is not the purpose that it should be hidden that our patient has thyrotoxicosis, but rather that such information should be established and validated through the application of the principles of history taking and diagnosis. It is necessary that the parties 'go through the motions'. The information game serves to ensure that an orderly transfer of information occurs in accordance with the rules of clinical procedure.

In the course of information games, the parties become involved in sequences of moves aimed at the management and control of information. Thus one may initiate *covering moves* when he becomes aware that knowledge is being sought which he himself wishes should remain private. In some varieties of encounter such covering moves will imply surreptitious work, the erection of false fronts, trailing red herrings or whatever. In the context of the bedside encounter, such covering may take a more straightforward form – questions and answers being ruled out of court as contravening the conventions of the diagnostic exercise. The bedside interaction is openly defined as an information-seeking situation, and to that extent, the frank vetoing of lines of inquiry are appropriate moves. Similarly, when the smooth progress of the history and diagnosis is at stake, *uncovering moves* may be brought into play. As I have pointed out, it is not the case that information should be permanently irretrievable, but should come into the open at the right time.

Information which is not forthcoming may be prompted – its divulgence may be declared legitimate and its appearance facilitated.

In the triadic situation that I have sketched, the major work of information management is the task of the teaching doctor. On the basis of his previously acquired information about the patient, he is in a position to monitor the flow and disclosure of information. Thus, rather differently from the two-party information game, it is not the questioner alone who makes uncovering moves, nor the respondent who seeks to cover. The third party is in a position to interject such items into the talk and thus to 'cue in' the other parties to their place in the game.

The discussion may appear to have taken us some way from the observation of teaching – and particularly far from considerations of research in school classrooms. In one sense this is deliberate. I believe that there is a danger in pursuing 'classroom' (or similar) research of assuming that the *locale* of the research provides a rationale and justification for the work which is done. But because educational research has begun to move nearer to 'where the action is', that does not guarantee that we shall necessarily understand *what* the action is. Having opened up the classroom and stepped inside, we should not always confine our attention to that small world. Theories which emerge from classroom research should draw on the observation of everyday life in other settings as well. Hence, the problems of race-goers, homosexuals and so on may be fruitfully inspected for parallels, contrasts and insights.

On the other hand, the issues that I have briefly raised are not without direct application to school-based teaching. Arguably, like the bedside situation, the 'guided discovery' approach in contemporary teaching practices depends on a 'mock up'. For instance, in the arena of science teaching, students' work and 'experiments' are designed to produce a workable account of 'real' science. Yet the successful accomplishment such a mock-up may depend on a degree of stage-management on the part of the teacher (cf. Delamont, 1973). Again, at a more general level, there is the situation of mutual pretence involved when teachers ask 'questions', when it is apparent that the answer is already well known (cf. Stubbs, this vol.). This clearly resonates with the bedside material I have presented above. The maintenance of reality based on the principle of discounting, suppressing or covering previously acquired knowledge may turn out to be a fundamental feature of instructional situations. Bedside teaching encounters may be, after all, less idiosyncratic than they first appear.

## Acknowledgements

I must thank Professor Liam Hudson and Mr Peter Sheldrake, both of the Centre for Research in the Educational Sciences, University of Edinburgh, for their support, help and advice in the course of my research. I am deeply indebted to Professor A. S. Duncan and Professor H. J. Walton, both of the Edinburgh medical school, for their encouragement and understanding. The staff and students of the medical school not only made the research possible, but contributed in great part to making it a very enjoyable experience. Individually they must remain anonymous; collectively, they have my grateful thanks. The financial support for my work came originally as a research studentship from the SSRC, and subsequently as a Small Grant from the Nuffield Foundation.

## References

ANDERSON, A. S. (1966). 'An analysis of instructor-student classroom interaction', *J. Med. Educ.*, **41**, March, 209–14.

ATKINSON, P. A. (1973). 'Worlds apart: learning environments in medicine and surgery', *Brit. J. Med. Educ.*, **7**, 4, 218–24.

BECKER, H. S. *et al.* (1961). *Boys in White.* Chicago: University of Chicago Press.

BLOOM, S. W. (1973). *Power and Dissent in the Medical School.* New York: Free Press.

BUCHER, R. (1970). 'Social process and power in a medical school'. In: ZALD, M. N. (ed.) *Power in Organizations.* Nashville: Vanderbilt University Press.

DELAMONT, S. (1973). *Academic Conformity Observed: Studies in the Classroom.* Unpublished PhD thesis, University of Edinburgh.

FLANDERS, N. A. (1955). *Teacher Influence, Pupil Attitudes and Achievements.* Co-operative Research Monograph, University of Michigan.

FLANDERS, N. A. (1970). *Analysing Teaching Behaviour.* London: Addison-Wesley.

FOX, R. (1959). *Experiment Perilous.* Glencoe: Free Press.

GARFINKEL, H. (1967). *Studies in Ethnomethodology.* Englewood Cliffs: Prentice-Hall.

GARFINKEL, H. and SACKS, H. (1970). 'On formal structures of practical actions'. In: MCKINNEY, J. C. and TIRYAKIAN, E. A. (eds.) *Theoretical Sociology: Perspectives and Developments.* New York: Appleton-Century-Crofts.

GLASER, B. and STRAUSS, A. (1965). *Awareness of Dying.* Chicago: Aldine.

GOFFMAN, E. (1955). 'On face work', *Psychiatry*, **18**, August, 213–31.

GOFFMAN, E. (1961). *Encounters: Two Studies in the Sociology of Interaction.* Indianapolis: Bobbs-Merrill.

GOFFMAN, E. (1967). *Interaction Ritual: Essays on Face-to-Face Behaviour.* Garden City: Doubleday.

HAMILTON, D. and DELAMONT, S. (1974). 'Classroom research: a cautionary tale', *Research in Education*, **11**, May, 1–15.

JASON, H. (1962). 'A study of medical teaching practices', *J. Med. Educ.*, **37,** Dec., 1258–84.

JASON, H. (1964). 'A study of the teaching of medicine and surgery in a Canadian medical school', *Canad. Med. Ass. J.*, **90,** April 4, 813–19.

LEACH, E. R. (1961). *Rethinking Anthropology.* London: Athlone.

LEWIN, K. *et al.* (1939). 'Patterns of aggressive behaviour in experimentally created "Social Climates",' *J. Soc. Psychol.*, **10,** 271–99.

LYMAN, S. M. and SCOTT, M. B. (1970). *A Sociology of the Absurd.* New York: Appleton-Century-Crofts.

MCINTOSH, J. (1974). 'Processes of communication, information seeking and control associated with cancer', *Soc. Sci. & Med.*, **8,** 167–187.

MERTON, R. K., *et al.* (1957). *The Student Physician.* Cambridge, Mass: Harvard University Press.

PARLETT, M. R. and HAMILTON, D. (1972). *Evaluation as Illumination: A New Approach to Innovatory Programs.* Occasional Paper No. 9, Centre for Research in the Educational Sciences, University of Edinburgh.

PAYSON, H. E. and BARCHAS, J. D. (1965). 'A time study of medical teaching rounds'. *New Eng. J. Med.*, **273,** 1468–71.

PIKE, K. (1954). *Language in Relation to a Unified Theory of Human Behaviour, Part 1.* Glendale, California: Summer Institute of Linguistics.

ROYAL COMMISSION ON MEDICAL EDUCATION (1968). *Report* 1965–68. Cmnd. 3569. London: HMSO. (The Todd Report).

SACKS, H. (forthcoming). *Aspects of the Sequential Organization of Conversation.* Englewood Cliffs: Prentice-Hall.

SCOTT, M. B. (1968). *The Racing Game.* Chicago: Aldine.

SIMPSON, M. A. (1972). *Medical Education: A Critical Review.* London: Butterworths.

STUBBS, M. (forthcoming). 'Keeping in touch: some functions of teacher-talk'. In: STUBBS, M. and DELAMONT, S. (eds.) *Explorations in Classroom Observation.* London: Wiley.

WALKER, R. and ADELMAN, C. (n.d.). 'Flanders system for the analysis of classroom interaction – comments on the limitations of research technology' (mimeo).

WALKER, R. and ADELMAN, C. (forthcoming). 'Strawberries'. In: STUBBS, M. and DELAMONT, S. (eds.) *Explorations in Classroom Observation.* London: Wiley.

# CHAPTER 10

# Systematic Observation in Informal Classrooms

*Deanne Boydell, University of Leicester School of Education*

## Introduction

Informal primary school classrooms provide special opportunities and problems for the classroom observer and highlight a number of the fundamental issues of classroom observation. The purpose of this paper is to illustrate some of these issues with reference to two observation instruments which have been developed for use in informal junior classrooms. One of these instruments focuses on the teacher (Boydell, 1974) and the other on pupils (Boydell, 1975). They are summarized in Tables 1 and 2. Parts of the observation sheets are reproduced in Figures 1 and 2.

## Observational focus

One of the most basic questions is the selection of an observational focus: what should be observed? The sheer mass and complexity of data which impinge on the observer's senses force him to make a choice. The foci of the overwhelming majority of observational techniques reflect a formal model of teaching in which verbal interaction is public to the whole class and teacher-dominated in terms of both the quantity and nature of the contributions (Amidon and Hough, 1967). Less than a quarter of the instruments in the anthology of Simon and Boyer (1970) contain categories which relate to psychomotor functioning and only seven focus on pupils as distinct from teachers or teacher-pupil contacts. In informal classrooms, where children interact with each other, and there is an increased emphasis on independent and group work and 'learning by doing', the relevance of instruments steeped in the traditions of formal classrooms must be called in doubt. In the first place the bias towards teacher talk will tend to alienate part of the audience to which the findings of observational research in informal classrooms should be addressed, namely the teachers implementing innovatory practices. In the second place profiles of teachers' verbal behaviour only provide a partial view of observable classroom events. In formal classrooms, pupils generally adopt a stereotyped and outwardly passive role which makes it extremely difficult for an observer to gauge their level of understanding and involvement in a detailed way. Informal classrooms provide fewer constraints on the overt expression of thoughts and feelings, and offer a mass of behavioural clues about children's learning and motivation. In order to capitalize on these data and provide information which is relevant to the aims of informal classrooms, the traditional focus of systematic observation must be extended to pupils.

The need for a broader focus raises a number of problems. The complexity of events in informal classrooms with children moving, changing tasks, talking to their neighbours, receiving individual attention from the teacher and so on, makes it impossible for the observer to keep track of all the children and their teacher simultaneously. If a pupil-oriented approach is chosen, two main issues emerge. In the first place, it is not feasible to use the conventional type of scanning procedure in which, for example, every pupil is coded once every two minutes, as in the schedule of Lindvall *et al.* (1970). Even when children can be located quickly it is frequently impossible to see and hear them clearly from a distance. One answer is to focus on a sample of children one at a time. This is the procedure adopted by Medley *et al.* (1973) in PROSE (Personal Record of School Experience) and followed in the pupil instrument (Pupil Record). Each child's name is entered on a separate record sheet together with some means of identification like 'red jumper'. The sheets are placed in an arbitrary order which has been determined beforehand from the class register by alternating boys and girls alphabetically. Both PROSE and the Pupil Record provide a sample of the situations in which children find themselves – on their own, interacting with other children, interacting with the teacher and so on – and enable multiple coding, thereby preserving more of the detail contained in the original event. With the pupil record three codings are made when the child is not interacting with anyone (categories 8, 9a and 9b), seven are made when he is interacting with the teacher (categories 1, 2, 3a, 3b, 8, 9a and 9b) and nine when he is interacting with another child (categories 4, 5, 6, 7a, 7b, 7c, 8, 9a and 9b). The observer ticks the one appropriate item within each relevant category. The data from each lesson are processed by computer to give the percentage incidence of each item and cross-tabulations of selected categories using SPSS (Nie, Bent and Hull, 1970). The second main problem with a pupil-oriented approach is the incidence of observed teacher-pupil contact. If the teacher relies heavily on individual attention, the chances of the child under observation interacting with the teacher are very slim: the average child in a class of 30 can expect two minutes' contact an hour. If a comprehensive picture of the classroom is required, a teacher-oriented instrument is also needed. The use of two instruments raises the question of how to conceptualize differing pupil and teacher perspectives on teacher-pupil contacts. This problem came to light following the initial analysis of the pilot project data collected with the teacher instrument (teacher record). It was found that about three-quarters of the teachers' time was spent in work-oriented contacts (task and task supervision). This high proportion seemed to be at variance with the subjective impression gained when observing children informally. Further analysis was then carried out to estimate the incidence of the different types of teacher talk pupils experienced. By analysing the same data from two different viewpoints – what the teacher said and what the children experienced – it was found that whereas teachers only spent about a quarter of their time on routine matters like classroom organization and discipline, the average child was likely to hear this type of comment on about two occasions out of five. This was because children received such a small amount of teacher contact that the few remarks about routine matters which were addressed to the class as a whole constituted a relatively large proportion of what they heard the teacher say (Boydell, 1974).

**Permanent records**
The need for a broad focus, and the problems of a pupil-oriented approach, make frozen records like sound recordings, films or videotapes a very attractive proposition. As Kounin (1970) has said of videotapes, they record 'without forgetting, exaggerating, theorizing, judging, interpreting, or eliminating'. Their relative permanency makes it possible to extract more information than is possible at one session, to code non-verbal behaviour with and without the accompanying speech, to invent or modify coding systems and obtain measures of inter-observer reliability.

Unfortunately tape recording, filming and videotaping in informal classrooms suffer from serious technical problems associated with sound recording. During the pilot work associated with the early development of the pupil and teacher instruments, attempts were made to videotape children engaging in group work using a stationary camera and suspended unidirectional microphones (with the leads fixed at ceiling level because of the amount of pupil mobility). The voices of many junior children are relatively weak, so sensitive microphones were used. However, the more sensitive the microphone the better it became at picking up unwanted ambient noise, particularly during practical work. Large portions of the tapes were rendered unintelligible.

Only partial solutions are available. Radio microphones, for instance, are expensive and cumbersome. Moreover there are legal problems associated with their transmitters, and the quality of the recording is not consistently good. Even the BBC cannot cope adequately with the problem: when recording the speech of young children in informal classrooms a buzz of background chatter is often superimposed afterwards. At present videotaping is unable to contribute as much to the study of informal classrooms as to the analysis of more formal teaching situations of the type investigated by Adams and Biddle (1970). It can only be used satisfactorily to collect data about teachers (Hilsum and Cane, 1971) and children in contrived situations outside the classroom (Worthington, 1973). However it has an important role to play where editing is permissible, for instance in the production of tapes for training observers, testing observer agreement and inventing and modifying coding systems.

### Conceptual framework

The selection of an observational focus and the need to invent and modify coding systems are related to another major issue in observational research, namely the nature of the conceptual framework. This will be examined from three interdependent aspects – the selection of variables, the adoption of a conceptual stance and the nature of the observational unit. What is observed, and how it is observed, reflect the observer's theoretical interests. As Popper (1962) has contended, all observation involves interpretation in the light of theoretical knowledge.

To argue that observation can never be entirely theoretical and value-free is not to deny that some techniques are less theoretical and value-laden than others. Ratings, for instance, require the observer to make inferences from a series of events and may be distinguished from low-inference measures like sign and category systems which 'focus upon specific, denotable, relatively objective behaviours' and record such events as frequency counts (Rosenshine and Furst, 1971). Despite the fact that the high-inference measures used in process-product studies tend to have greater predictive validity than most low-inference measures, Rosenshine and Furst (1971) point out the need to seek the low-inference measures which comprise high-inference measures like clarity of presentation and enthusiasm. Medley (1969) goes even further. He argues that it is necessary to move to a more 'primitive' level than the conventional low-inference sign and category systems in which the selected variables reflect definite hypotheses about important teacher behaviours. He contends that it is not necessary for the categories to relate to important dimensions or to discriminate among classes. The only requirement is that different observers agree about the frequency of events in each category, in which case 'if the number and variety of categories was sufficient it should be possible to combine categories (with or without varying weights) into super-categories which would discriminate teachers along psychologically or pedagogically relevant dimensions'.

In view of the lack of knowledge about the important dimensions of informal classrooms, both with respect to the processes of ongoing interaction and their relationships to children's learning, the pupil and teacher instruments are characterized by an extensive range of low-inference measures. Quite apart from the long-term objective of combining categories to produce discriminating dimensions, this inductive approach has two other advantages. It enables the instruments to be used by investigators with varying theoretical interests, and it increases the relevance of the data to teachers who can interpret the findings from their own particular pedagogical standpoint.

Biddle (1967) identifies three approaches to the issue of conceptual posture, that is to say the question of what should be coded about any selected behavioural event: its objective characteristics, the person's intent or the effect of what is said or done. As an example of the distinction, consider the case of a child helping the teacher tidy the store cupboard. The objective characteristic of the child's action might be described as cooperative, his intent may be inferred as trying to please the teacher but the effect on the teacher may be visual signs of exasperation that the child has yet again opted out of the reading corner. As intentions are notoriously difficult to impute, the emphasis in both the pupil and teacher instruments was on an objective description of events or their observable effects.

Systematic observation is sometimes criticized for focusing on the surface aspects of interaction and neglecting underlying features which may be more meaningful (Hamilton and Delamont, 1974). However, informal classrooms are characterized by a wide range of observable responses, and by observing an events' effect it is possible to gain some understanding of what it meant to the teacher or child. This approach seems particularly useful in the analysis of teacher-pupil contacts, where there is growing awareness of the gulfs that sometimes exist between, for example, the teacher's intent in using a particular word or posing a certain question, and what children take it to mean (Barnes, 1969). In the teacher record, the major distinction between questions and statements was made on the basis of whether the child replied. This meant that certain utterances which would carry a question mark when written down were coded as statements if they did not elicit replies; and conversely, statements like 'give me your suggestion' or 'tell me the answer' which elicited pupil replies were treated as questions. In addition, questions were allocated to their respective categories in terms of how they were interpreted and answered. Thus a question like 'what should you weigh next?' would be coded as a factual recall question (1 (a)) if the child simply recalled the teacher's earlier instructions; a closed task question (1 (b)) if the child paused to work out an answer and the teacher indicated that it was the particular response she wanted; and an open task question (1 (c)) if the child proffered a suggestion and the teacher showed by her reaction that she was willing to accept a wide range of ideas. Task directives (5 (b)) were also distinguished from routine directives (6 (a)) in terms of the child's reaction rather than the content of what was said. Thus if the teacher asked a child to 'get a book' and the child brought one back to the teacher it would be coded as a management command (6 (a)). If the child understood the instruction to mean that he should get on with some reading, and behaved accordingly, it would be coded as a task supervision command (5 (b)). Utterances other than questions and directives were coded in terms of their objective characteristics because their effects were not consistently observable. Most of children's behaviour was coded in terms of its objective characteristics on the pupil record, for the same reason.

The choice of measures (variables) and the adoption of a stance (conceptual posture) are related to the question of how to break up the flow of classroom events (units of analysis). There are three common types of unit-arbitrary time: units like Flanders' three second intervals (Amidon and Hough, 1967); phenomenal units which are assumed to be recognized by the classroom participants, like Gump's segments (1969); and analytic units which are defined in abstract terminology, such as the strategies and ventures of B. O. Smith *et al.* (1970). Informal classrooms highlight the deceptive simplicity of the unit problem. There is a paucity of suitable statistical models. In addition, theoretical rationales for the definition of analytic units are lacking, and the emphasis on individual work and individual attention means that only natural breaks of the grossest kind are recognized by all the classroom participants. However, phenomenal units, defined in terms of the experience of a selected individual (or individuals), raise problems of generalization. Whilst acknowledging that any comprehensive understanding of informal classrooms must take account of the continuous and interweaving nature of classroom events, arbitrary time units were used in both the pupil and teacher instruments because the aim was to give an overall view of the lesson as a whole rather than a longitudinal perspective. Observers coded at the precise moment of time signals which were fed into their ear every 25 seconds from a portable cassette tape recorder. In the case of the pupil record, observers shifted their attention to a new target child after five sets of coding. The demands of multiple coding made it impossible to code at a faster rate. The use of arbitrary time units may be justified on two grounds. It allows for the possibility that informal classrooms can be characterized in terms of the overall frequencies of categories (or super-categories) of classroom behaviour which are pedagogically meaningful; and it facilitates the comparison of actual events with the image of the informal classroom in terms which are widely used by its advocates and critics.

Claims are often made, for instance, about the levels of children's involvement and the nature of group functioning. When a pilot study was undertaken with the pupil record in six junior classrooms, it was found that children were involved in work or waiting to see the teacher for almost three-quarters of each lesson. The evidence on children's interactions with each other revealed a bias for contact between children of the same sex, a lower level of involvement than when children were not interacting, and the relative infrequency of contact more than 25 seconds long (Boydell, 1975). The teacher record was piloted simultaneously in the same six classrooms. The results highlighted the teachers' preference for talking to children privately one at a time, and revealed that teachers spent about half the lesson on task supervision. The remainder of their time was split almost equally between routine and task matters. Most of the task contact was low-level and factual (Boydell, 1974).

Informal primary classrooms have been so little investigated that even comparatively unsophisticated techniques can provide information which is relevant in certain contexts. The growing dialogue among classroom observers, including those who reject systematic observation in favour of techniques rooted in the traditions of sociology and anthropology (for instance Nash, 1973), has resulted in a broader-based discussion of the underlying issues. Such debate takes on added importance in view of the increasing interest of curriculum evaluators in classroom process (American Educational Research Association, 1970). Informal classrooms highlight some of the major issues to be solved.

**Table 1: Summary and brief definitions of the Teacher Record categories and items**

| Category | Item |
| --- | --- |
| Interaction | 1. *Task questions* answered by child – |
| | (a) recalling facts |
| | (b) offering ideas, solutions (closed-one acceptable answer) |
| | (c) offering ideas, solutions (open-more than one acceptable answer) |
| | 2. *Task supervision questions* answered by child – |
| | (a) reporting progress |
| | (b) choosing another task |
| | (c) evaluating own task |

*continued on next page*

| Category | Item |
| --- | --- |

3. *Routine questions* answered by child – referring to matters of classroom management, behaviour or small talk

4. *Task statements* –

   (a) of facts
   (b) of ideas, explanations

5. *Task supervision statements* –

   (a) of written instructions or words or spellings child does not know
   (b) which tell child which task to do or how to do it
   (c) which tell child to choose task
   (d) which grant or refuse task request
   (e) which praise child's work or effort
   (f) which provide neutral or critical feedback on child's work or effort

6. *Routine statements* –

   (a) of information, directions, permissions to do with classroom management
   (b) which provide positive or neutral feedback on routine matters
   (c) of critical control
   (d) of small talk

7. *Other contracts* and situations in which teacher –

   (a) interacts silently by demonstrating, smiling, nodding, pointing etc.
   (b) marks or checks child's work in front of him
   (c) tells or reads a story
   (d) listens to a child read
   (e) interacts with visiting pupil from another class
   (f) interacts with visiting adult (such as the head or secretary)
   (g) cannot be heard or seen
   (h) cannot be coded
   (i) does not interact with anyone
   (j) is out of the room

| | |
| --- | --- |

Audience     *Teacher interacts with* –

   (a) whole class or single child in class setting
   (b) group of children or single child in group setting
   (c) single child privately, giving individual attention

Activity     Open-ended category in which investigator can insert own items, for instance the activity of the child with whom the teacher interacts.

**Table 2: Summary and brief definitions of the Pupil Record categories and items**

| Situation | Category | Item | |
|---|---|---|---|
| Pupil – Adult Interaction | 1. *Target's role* | INIT | Target initiates to adult privately or publicly (focus) |
| | | STAR | Adult initiates or sustains contact with target privately or publicly (focus) |
| | | PART | Target part of adult's group or class audience (audience) |
| | | LSWT | Target listens/watches adult interact privately or publicly with other child (ren) (audience) |
| | 2. *Interacting adult* | TCHR | Target interacts with teacher |
| | | OBSR | Target interacts with observer |
| | | OTHER | Target interacts with any other adult (head, secretary, etc.) |
| | 3a. *Adult's interaction* | WORK | Adult interacts about a work matter |
| | | ROUTINE | Adult interacts about a matter of classroom routine (organization and management) |
| | | POS | Adult reacts positively (praises) |
| | | NEG | Adult reacts negatively (criticizes) |
| | 3b. *Adult's communication setting* | IND ATT | Adult gives private individual attention to target |
| | | GROUP | Adult interacts with group which includes target |
| | | CLASS | Adult interacts with whole class |
| | | OTHER | Adult gives private attention to another child or group and target listens in or eavesdrops |
| Pupil – Pupil Interaction | 4. *Target's role* | INIT | Target initiates contact with other pupil(s) |
| | | COOP | Target cooperates by responding to an initiation or by sustaining contact |
| | | IGN | Target ignores attempted initiation |
| | 5. *Role of other pupil(s)* | INIT | Other pupil initiates contact with target |
| | | COOP | Other pupil cooperates by responding to target's initiation or by sustaining contact |
| | | IGN | Other pupil ignores target's attempted initiation |
| | 6. *Mode of interaction* | CNTC | Non-verbal, mediated solely by physical contact, gestures, etc. |
| | | MTL | Non-verbal, mediated solely by materials, apparatus, etc. |
| | | VRB | Verbal (may be accompanied by non-verbal interaction) |

*continued on next page*

| Situation | Category | Item | |
|---|---|---|---|
| | 7a. *Task of other pupil(s)* | S TK | Same or similar to target's |
| | | D TK | Different to target's task |
| | 7b. *Sex & number of other pupil(s)* | SS | Target interacts with one pupil of same sex |
| | | OS | Target interacts with one pupil of opposite sex |
| | | SV | Target interacts with several pupils of same sex |
| | | BG | Target interacts with boy(s) and girl(s) |
| | 7c. *Group of other pupil(s)* | OWN GP | From target's own base group |
| | | OTH GP | From another base group |
| All (Pupil – Adult Interaction, Pupil – Pupil Interaction & No Interaction) | 8. *Target's activity* | COOP TK | Involved and cooperating on task work (e.g. reading) |
| | | COOP R | Involved and cooperating on routine work (e.g. sharpening a pencil) |
| | | MOB (WK) | Involved and mobile/work-oriented |
| | | DSTR | Non-involved and distracted from work |
| | | DSRP | Non-involved and disrupting another child's work |
| | | HPLY | Non-involved and engaging in horse-play with other pupil(s) |
| | | MOB (DSTR) | Non-involved and mobile/distracted |
| | | WAIT TCHR | Waiting to see the teacher |
| | | CODS | Partially distracted and partially cooperating on work |
| | | DSTR TCHR | Distracted by teacher's activity or interaction with other pupil(s) |
| | | RIS | Responding to internal stimuli (e.g. daydreaming) |
| | | WOA | Working on a work activity which is not approved work |
| | 9a. *Target's location* | P IN | Target in base group |
| | | P OUT | Target out of base group |
| | | P OUT RM | Target out of room |
| | 9b. *Teacher activity & location* | T PRES | Teacher physically present or interacting with target, his seated group or class |
| | | T ELSE(I) | Teacher elsewhere interacting with other pupils |
| | | T APART(W) | Teacher apart and waiting/watching (not interacting) |
| | | T REM(H) | Teacher removed and housekeeping (not interacting) |
| | | T OUT RM | Teacher out of room (not interacting) |

**Figure 1: Part of the Teacher Record observation sheet**

THE TEACHER RECORD        Ref. No.......................

CONVERSATION

*Teacher questions answered by —*

| | | |
|---|---|---|
| TASK | 1a. | recalling facts |
| | 1b. | offering ideas, solutions (closed) |
| | 1c. | offering ideas, solutions (open) |
| | | |
| TASK | 2a. | reporting progress |
| SUPVN | 2b. | choosing another task |
| | 2c. | evaluating own task |
| | | |
| ROUTINE | 3a. | referring to routine matter |

One observation sheet provides space for 15 sets of codings (one per column). The columns are grouped in fives for ease of recording. Nine to ten sheets will be completed in a lesson of approximately an hour's duration.

The Teacher Record instrument must only be used in conjunction with *The Teacher Record: A Manual for Observers*. The manual explains the observation procedure in full and gives detailed category definitions (available from University of Leicester School of Education).

**Figure 2: Part of the Pupil Record observation sheet**

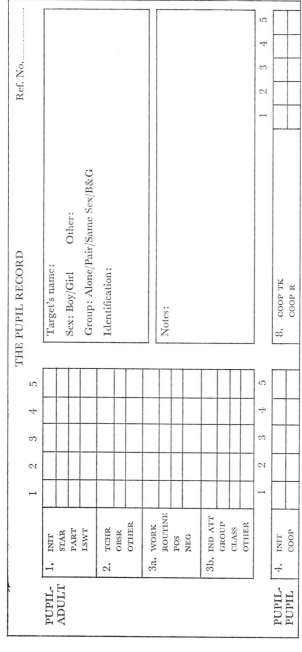

One observation sheet provides space for five sets of codings (one per column) for a single child. About 24 sheets will be completed (i.e. 24 children will be observed) in a lesson of approximately an hour's duration.

The Pupil Record instrument must only be used in conjunction with *The Pupil Record: A Manual for Observers*. The manual explains the observation procedure in full and gives detailed category and item definitions (available from University of Leicester School of Education).

**Acknowledgement**

The Teacher and Pupil Records were developed during Professor Brian Simon's SSRC funded project at the University of Leicester on 'the nature of classroom learning in primary schools'.

**References**

ADAMS, R. S. and BIDDLE, B. J. (1970). *Realities of Teaching: Explorations with Video Tape*. New York: Holt, Rinehart and Winston.

AMERICAN EDUCATIONAL RESEARCH ASSOCIATION (1970). *Classroom Observation*. Monograph Series on Curriculum Evaluation No. 6. Chicago: Rand McNally.

AMIDON, E. J. and HOUGH, J. B. (eds.) (1967). *Interaction Analysis: Theory, Research and Application*. Reading, Mass.: Addison-Wesley.

BARNES, D., BRITTON, J., ROSEN, H. and the LONDON ASSOCIATION FOR TEACHING OF ENGLISH. (1969). *Language, the Learner and the School*. Harmondsworth: Penguin Papers in Education.

BIDDLE, B. J. (1967). 'Methods and concepts in classroom research', *Rev. Educ. Res.*, **37,** 337–57.

BOYDELL, D. (1974). 'Teacher-pupil contact in junior classrooms', *Br. J. Educ. Psychol.*, November.

BOYDELL, D. (1975). 'Pupil behaviour in junior classrooms', *Br. J. Educ. Psychol.*, in press.

GUMP, P. V. (1969). 'Intra-setting analysis: the third grade classroom as a special but instructive case.' In: WILLEMS, E. P. and RUSSELL, H. L. (eds). *Naturalistic Viewpoints in Psychological Research*. New York: Holt, Rinehart and Winston.

HAMILTON, D. and DELAMONT, S. (1974). 'Classroom research: a cautionary tale', *Res. in Educ.*, No. 11, 1–15.

HILSUM, S. and CANE, B. S. (1971). *The Teacher's Day*. Slough: NFER.

KOUNIN, J. S. (1970). *Discipline and Group Management in Classrooms*. New York: Holt, Rinehart and Winston.

LINDVALL, C. M. *et al.* (1970). 'Students observation form.' In: SIMON, A. and BOYER, E. G. (eds.) *Mirrors for Behaviour*. Philadelphia: Research for Better Schools.

MEDLEY, D. M. (1969). 'Oscar goes to nursery school: a new technique for recording pupil behavior.' Paper presented at the meetings of the American Educational Research Association, Los Angeles, California, February 8.

MEDLEY, D. M. *et al.* (1973). 'The personal record of school experiences (PROSE).' In: BOYER, E. G., SIMON, A. and KARAFIN, G. (eds). *Measures of Maturation: An Anthology of Early childhood observation instruments, vol. II*. Philadelphia: Research for Better Schools.

NASH, R. (1973). *Classrooms Observed*. London and Boston: Routledge and Kegan Paul.

NIE, N. H., BENT, D. H. and HULL, C. H. (1970). *The Statistical Package for the Social Sciences*. McGraw-Hill.

POPPER, K. R. (1962). *Conjectures and Refutations*. New York, London: Basic Books.

ROSENSHINE, B. and FURST, N. (1971). 'Research on teacher performance criteria.' In: SMITH, B. O. (ed.) *Research in Teacher Education: A Symposium*. Englewood Cliffs, New Jersey: Prentice-Hall.

SIMON, A. and BOYER, E. G. (eds.) (1970). *Mirrors for Behaviour*. Philadelphia: Research for Better Schools.

SMITH, B. O., MEUX, M. O. *et al.* (1970). *A Study of the Logic of Teaching.* Urbana: University of Illinois.

WILLEMS, E. P. and RAUSH, H. L. (eds.) *Naturalistic Viewpoints in Psychological Research.* New York: Holt, Rinehart and Winston.

WORTHINGTON, F. (1973). *A Theoretical and Empirical Study of Small Group Work in Schools.* Unpublished PHD thesis. University of Leicester.

CHAPTER 11

# Teachers' Questions and Reactions: A Microteaching Study

*Gordon MacLeod, Stirling University, Donald MacLennan, Callendar Park College of Education, and Donald McIntyre, Stirling University*

## The study of teaching effectiveness

Despite its obvious importance and the efforts of generations of researchers, the question 'What characterizes effective teaching?' remains one to which only very inadequate answers can be given. And, as non-significant and apparently inconsistent research results have accumulated, researchers have gradually come to realize that we should not expect much success so long as we seek widely generalizable answers to this question. There is, of course, nothing very original about this realization, since every practising teacher demonstrates many times each day his implicit knowledge that to have any chance of teaching effectively one must be prepared to change one's behaviour according to the subject matter one is dealing with, the previously acquired knowledge, skills, attitudes and experience of one's pupils, the size and mood of one's class, and what one is hoping to achieve at any particular moment.

To know that the answers which we seek must generally be conditional upon such factors does not, however, remove the need to ask the question. The knowledge *that* one needs to adapt one's behaviour to different circumstances does not imply any knowledge of *how* one's behaviour can be adapted to greatest effect. All we have gained is the awareness that the research required will have to be more extensive than our predecessors imagined, and that we shall have to use more sophisticated research strategies.

The first and most obvious requirement of such strategies is the need to *specify* the situations and behaviour studied more fully than has been common in the past. Generalization can only be justified in so far as similar findings are obtained for different samples in different contexts; and the range of any generalization can only be identified if the features of every study undertaken are specified in terms of several dimensions. Thus Flanders (1973) suggests that the results of different studies can only be compared in relation to: the school settings involved; the subject matter taught; the samples of teachers and pupils; conceptual definitions of predictor and outcome variables; operational definitions of the outcome variables, e.g. the specific achievement tests used; the observation system used; the length of time for instruction; and the sample of instruction time observed. In addition, it would seem important to specify at least two other features of any study. In what way is the selection of outcome variables related to the teachers' objectives or intentions? And, if the predictor variables studied are concerned with teachers' tactics, within what strategic contexts are these tactics used?

At this stage, one can only speculate as to which of these or other features, and which aspects of them, will turn out to be important in limiting the range of generalizability about effective teaching. In particular, we are almost entirely ignorant about the aspects of school settings, of subject matter, and of teacher and pupil characteristics which may influence relationships between teachers' behaviour and pupils' learning. But without specification in terms of such features, little progress can be expected.

A second requirement of adequate research strategies is the need to *control* variations among the situations and the behaviours of teachers whose teaching is being compared. The premise that effective teaching is likely to depend on adaptation to circumstances implies that it will only be possible to relate specified aspects of teachers' behaviour to outcomes where the teachers are faced with similar situations and other aspects of their behaviour, such as their choice of content, are similar. It may well be, for example, that the most effective kinds of questioning differ according to the teaching strategies within which they are used: only when there are no variations in such other respects can one hope unambiguously to identify effects of variations in questioning behaviour.

The case for controlled studies does not depend, however, on the assumption of such interactions between variables. If there are variations between classes in the initial abilities of pupils, or in the opportunities which pupils are given to acquire the knowledge on which criterion tests are based, the effect of these variations will be to diminish or even entirely obscure the effects of those aspects of teaching which are being studied. We should by now have sufficient experience of unproductive research to know that it is hopeless to look for ways in which, *other things being unequal*, teachers vary in their effectiveness.

A third requirement of research strategies is that the ambitiousness of our research questions should not exceed the sophistication of our research designs. As Gage has commented, a great deal of past research has consisted of 'hopelessly ambitious attempts to predict teacher effectiveness over vast arrays and spans of outcomes, teacher behaviours, time intervals and pupil characteristics, all on the basis of predictive variables that had only the most tenuous theoretical justification in the first place' (Gage, 1968, p. 602). In particular, the length of the time intervals over which we attempt to relate teaching behaviours to learning outcomes merits attention. The longer the interval, the more complex the processes of teacher influence are likely to be and, although long-term outcomes are the ones which it is most useful to predict, 'long-term outcomes which cannot be explained are not very useful in understanding teaching and learning' (Flanders, 1973, p. 41). Thus investigations relating teacher behaviours to learning outcomes after a period of months, or even of days, may be of little value unless demanding controls are maintained, extensive observations undertaken, and predictions derived from sophisticated multivariate models confirmed.

An alternative strategy, suggested by Gage as long ago as 1963, is to focus attention upon teachers' behaviour and short-term outcomes within highly circumscribed situations. Such research would not in itself allow us to develop an understanding of effective teaching, but the problems of design which it presents are much more manageable, and an established body of knowledge about the predictors of short-term 'microcriteria' would make research relating teaching behaviour to long-term outcomes very much easier to plan. As a relatively low-risk and low-cost strategy, it would seem to merit wider use. One feature of this strategy is that it highlights the need to identify the processes whereby teaching behaviours are related to long-term outcomes. It is not enough to measure those outcomes which correspond to the immediate objectives towards which the teaching is directed. Instead, one has to attempt to measure all those outcomes which can be hypothesized to contribute towards (or to inhibit) the achievement of long-term objectives; in particular, it is desirable to measure characteristics of pupils' classroom behaviour, a much neglected type of criterion variable.

The investigation reported in this article is one attempt to conduct research into teaching effectiveness with adequate specification of the context and control over contingent variables, and in which the questions asked are not too ambitious. The context in which the research was carried out was that of microteaching, with student-teachers teaching short lessons to small classes of pupils whom they had not previously met, all the lessons being videotaped for later analysis. In this context, a high degree of specification and control is possible. For example, it is relatively easy to ensure that all teachers are dealing with the same subject-matter, using the same broad strategy of teaching and the same materials, and aiming towards the same objectives. These are factors which it is often extremely difficult to control in 'natural' school settings.

One set of factors which it is almost impossible to control in natural settings is that of the initial characteristics of pupils. If pupils are not allocated to classes at random, the researcher loses the basis upon which any reliable comparison among teachers and classes depends, and is forced to depend upon such inappropriate techniques as analysis of covariance or the use of gain scores. In a microteaching context, on the other hand, it is possible to use 'the ideal experimental design, which is usually beyond the reach of the researcher . . . . . the random assignment of pupils to classes from strata based on ability' (Flanders, 1970, p. 382). In addition, the microteaching setting ensures that comparisons between the teacher-pupil interactions in different classrooms are not complicated by the expectations and mutual understandings which inevitably develop in an ongoing relationship, and influence communication in ways which the observer cannot easily detect.

'Laboratory' research of this kind is commonly criticized on the grounds that it is artificial and therefore, it is argued, not relevant to 'the real classroom'. Such criticism is, however, misguided because:

(a) however atypical the context may be, teachers and pupils are faced with meaningful tasks of teaching and learning, tasks which are closely similar to many of those with which they are faced in more normal contexts;

(b) although it would be impermissible to generalize from micro-teaching to school settings, the disadvantage of this is minimal since the degree of permissible generalization from research in any one type of school setting is also severely limited;

(c) research in the microteaching context is not undertaken with the intention that the results should be immediately applicable to educational practice, but rather as the first stage of a realistically long-term strategy to inform educational practice;

(d) whilst it is important that research designs should involve the maximisation of both internal and external validity, it is the former which is the 'basic minimum without which any experiment is uninterpretable' (Campbell, 1963, p 214),

Previous research on teaching effectiveness using the microteaching context appears to have been exclusively concerned with teachers' presentation behaviours (Gage, *et al.*, 1968; Fortune, 1967). It was in the belief that the advantages of the microteaching context justify its use for research into other strategies of teaching, involving teacher-pupil interaction, that we undertook the investigation reported here, into the effects of variations in teachers' questioning and reacting behaviours.

## The study of teachers' questions and reactions

### Questioning

Prescriptions about the nature of effective questioning are far from rare in the world of teacher-education, but most of these prescriptions are based on intuitive impressions, not on empirical evidence. This reflects not a neglect of research findings but rather the fact that, despite the several significant relationships between teachers' questioning and pupil outcomes found in recent studies, few consistent and meaningful conclusions have emerged.

One reason for this, suggested by Rosenshine and Furst (1971), may have been researchers' over-reliance on dichotomous classifications of questions, and it certainly seems likely that more complex systems of categorization will be necessary to cope meaningfully with the diversity of teachers' questions. As Rosenshine and Furst

(1973) themselves point out, however, the mere generation of categories is not in itself likely to be profitable; more fundamental is the clarity and explicitness with which the dimensions underlying the categories are conceptualized. The lack of such clarity, and also of consistency among researchers, has been a source of considerable semantic confusion in the study of teachers' questioning. One can never be sure whether the 'factual' category used by one investigator is conceptually related to the category of 'closed' used by another, or whether one man's 'open' question is another man's 'divergent' question. In particular, there appears to have been a frequent confusion of the following three dimensions which are the three differentiated for use in this study:

(a) the kinds of cognitive demands being made from pupils classified in terms of the 'substantive-logical' meanings of questions (derived mainly from Bellack *et al.*, 1966);

(b) the extent to which pupils are being asked to produce divergent thinking; and

(c) the degree of structure in the question, i.e. the extent to which the teacher limits the range of appropriate answers by providing information in the question which explicitly or implicitly specifies the conditions or criteria in terms of which the answer should be given.

Before elaborating on these three dimensions and relating them to previous research, we may note that the use of them in combination allows the multiple categorization of questions as shown schematically in Figure 1.

*Cognitive demands being made from pupils*

Studies of questions coded according to cognitive demand have been much the most common in the literature, and within this general area the most common basis for classifying questions has been a higher-order/lower-order distinction, deriving from Bloom's (1956) taxonomy of objectives. Probably the most commonly supported finding is that teachers' use of higher-order questions is associated with a raised level of classroom discourse (e.g. Bellack *et al.*, 1966; Davis and Tinsley, 1968; Gallagher, 1965; Hudgins and Ahlbrand, 1969; Taba *et al.*, 1964). There is less consistency, however, in the results of studies relating higher-order questions to pupil-achieve-

**Figure 1: Questioning system**

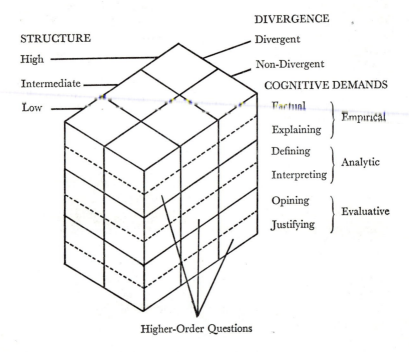

Higher-Order Questions

ment, some studies finding negative (e.g. Spaulding, 1965), some positive (e.g. Kleinman, 1964), and other non-significant relationships (e.g. Rogers and Davis, 1970).

Surprisingly little use appears to have been made, in process-product studies, of systems like that of Bellack *et al.* (1966) which differentiate questions into categories which *describe* the nature of the demand being made rather than into categories which merge questions of several kinds assumed to be comparable in the 'level' of their demands. However, the basis of classification is in many cases far from clear or so idiosyncratic that it is impossible to know how to relate the results of different investigations. 'Factual' questions, for example, have been differentiated from others in several studies – Soar (1966) and Spaulding (1965) found the use of such questions to be correlated with attainment in mathematics and arithmetic – but the definition of 'factual' tends to vary from one study to another. Idiosyncrasies of definition and terminology also lead to difficulties in differentiating between studies which categorize questions in terms of the nature of the cognitive demands and those which are concerned with the extent to which pupils are free to choose the kind of response they make. Thus Wright and Nuthall (1970), in categorizing questions as open or closed, appear to be concerned with the latter distinction; but closer examination of their definition shows that it relates much more closely to the higher-order/lower-order dichotomy.

*Structuring*

The open-closed dichotomy, applied to teachers' questions, appears to be used in various different ways, often with evaluative overtones (e.g. Barnes, 1969). The dimension of structuring used in this investigation is an attempt to make more precise one of the distinctions implicit in this dichotomy. The closest approximation in the research literature to our meaning of 'structuring' (cf. p. 203) appears to be that of Nuthall and Church (1971), who report that closed questioning appeared to lead to greater pupil knowledge and comprehension than more open (i.e. 'less structured, vague') questioning, when the time was held constant.

*Divergence*

Divergent questions are defined in this study as those which appear to be asking for divergent thinking from pupils. Previous studies using similar conceptual definitions (Gallagher and Aschner, 1963; Gallagher, 1965; Hudgins and Ahlbrand, 1969) have found positive relationships between teachers' use of divergent questions and divergent thinking on the part of the pupils. Like previous investigators, however, we are unable to provide any adequate operational definition of divergent questioning. But since the lack of differentiation between 'divergent' questions, 'open-ended' or 'unstructured' questions, and 'opining' or 'evaluative' questions appears to us one of the major sources of confusion in discussions of classroom questioning, and since we have found our intuitive ratings of the divergence of questions to be fairly reliable (coefficient of concordance among four observers $=\cdot75$), we have considered it useful to categorize questions on this third independent dimension.

### Reacting

In common with studies of teachers' questioning behaviours, the study of teachers' reactions has generated a substantial amount of published literature but has often lacked clear conceptualization and has focused on only limited aspects of teacher reacting behaviour.

Rosenshine and Furst (1971) and Rosenshine (1971), in reviews of correlates of 'effective' teaching demonstrate at one and the same time, both the difficulties involved in grouping and reviewing studies involving teacher reacting behaviour and the plethora of *empirical* data which suggest why teachers' reacting behaviours should be a source of interest. As with questioning, we have in this study attempted to distinguish clearly among three dimensions of reacting behaviour (Figure 2) which appear to cover most of the variables examined in previous research, but which have not always been differentiated.

A reaction may be defined as a teacher behaviour elicited but not solicited by a previous pupil contribution and directly related to that pupil contribution and whose pedagogical function 'is to rate (positively or negatively) and/or to modify (by classifying, synthesizing, or expanding)' (Bellack *et al.*, 1966, p. 165) the pupil behaviours which occasioned them.

### *Rating reactions (critical and evaluative)*

Although Bellack notes Wellman's (1961) distinction between 'critical' meaning and 'evaluative' meaning, he does not operationalize the distinction in his coding system but suggests that opera-

**Figure 2: Reacting system**

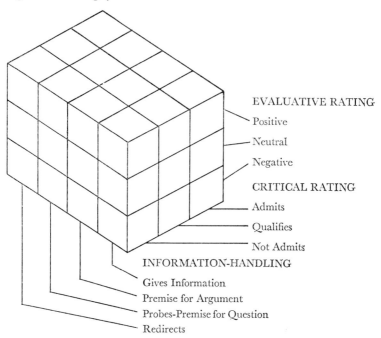

EVALUATIVE RATING
Positive
Neutral
Negative

CRITICAL RATING
Admits
Qualifies
Not Admits

INFORMATION-HANDLING
Gives Information
Premise for Argument
Probes-Premise for Question
Redirects

'Repeats' may be coded with any of the other cells.

tional differentiation might be valuable for future study. In this study the attempt was made to separate the evaluative ('being pro or con, being partial') from the critical ('accepting, qualifying or rejecting the claim of a given statement to be rationally justified') (Bellack, p. 170). This separation was thought valuable for both theoretical and empirical reasons. On theoretical grounds much debate has taken place between the proponents of two theories of human behaviour – those supporting the efficacy of information feedback and those supporting the efficacy of reinforcement (e.g. Annett, 1969; Bilodeau, 1966; Skinner, 1968). On empirical grounds, although ratings have often been embedded in broader categories, as in the use of Flanders' basic system, there are indications of the predictive power of both evaluative ratings (e.g. Spaulding, 1965, Ward and Baker, 1968) and of critical ratings (e.g. Flanders, 1970; Soar, 1966; Wright and Nuthall, 1970)

*Modifying reactions (information-handling)*

Modifying reactions are those which refer to the cognitive process or information-handling involved in dealing with the subject-matter under study. These are exemplified most commonly in teacher effectiveness research in terms of sub-categories of Flanders (1965) category 3 (Use of Pupil Ideas) which as a single category may involve as little as simple repetition of pupils' ideas, or may involve the use of pupils' ideas as the basis for advancing an argument or as the basis for a new or probing question. Although Rosenshine and Furst (1971) subsume use of pupil ideas under the more general category of teacher indirectness, there does seem a need to differentiate among the several cognitive processes involved in this variable (cf. Flanders, 1970) and to relate these to the cognitive behaviours of pupils. There are indications in the research literature that such modifying reacting behaviours, including reacting-by-questioning or probing may be powerful predictors of pupil achievement and attitudes (Bellack *et al.*, 1966; Flanders, 1970; Hughes, 1973; Wright and Nuthall, 1970).

## Design of the study
*Subjects*

(i) Teachers. The teachers in this study were 33 second-year undergraduates at the University of Stirling, all studying Education concurrently with other academic subjects. This group consisted of nineteen History/Education students and fourteen English/Education who constituted the two largest subject-groups which met the criteria for selection for further study (i.e. appropriate preparation and random assignment to classes) from a year-group of approximately 120 students.

(ii) Pupils. The pupils in this study were drawn from all eight mixed-ability first secondary year classes of a large comprehensive school and assigned randomly to 'micro-classes' of five pupils from three strata based on their ability groupings on entry to secondary school, but with the further constraint that no class should contain more than three pupils of either sex.

*Preparation of lessons and associated test materials*

The specification of content, aims and objectives for the experimental lessons was carried out by departmental lecturers specializing in the teaching of History and English. The criteria for selection of subject-matter were that it should be suitable for a 20-minute 'questioning' lesson to first-year pupils and unlikely to have been previously taught to them.

Tests relating to the specified content and objectives for each subject-area were then devised by the experimenters. One of these tests was of the multiple-choice type, containing convergent questions designed to assess pupils' knowledge and comprehension of the convergent objectives specified by the subject-specialist. The second test was designed to assess pupils' divergent thinking arising from the taught lessons, and the third was a short attitude-test to gauge the affective reactions of the pupils to the particular lessons they had been taught.

To assess the suitability of lesson contents, aims, objectives and tests, several trial lessons were taught by the subject-specialists and by one of the experimenters, both in the microteaching context and in a large comprehensive school. Pupil test scores arising from all of these lessons were scrutinized to ensure appropriateness of test items and approximately normal distribution of scores.

*Preparation of teachers*

All student-teachers in this study had previous experience of microteaching and all were asked to participate in a research project involving their teaching of specified content over a longer period than previously (twenty minutes for the History lessons;

twenty-five minutes for English to allow reading of a prose extract). The general strategy to be followed for both sets of lessons was 'question-and-answer' and all subjects were given an introductory lecture on the possible uses of questioning in teaching, with some emphasis being laid upon using questions to produce divergent thinking, and on teachers' reactions to pupils' responses to questions.

Subjects then attended separate curriculum-seminars conducted by appropriate subject-specialists and attended by the experimenters. Model tapes of the trial lessons taught by the subject-specialists were shown and discussed, the content, objectives, materials and strategy for the lessons were described and any queries were answered. The pupil criterion measures were described and two of the convergent-test items and one of the divergent-test items were read out.

### Lesson and testing arrangements

All micro-classes were to participate in two lessons, so the lessons were timetabled so that each class received their English lesson and tests before their History lesson and tests. All lessons took place in studio-classrooms and were video-recorded. The testing of pupils was carried out by the experimenters in rooms adjacent to the classrooms, with the sequence of test administration being convergent test, followed by divergent test, followed by attitude test.

### Categorization of questions and reactions

The categorization of the teacher behaviours was carried out from lesson transcripts and videotape by two of the investigators, one using an observational instrument for the coding of teachers' questions, the other using an instrument for the coding of teachers' reactions. Combined question-reaction codings were then formed on the basis of the initial individual codings.

Previous large-scale studies of inter-observer agreement in the use of the instruments by four trained observers on a sample of videotaped microteaching lessons indicated very satisfactory correlations among observers for their total lesson codings for each category (MacLennan, 1973; MacLeod, 1972). As a measure of agreement in the coding of specific questions and reactions, the overall agreement of the three independent observers with the appropriate investigators was found to be 65 per cent for use of the questioning instrument and 73 per cent for use of reacting instrument.

*Criterion variables*

All criterion measures refer to class-scores, based on the performance of the five individuals within each class.

The post-lesson divergence measures were derived from pupils' written responses to the divergent-test questions. Divergent Length is the mean length (in words) of these responses; Divergent Originality is a weighted measure based on scores assigned to those responses which were shown by frequency count to have occurred rarely, and Divergent Rating is the average rating by two observers on a seven-point scale of the divergence of the responses (Pearson r for English rating agreement is ·58 ($p<$ ·05), for History $r=$·83).

The Attitude Scale score consisted of the summated scores of the classes on two sections of an attitude scale, the first section attempting to assess pupils' attitudes to the content of the lesson; the second section, the pupils' attitudes towards the teaching. The two sections were not differentiated as criterion measures because the scores on them were highly inter-correlated.

The during-lesson pupil behaviour measures were assessed during the second half of the lesson, when, it was hypothesized, the effects of the teachers' behaviours would become apparent. Proportion of Divergent Responses was the proportion of all second-half pupil responses rated as divergent by two observers for the English lessons ($r=$·51) and by three observers for the History lessons (average $r=$·47). Proportion of Causal Links consisted of the proportion of pupil responses in the second half of the lesson which contained one or more causal links. Following Rosenshine (1968), it was hypothesized that such a measure would reflect the adequacy and effectiveness of explanations being offered by the pupils, and that such adequacy of explanation might in turn be related to specific teaching behaviours. Length of Pupil Response is a measure of the average number of words used by each class of pupils in their responses during the second half of the lesson.

The attainment measures all relate to class scores in the convergent test designed to assess knowledge and comprehension of the pre-specified convergent objectives. Mean Attainment is the average score of each class, Standard Deviation Attainment reflects the spread of scores within each class, whilst Mean plus one Standard Deviation and Mean minus one Standard Deviation reflect respectively attainment at approximately the 83rd percentile and attainment at approximately the 17th percentile.

## Analysis of data

For each lesson, counts were made of the coded questions, reactions and question-reactions as well as of several global extra-system measures (e.g. proportion of teacher talk). In all, there were six kinds of independent variables, each of which is exemplified in Figure 3.

**Figure 3: Categories and Examples of Independent Variables**

|         | Questioning                   | Reacting                         |
|---------|-------------------------------|----------------------------------|
| Simple  | Propn. of Defining Qs         | Propn. Admits Rs                 |
| Complex | Propn. Defining/Hi. Structure | Propn. Admits/ Repeats/Probes Rs |
|         | Combined Q/R                  | Propn. Defining/ Admits          |
|         | Global                        | Propn. Teacher Talk              |

Because of the large number of variables generated by these procedures, a first priority for data analysis was to reduce the number of variables. This reduction was carried out through a two-stage procedure, firstly excluding those variables with a low frequency of occurrence, and then excluding those variables which did not correlate at least at the 10 per cent level of significance with any of the dependent variables. There remained 62 independent variables for History and 47 for English.

The final stage of the analysis was to carry out a multiple stepwise regression analysis for each of the dependent variables, with only the significant ($p < \cdot 10$) independent variables being allowed to enter the regression equation. This procedure allowed the choosing of a set of independent variables to give the best possible prediction of each dependent variable. In each case, the regression analysis was stopped at the point where the next variable was accounting for less than one per cent of the variance.

## Results and discussion

Whilst it is not possible here to deal individually with all the criterion variables' correlates, it is possible to consider some of the more general features of the results.*

*Fuller details of the coding procedures, data analysis and results are available from the authors.

One striking feature is the magnitude of the multiple correlation coefficients, the average of which over all twenty-two dependent variables was ·88; even after only two steps the average multiple correlation was ·77. That high proportions of the variance of outcome measures can thus be accounted for is of particular interest in view of the fact that the investigation was deliberately designed to minimize the effects of variables other than those being studied and thus to maximize their effects. The results appear to suggest the power of the control measures taken.

A second striking feature of the results is the lack of consistency across the two subjects in the relationships between predictor and criterion variables: the proportion of significant correlations common to the two subjects is no greater than one might expect by chance. There are, however, interesting patterns of similarity and dissimilarity between the two subject-areas at a more general level. The same teaching behaviour variables tend to be good predictors of criterion variables in both subject areas, although in many cases they do not relate to the *same* criterion variables in the two subjects.

There is, indeed, evidence to suggest that the three ways in which teachers' questions were categorized, and also the three ways in which their reactions were categorized, all have their distinctive value in predicting the outcomes of teaching:

*Questions, cognitive demands:* The proportion of questions classified as Opining is significantly and positively correlated with three criterion variables for English and six for History. In contrast, the proportion of Factual questions is negatively correlated with five of these nine criterion variables and with one other. In both areas, the proportion of Opining questions is related to pupils' post-lesson divergence. For History, however, but not for English, the Opining-Factual opposition is most closely related to pupils' attitudes and to the attainments of the more able.

*Questions, degree of structuring:* For English, the structuring of questions is highly correlated with all three measures of pupils' within-lesson behaviour and with all three measures of post-lesson divergence. A similar but weaker and less consistent pattern is apparent for History.

*Questions, divergence:* The divergence of teachers' questions was one of the best predictors of attainment in English, and the best for the attainment of the more able pupils ($r = \cdot 67$). In History, it was not pupils' attainments but their attitudes which were significantly correlated with the divergence of teachers' questions. Different aspects of pupils' within-lesson behaviour were also associated with the divergence of questions in the two subject areas.

*Reactions, evaluative ratings:* Since there were relatively few such ratings, the measure used was 'positive minus negative ratings'. In History, the use of praise appeared to have an inhibiting effect upon pupils, being negatively correlated with measures of divergence both during and after the lesson. In English, 'positive minus negative' was correlated positively with mean attainment and negatively with the standard deviation of attainment; correspondingly, it was not significantly correlated with the attainment of the more able pupils, but was the variable most highly correlated with the attainment of the less able ($r = \cdot 61$).

*Reactions, critical ratings:* The great majority of pupils' responses were admitted by the teachers, so significant variables tended to be those associated with the lack of admission. In English, the length of pupils' responses during lessons, their divergence after lessons, and their attitudes were all negatively correlated with the proportion of reactions which did not admit responses or which admitted them only with qualification; and the variable most highly correlated with the spread of attainment within classes was the proportion of qualifying reactions. These critical rating variables were not, however, significantly correlated with any criterion variables in History.

*Reactions, information-handling:* The two most frequent types of information handling were for the teacher to give information to supplement that given by the pupil or, on the other hand, for him to probe the pupil's response or use it as a premise for a further question. Pupils' attitudes in both subject-areas and their post-lesson divergence in History were correlated positively with Probes/ Premise for Question reactions and negatively with Gives Information reactions. These two types of information-handling were also important in defining several categories of question-reaction sequences which were highly correlated with criterion variables. A less frequent type of information-handling, using the pupil's response as a premise for argument, was positively and significantly correlated with pupils' use of causal links during lesson in History.

Each of the six ways of categorizing questions and reactions thus appears to have some predictive power. This power is significantly increased when they are used in combination. In English, for example, the highest correlate of Divergent Length, Divergent Rating, and of Divergent Responses (during lessons) was *Mean Structure of Opining Questions* (average $r = \cdot 78$); and the highest correlate of Mean Attainment was Proportion of Question-Reaction Units coded as *Divergent/Probes-Premise for Question* ($r = \cdot 63$). In History, similarly, the highest correlate of all three post-lesson divergency measures was *Proportion of Reactions coded as Probes-Premise for Question not preceded by Admits* (average $r = \cdot 68$) and the highest correlate of pupils' attitudes was *Proportion of Question-Reaction Units coded as Factual/Gives Information* ($r = -\cdot 78$).

The other, more global, measures of teacher behaviour were of very little importance in accounting for variation on the criterion variables in English. In History, on the other hand, these variables were of considerable importance. Pupils' attitudes and their divergence during and after the lessons were significantly correlated with the proportion of pupil, as opposed to teacher, talk, but also with the number of teachers' questions and reactions and, with the proportion of questions which dealt with substantive issues. There was also an interesting negative correlation between the average number of words spoken by teachers immediately after asking a question and the spread of attainment within classes, so that while this was negatively associated with the attainment of the more able pupils, the tendency to ask more than one question in a single utterance was positively correlated with the attainment of the less able.

It has only been possible, in the space available, to provide a brief summary of our findings, but enough may perhaps have been said to demonstrate that the investigation has generated a large number of plausible and testable hypotheses. Of particular interest are the hypotheses suggested about the differential effects of praise, and also about the elaborating on questions after they have been asked, on more and less able pupils. Also important is the evidence indicating the need to distinguish clearly between divergent questions and unstructured questions: not only do the divergence and structure of questions differ considerably in the outcomes with which they are associated, but it is the frequencies of divergent questions and of *high* structured questions – types generally seen to be opposed – which are the positive predictors.

The lack of correspondence between the results for the two subject areas merits some consideration. The investigation was designed with the intention that both the strategies of teaching being used and the types of outcome variables being measured should be clearly specified and the same for the two sets of lessons, except that they were in different subject areas. The obvious conclusion, therefore, is that the differences in results are due to the differences between the two subjects. But to say that one set of lessons was in English and the other in History is not sufficient to indicate the kind and structure of knowledge being dealt with, nor does it necessarily imply that there were any differences at all. If the different results are indeed due to differences in subject matter or to differences in teaching or testing which resulted from the subject matter, adequate specification of the strategies and outcome variables should have indicated the nature of these differences. That this was not done was not simply a methodological weakness: it arose rather because we did not know how to specify the strategy in generalizable terms more precisely than as 'teaching by questioning', nor how to specify the nature of the objectives more precisely than in terms of Bloom's (1965) categories. In retrospect it seems likely that an analysis of the lesson content, and of any inherent structure it may have had, would have helped towards a fuller specification both of the strategies and of the objectives.

At a more general methodological level, note should also be made of the correlational approach to process-product study and its disadvantages. It probably remains worth saying that correlation does not imply causation and that a further danger lies in the multiple correlation approach, where selected variables are drawn from a pool. The resultant multiple correlation 'is not an unbiased estimate of the correlation between the selected items and the criteria – it is, in fact, an estimate of the highest correlation that can be obtained with that many items from that pool. In another sample it is not inconceivable that an entirely different set of items might be the ones to yield the highest correlation' (Medley and Mitzel, 1963, p. 89). Another disadvantage of such approaches is that implied by Alkin and Johnson (1971) in their use of the term 'correlational fishing-trips'. Such investigations, when unguided by theory or model may end up showing which empirical relationships can be 'caught', and for which, *post hoc* explanations can take place, rather than pointing up those aspects of a model or theory which can be supported by empirical evidence. It is this last point which seems to us to be one of the major weaknesses of the study reported here. Although the teaching situation was rigorously controlled, and the coding of teacher behaviour was to some extent based on existing theoretical or conceptual models, the degree of hypothesis testing was very low. This situation is particularly hazardous when large numbers of both independent and dependent variables are being employed, and when the statistical approach being used is one which relies upon probabilistic statements of significance, thus allowing the possible appearance of significant relationships explicable by the laws of probability alone. Only when studies of similar design to the one reported here are replicated at the hypothesis testing level will it be possible to begin to construct models of the teaching process in which measures of teaching behaviour can be confidently related to measures of pupil behaviour and outcomes in a causal way.

## Acknowledgements

The authors wish to express their gratitude to the Leverhulme Trust, who funded the research programme of which this study was part; to their colleagues on the academic and technical staff of Stirling University Department of Education; to the headmaster and staff of Lornshill Academy, Alloa; to Miss Kathleen Dobbie, who typed our many drafts of this paper; to the programming staff of Stirling University Computer Unit; and, most of all, to the students and pupils who participated in this study.

## References

ALKIN, M. C. and JOHNSON, M. (1971). 'Comments on the research and development program of Byro L4:1', *Newsletter School Research*, **24**, National Board of Education, Stockholm, Sweden (mimeo).

ANNETT, J. (1969). *Feedback and Human Behaviour*. London: Penguin Books.

BARNES, D. *et al.* (1969). *Language, the learner and the school*. London: Penguin Books.

BELLACK, A. A. *et al.* (1966). *The Language of the Classroom*. New York: Teachers' College Press, Columbia University.

BILODEAU, E. A. (ed.) (1966). *Acquisition of Skill*. Academic Press.

BLOOM, B. S. (ed.) (1956). *Taxonomy of Educational Objectives Handbook I: Cognitive domain*. New York: David McKay.

CAMPBELL, D. T. (1963). 'From description to experimentation.' In: HARRIS, C. W. (ed.) *Problems in Measuring Change*. The University of Wisconsin Press.

DAVIS, O. L. and TINSLEY, D. C. (1968). 'Cognitive objectives revealed by classroom questions asked by social studies student teachers.' In: HYMAN, R. T. (ed.) *Teaching: Vantage Points for Study*. Philadelphia: Lippincott.

FLANDERS, N. A. (1965). *Teacher influence, pupil attitudes and achievement*. Coop. Res. Monograph No. 12 (OE-25040), US Office of Education.

FLANDERS, N. A. (1970). *Analyzing Classroom Behaviour*. New York: Addison-Wesley.

FLANDERS, N. A. (1973). *Knowledge about Teacher Effectiveness*. Paper presented to the American Educational Research Association, New Orleans. Report 1973-17, Far West Laboratory for Educational Research and Development.

FORTUNE, J. C. (1967). *A study of the generality of presenting behaviours in teaching pre-school children*. Memphis, Tenn.: Memphis State University, 1967. (USOE Project No. 6-8468).

GAGE, N. L. (1963). 'Paradigms for research on teaching.' In: GAGE, N. L. (ed.) *The Handbook of Research on Teaching*. Chicago: Rand McNally and Co.

GAGE, N. L. (1968). 'An analytical approach to research on instructional methods', *J. Exp. Educ.*, **37**, 119-125.

GAGE, N. L. et al. (1968). *Explorations of the Teacher's Effectiveness in Explaining*. Technical Report No. 4, Stanford Center for Research and Development in Teaching, Stanford University.

GALLAGHER, J. J. (1965). *Productive Thinking of Gifted Children*. USOE Coop. Research Project No. 965. Urbana: Institute for Research on Exceptional Children, College of Education, University of Illinois.

GALLAGHER, J. J. and ASCHNER, M. J. (1963). 'A preliminary report on analyses of classroom interaction.' *Merrill-Palmer Quarterly*, **9**, 183-194.

HUDGINS, B. B. and AHLBRAND, W. P. (1969). *A Study of Classroom Interaction and Thinking*. Technical Report Series No. 8. St Ann, Missouri: Central Midwestern Regional Educational Laboratory.

HUGHES, D. C. (1973). 'An experimental investigation of the effects of pupil responding and teacher reacting on pupil achievement', *American Educational Research Journal*, 10, 1, 21-37.

KLEINMAN, G. (1964). *General Science Teachers' Questions, Pupil and Teacher Behaviours, and Pupils' Understanding of Science*. Unpublished doctoral dissertation, University of Virginia. University Microfilms No. 65-3961.

MACLENNAN, D. J. (1973). *The Effects of Teachers' Questions on Pupils' Attitudes and Achievements: A Study in the Microteaching Context*. Unpublished MSC thesis, University of Stirling.

MACLEOD, G. R. (1972). *The Effects of Teachers' Reactions to Pupils' Responses: A Study in the Microteaching Situation*. Unpublished MSC thesis, University of Stirling.

MEDLEY, D. M. and MITZEL, H. E. (1963). 'Measuring classroom behaviour by systematic observation.' In: GAGE, N. L. (ed.) *Handbook of Research on Teaching*. Chicago: Rand McNally and Co.

NUTHALL, G. A. and CHURCH, J. (1971). *Experimental Studies of Teacher Behaviour*. Paper presented to the 43rd Congress of the Australian and New Zealand Association for the Advancement of Science.

ROGERS, V. M. and DAVIS, O. L. (1970). *Varying the Cognitive Levels of Classroom Questions: An Analysis of Student Teachers' Questions and Pupil Achievement in Elementary Social Studies*. Paper presented to the American Educational Research Association.

ROSENSHINE, B. (1968). *Objectively measured behavioural predictors of effectiveness in explaining*. Paper presented to the American Educational Research Association Chicago.

ROSENSHINE, B. (1971). *Teaching Behaviours and Student Achievement.* Slough: NFER.
ROSENSHINE, B. and FURST, N. (1971). 'Research on teacher performance criteria.' In: SMITH, B. O. (ed.) *Research on Teacher Education: A Symposium.* Englewood Cliffs, New Jersey: Prentice-Hall.
ROSENSHINE, B. and FURST, N. (1973). 'The use of direct observation to study teaching.' In: TRAVERS, R. M. W. (ed.) *Second Handbook of Research on Teaching.* Chicago: Rand McNally.
SKINNER, B. F. (1968). *The Technology of Teaching.* New York: Appleton-Century-Crofts.
SOAR, R. S. (1966). *An Integrative Approach to Classroom Learning.* Final Report. Philadelphia, Pennsylvania: Temple University.
SPAULDING, R. L. (1965). *Achievement, Creativity and Self-Concept Correlates of Teacher-Pupil Transactions in Elementary Schools.* USOE Coop. Research Project No. 1532, Hofstra University, New York.
TABA, H. *et al.* (1964). *Thinking in Elementary School Children.* USOE Coop. Research Project No. 1574, San Francisco State College.
WARD, M. H. and BAKER, B. L. (1968). 'Reinforcement therapy in the classroom', *Journal of Applied Behaviour Analysis*, 1, 4, 323-8.
WELLMAN, C. (1961). *The Language of Ethics.* Cambridge, Massachusetts: Harvard University Press.
WRIGHT, C. J. and NUTHALL, G. (1970). 'Relationships between teacher behaviours and pupil achievement in three experimental elementary lessons', *American Educational Research Journal*, 7, 4, 477-91.

# CHAPTER 12

# Developing Pictures for Other Frames: Action Research and Case Study

*Clem Adelman and Rob Walker, University of East Anglia*

## Research in the classroom

*Clem Adelman*

The view of classroom research presented here arises from our experience at the Centre for Science Education, Chelsea College, and at our current location, the Centre for Applied Research in Education, University of East Anglia. The aim is not to present alternatives to interaction analysis. An alternative presumes some sharing of the same assumptions. We do not consider that interaction analysis provides information appropriate or adequate for any but the most limited of educational ideologies.[1]

Before presenting something of our current work, a synopsis of our earlier research is pertinent. Early in 1969, Rob Walker began long term observation in science classrooms, one classroom being particularly intensively studied. The research brief was to find out how the role of the Nuffield teacher differed from that of the non-Nuffield.

During initial observation Walker delved into the literature and emerged with a range of applicable methods and instruments namely those of Medley and Mitzel, Flanders, and Withall. He found that although the instruments were useful for roughly locating differences among centralized, formal classrooms, they were virtually unusable in informal contexts.[2] Even with centralized,

[1]Our critique of Flanders' system is 'Flanders' system for analysis of classroom interaction – comments on the limitation of a research technology', forthcoming in *British Journal of Educational Psychology*. See also R. Walker 'Some problems that arise when interaction analysis is used to assess the impact of innovation' published in *Classroom Interaction Newsletter*, 1972.

[2]The attempt to categorize and classify classroom contexts as communication situations was an early concern which developed from problems in using interaction analysis. An early paper made this clear: 'A sociological language for the description of the stream of classroom behaviour'. (1969) mimeo, CARE.

formal classrooms, what was not collected by the instruments was often more interesting and seemingly more representative of the essential qualities of that classroom.

The referents of utterances in the informal context were not always clear, even with the recording assistance of a radio mike. Often the intention of the utterance, by which it had to be assigned to a category, was hidden from the observer. Supplementing or refining Flanders' categories was not the answer – the decentralized, informal classroom has cultural rules inaccessible to the Flanders system. These problems engendered a renewed search in the literature which led to the work of P. Jackson, J. Henry, Smith and Waller, amongst others. From them emerged new perspectives, technologies and techniques.[1]

In 1969, I joined the educational technology section of the Centre for Science Education. The problems of observation that Rob Walker had articulated overlapped with my interests in the application of recording technology. One major problem was the lack of visual recordings which would retain sufficient social context of the talk – who, where, when? A technology which would provide stop-frame cinematography with synchronized sound was constructed and was tried out in 1970. Even our first results indicated that this was not only a satisfactory technology for a classroom observation but also had implications for methodology.[2]

The original research produced the conclusion that there was as much variation and innovation within non-Nuffield classrooms as in Nuffield ones, using what criteria could be found in the Nuffield curriculum texts. We now had access to the front door. The interior, its inhabitants and its boundaries were beginning to be perceived. We had become very interested in the 'open' or 'informal' classroom especially in the secondary school. For instance, the Goldsmiths' College interdisciplinary inquiry in secondary schools scheme (IDE) presented a teacher with pedagogic problems of a kind amenable to our methods. (One school was studied intensively in 1969/70.)

[1] An account of these explorations is in R. Walker, MPhil thesis, Chelsea College, London University, 1971. A brief summary is 'The sociology of education and life in school classrooms' published in *Interactional Review of Education* xviii 1972/1 UNESCO Nijhoff, The Hague.

[2] For instance whereas the 3 second observation interval for FIAC is arbitrary, the 2 second photographic interval provides the minimum of visual reference necessary as context for the talk. The interval in informal primary classrooms is about 1 second.

In 1971 we received a grant from the Social Science Research Council to study informal and open classrooms using the technology as an aid to our participant observation.[1] Our selection of classrooms was mainly based on recommendations from curriculum designers, colleagues and teachers. We replayed the recordings to the teachers, sometimes to the children and sometimes to the teacher and his colleagues. We used unstructured interviews with the teachers and pupils but did not record these, although what was said was noted and often used. The archive of recordings was analysed by various techniques, our basic methodology being that of 'analytic-induction'.[2]

Some time later we began to realize connections between our data, methodology and Bernstein's ideas about 'classification and framing'.[3] Bernstein's theory provided us with criteria for selection of further types of 'open' and informal classrooms for recording. We wanted to find out to what extent the characteristics of the classroom types implied by the theory could be located and recorded. We found examples of all four types each with their own cultural rules for actions. One of the types, 'the integrated code' was exemplified by only one classroom. Most of the 'open', informal classrooms, no matter what the context of the curriculum innovation, were strong-frame weak classification, or weak-frame strong classification.[4] We developed a 'grounded theory' of classrooms from our explorations.[5]

The Ford Teaching project, which began in 1973, is action research based,[6] monitoring the practices of forty teachers in

[1]The technology is described in Adelman and Walker 'Stop-frame cinematography with synchronized sound: a technique for recording in school classrooms', *Journal of the Society of Motion Picture and Television Engineers*, volume 83 number 3, Scarsdale, New York.

[2]Analytic induction is described briefly in Howard S. Becker *Sociological Work* published by Allen Lane, 1971, Chapter 2.

[3]In Bernstein, B. *Class Codes and Control*, vol. 1, Paladin edition, 1973.

[4]A report of this work is Walker and Adelman 'Towards a sociography of classrooms' 1972, available from British Library, Boston Spa, Yorkshire. Subsequent articles arising from this research include:
(i)  'Strawberries' – critical incidents in the evolution of children's classroom identities, in *Explorations in Classroom Observation* edited by M. Stubbs and S. Delamont, published by Wiley, 1975.
(ii)  'Open-space – open classrooms?' *Education* 3–13, November 1974.
(iii)  'Communication games', *Classroom Interaction Newsletter*, December 1973.
(iv)  'Teaching, that's a joke', mimeo, CARE.

[5]Unpublished, CARE. See also *The Discovery of Grounded Theory*, by R. Glaser and A. Strauss, Aldine, 1968.

[6]Rappaport, R. N. *Three dilemmas in action-research*, mimeo given to the Social Science Research Council Conference, York, 1970.

fourteen East Anglian schools.[1] This is a cooperative enterprise
which involves John Elliott and myself in sustained relationships
with the teachers. The project is concerned to make explicit from
the teachers' and pupils' viewpoints the problems inherent in
attempting inquiry/discovery pedagogy. The teachers and schools
are widely representative of the state system. The one particular
characteristic shared by the teams of project teachers is that they
aspire to being practitioners of inquiry/discovery approaches.

At the commencement of the project a conference consisting
mainly of small discussion groups attempted to clarify notions of
inquiry/discovery pedagogy. The misunderstandings between the
teachers seemed to arise from the use of different terminology
to refer to the same actions and ideas and the same terminology to
refer to different actions and ideas. We hoped that the teachers
would quickly devise their own research instruments for monitoring
the effects on pupils of their teaching actions.[2] Before they could
communicate adequately about their problems, practices and ideals,
across subject, school and pupil-age boundaries, there had to be
some sharing of essential language. We noted from the recordings of
the classrooms that certain terms recurred. We considered that the
terms would have particular relationships to each other as a whole,
and that these relationships might be hierarchically inclusive to form
a taxonomy. There was also the possibility that these terms might be
the key to the 'theory' of pedagogy that teachers use to sustain sets
of teaching actions. These notions were influenced by our reading of
ethnosemantic and philosophic literature. In the background was a
statement by Goodenough:

> As I see it a society's culture consists of whatever it is one has
> to know or believe in order to operate in a manner acceptable to
> its members, and do so in any role that they accept for any one
> of themselves. But there remains the problem of 'what any one
> has to know or believe'.[3]

We asked the teachers to discuss the meanings of these terms,
keeping their discussion close to the awareness arising from their

[1]An initial description is J. Elliott and C. Adelman, 'Reflecting where the action
is: the design of the Ford Teaching Project', *Education for Teaching*, Autumn 1973.
[2]See 'Teachers as evaluators', *The New Era*, December 1973.
[3]W. Goodenough (1957). 'Cultural anthropology and linguistics' reprinted in
D. Hymes, '*Language in Culture and Society*', Harper and Row, New York, 1964.

self-monitoring of their teaching actions.[1] We also interviewed teachers about general aspects of the project, interpolating at conversationally appropriate moments questions that attempted to test the referents of these terms. As a further check on the meanings for teachers of these terms, a set of polar lexical pairs, which included the terms already mentioned, were sent to school teams. Teachers were asked to rate themselves and their colleagues on a seven point scale – rather like one of the methods of collecting 'constructs'.[2] This was set out again towards the end of the project in an attempt to assess change. The responses corroborated the meanings emerging from the discussions and interviews.

About two months after this 'terminological enterprise' had begun, a recording of a school team in action was received. This provided the information which related and made sense (to us and we hoped to the teachers) of all the rest of the data. By taking the sets of terms whose references contrasted, a 'conceptual map' was constructed. It was not a taxonomy but a 'tree'.[3] (See Figure 1) The conceptual map was presented to teachers to allow them to evaluate its usefulness for describing their pedagogies.[4] The different pedagogic experience and expertise of the teachers at any one time made for differing degrees of acceptance of the conceptual map.[5] This problem – one of diachronic development – is a feature of this project and action research in general. In retrospect we realized that those who had experienced the range of pedagogy referred to by the conceptual map were those who found the conceptual map most immediately useful. Those whose experience was restricted to 1 and 2 often could not imagine how, 4 especially could be put into practice. In spite of the diachronic problem, the terms and the

---

[1] P. Winch, *The Idea of a Social Science and its Relation to Philosophy*, Routledge, Kegan and Paul, 1958.

[2] *The Evaluation of Personal Constructs* by D. Bannister and J. M. Mair, Academic Press, 1968, especially chapter 5.

[3] An extensive description and discussion of the techniques and methodologies involved in ethnosemantics is *Cognitive Anthropology*, edited by S. Tyler, 1969, Holt, Reinhart and Winston.

[4] A fuller account of this procedure is 'meanings and a derived schema', Ford Teaching Project, mimeo, CARE.

[5] Towards the end of the fieldwork period of the project the refined conceptual map was tested against the experience and knowledge of the teachers. The method was to present the 'tree' and ask for the difference/sameness between two pedagogic approaches that differed by one term. The sequence was, 1:2, 2:4, 4:5, 5:3.
Those teachers who used all the approaches (only two in the project) were able to make the distinctions between the types without much difficulty.

conceptual map were increasingly found to be more generally valuable for communication within the project.

**Figure 1: Conceptual map**

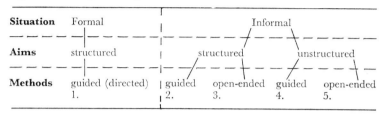

About eighteen months into the project we became aware that the evidence we had collected indicated that modifications had to be made to the conceptual map. The formal/informal distinction (which had included both social and spatial organization and dependence/independence on the teacher or his surrogates as the authoritative knowledge sources) was restricted to refer to the knowledge aspect only. 'Centralized/decentralized' labelled the spatial aspects. An additional distinction was made at the 'communication procedures' (methods) level, on the basis of transcript evidence, into person/means/ends. The pedagogic conceptual map was now as in Figure 2.

**Figure 2: Revised conceptual map**

| | |
|---|---|
| Formal instruction | Formal – structured – directed |
| 'Discovery' | Informal – structured – implicitly guided (person-ends) |
| | Informal – structured open-ended |
| 'Inquiry' | Informal – unstructured – guided (person-means) |
| | Informal – unstructured – open-ended |

Although we used a wide variety of methods and instruments, the major technique was that of 'triangulation'.[1] This involved collecting and analysing the viewpoints of representative participants. As the project attempted to encourage teachers to monitor their own actions, the choice of triangulation seemed appropriate.

[1]See for instance, H. Garfinkle, *Studies in Ethnomethodology*, published by Prentice-Hall, 1967 and A. Cicourel, *Cognitive Sociology*, Penguin, 1973, especially the chapter entitled 'Ethnomethodology'.

**H**

The teacher or pupils may intend an action (including talk) to have a particular meaning, but how the recipient interprets the action is another matter. In spite of miscommunication, the classroom inhabitants have a remarkable ability to 'remedy or 'fill-in' the action so that it makes 'sense' to them. Through recording lessons, selecting portions and playing them back to pupils with questions like 'what did you understand the teacher to mean?', and playing these back to the teacher, a simple but powerful technique was put into operation. The attempt to self-monitor one's pedagogy by identifying problems and devising experimental pedagogic strategies needed the detailed interpretative feedback from pupils and observers that the technique of triangulation provides. Misunderstandings and miscommunication are highlighted and corroborated from many points of view. Subsequent discussions take into account disparities of experience. The third viewpoint of the triangulation is that of the observer. Occasionally the observer's commonsense interpretation of the action is not that of the teachers and pupils. The pupils and teachers would then cite counter-examples. The selection of episodes for triangulation is obviously a significant way of constructing realities. The following list roughly corresponds (within diachronic variation) to duration in the project. The first mentioned tended to be the selector of episode.

1. Observer/Teacher as pedagogue/Pupils. *At commencement of project.*
2. A teacher as observer/Teacher as pedagogue/Pupils
3. Teacher as pedagogue/Observer/Pupils
4. Teacher as pedagogue/Teachers as observers/Observer. *Towards the end of project.*

A problem with this technique is when to stop eliciting interpretations. A tape-slide recording was made. This was the observer's interpretation. The recording was played back to the teacher. The observer asked the teacher if there were any episodes which he considered contained misunderstandings or miscommunication. Then the two pupils involved in the cited episode[1] were asked (without the

---

[1]The episode concerned the ambiguity of 'tin' (tin-can) and 'tin' (metal) in the context of a pupil constructed experiment on rusting. The miscommunication is recognizable in the transcripts of the lesson, but the teacher's and pupils' intended meanings could only be speculated upon until the triangulation was completed. 'Recordings, interviews and interpretations', Ford Teaching Project, mimeo, CARE.

teacher's presence) for their interpretation of that section. The pupils' account was played back to the teacher. At this third level from the original activity (1) recording, (2) teacher/pupil interviews, (3) playback interviews to teacher) I found it extremely difficult to keep all the interpretations in mind as a question agenda; but as it happened the second interview with the teacher clarified the problems.

About twenty-five of the forty teachers diligently worked with the project. Many of these have written remarkable case studies of their own teachings. They are now autonomously using the project's materials to create a training manual for any other teacher who wants to embark on inquiry/discovery pedagogy.[1]

We consider that the project exemplifies the fruitfulness of using an action-research methodology, with appropriately selected techniques, in the ideological minefield of research into educational issues. Although the Ford Teaching project had a different basis from the SSRC project, there are remarkable similarities between the 'conceptual map' and the classroom grounded theory, and between both and many of the ideas embodied in Bernstein's germinal essay.

## Case study research in education
*Rob Walker*

SAFARI, which stands for 'success and failure and recent innovation', is a three year research project investigating the medium term effects of four national curriculum development projects in British secondary schools. The projects we are tracking are: Nuffield Secondary Science, Humanities Curriculum Project, Geography for the Young School Leaver and Project Technology. Our aim is to assess the impact of these projects, not just in the classroom but in the educational system as a whole. Our audiences are those who make management decisions about innovation – teachers, head-teachers, LEA officers, DES staff, sponsoring bodies and those in teacher education.

It follows that relative to the research field our approach to classroom observation is highly focused – we are interested in the

[1]The Ford Teaching Project training manuals will be published by the Centre for Applied Research in Education at the University of East Anglia by early 1975. An extensive account of the project is to form a unit in the Open University, *Curriculum Context and Design*, 1975. See also 'Teacher Education for Curriculum Reform', *British Journal of Teacher Education*, volume 1, number 1, January 1975.

impact of certain curriculum development projects, and particularly in those effects that relate to management decisions. Teacher-pupil interaction is certainly of interest to us, but so too are the interactions of teachers with their heads of department, headmasters, LEA advisors, teacher centre wardens and curriculum development project teams. Our aim is to relate what happens inside the classroom in terms of curriculum to what happens outside. Our primary focus is not so much on learning but on teaching and management.

*Limits of the classroom*

Taking this perspective inevitably cuts us off from some of the current concerns and procedures of classroom research. On the other hand it opens up for us a range of data not normally considered in designing observational research projects. We find ourselves collecting a lot of information about what Philip Jackson has called pre-active (as opposed to interactive) aspects of teaching. For example, we are collecting teachers' life histories, case studying schools, documenting the histories of curriculum movements, studying conferences and training courses, looking at decision making at the LEA level and portraying the work of local advisors. These exercises fit comfortably within our design and involve things which relate directly to what happens in classrooms but are not the sort of things normally studied by classroom research. It is one of the implicit assumptions of classroom research that the classroom is a discrete unit, sealed-off from what happens in the rest of the school and relatively uninfluenced by 'outside' effects. Our assumption is in fact the opposite, that what happens outside the classroom does have effects that can be located and recognized in what happens inside, and this is something we hope to document more fully.

Although we start from this assumption, we also assume that we do not know and cannot predict the full range of effects on a classroom or a school that stem from the introduction of an innovation in curriculum. The SAFARI proposal makes the point strongly:

'We innovate in the dark. We know little about the nature of the impact that ... change-effects make, even less about whether that impact will endure. Our understanding of the educational process is so limited that we cannot anticipate the effects of intervening in it and so the current debate about the merits of alternative approaches and strategies is speculative in character.

This is not good enough. Because we have failed to use our experience of innovation cummulatively, each new project has to reinvent the wheel.'

We have, as a result, a strong commitment to forms of research that promise to discover and identify unknown and unpredicted effects of change initiatives.

*Research methods*

In terms of the repertoire of available methods in classroom research, the approach that seems most congruent with the SAFARI proposal lies in the tradition we usually call 'ethnographic' or 'descriptive', particularly as represented by the work of Willard Waller, Louis Smith, Philip Jackson and Jules Henry. The advantage of such an approach for our purposes is that it retains considerable flexibility, allowing the researcher to move from one hypothesis to another throughout the period of research. This freedom of movement is essential to an inquiry which aspires to be genuinely exploratory, and which makes few claims for highly generalizable findings.

As the research has progressed we have developed a commitment to a specific form of the 'ethnographic' or 'descriptive' observational tradition, a form we call the 'case study'. Case study research attempts to reach understanding through the detailed study and portrayal of individual instances, persons, ideas, institutions and events.

*Research and practice*

Our view is that educational research operates within a paradox. It aims for understandings which have been generalized *from* specific and localized information, and offers high levels of predictive reliability. Yet it also aims to inform practitioners who operate in the context of problems and decisions which are essentially idiosyncratic and unique. The problem *they* face is not how to generalize *from*, but how to infer from the general to the specific. In this context most research offers the practitioner trends and patterns, but little help with his particular case. In taking the next step, the practitioner tends to rely less on research and more on wisdom accumulated from past experience.

Our claim is that it is possible to envisage another form of educational research, a form which offers insight into the individual instance. This would start with, and remain close to, the common-

I

sense knowledge of the practitioner, and the constraints within which he works. It would aim to systematize and to build on practitioner lore rather than to supplant it.

An argument commonly advanced against case study methods is the severe restriction they impose on generalization from the case. Our point is that this conception of 'generalization' is one derived from a particular conception of scientific knowledge. We feel that there is a strong case for developing forms of educational research which accept practitioner lore as both a constraint and as a target but which attempts to retain from scientific method respect for systematic application of procedures. We see the aim of such research not so much in the production of facts or theories, but in the attempt to support the process by which professional judgement is gained from personal experience. To use Bob Stake's phrase the aim is to construct reports which provide *vicarious experience* for their audience.

If such a form of research is possible then perhaps what the researcher will report and transmit is not only his results, but also his methods and techniques. If a form of case study research such as we envisage can be made to work in educational contexts then the studies we, as researchers, make are exemplars. What we hope is that the kinds of understandings we are able to reach can be replicated by practitioners in the context of their own situations. Our case studies serve to validate the procedures and techniques we adopt as well as presenting data *per se*. What might be disseminated by our research would be not only the findings but the methods and procedures used to produce the study.

Perhaps we can clarify this by looking specifically at classroom research. As researchers we tend to think of classroom observation in terms of formal methods and procedures. The truth is that classroom observation is a form of research daily practised by pupils, teachers, teacher educators and advisors and inspectors. Their aims, criteria of significance and contexts of concern are perhaps very different to those of the professional research worker yet to a considerable extent they depend on their skill as observers in formulating next steps in terms of action.

In SAFARI we take this 'natural practice' of classroom research as a starting point. Our next question is then, in what ways can *we* practise classroom observation that offers means by which 'natural' observers can reflect upon, and perhaps improve their routine practices.

This may seem a simple statement, but the implications impose considerable constraints on how the researcher operates. First, the statement assumes that the research will start from the natural language of description of 'natural' observers and attempt to remain as close to them as possible. This is to say much more than that the research must simply avoid jargon and attempt to write lucidly. Nor does it imply inherent simplicity. The 'taxonomy of meanings' used by the Ford Teaching project illustrates something of the complexities of procedure and subtlety of conceptual analysis such a condition can involve.

Second, it assumes that research will remain as close as possible to the organizational constraints facing 'natural' observers. If a local adviser *can* only spend five minutes in each class there is little to be gained from telling him he would do better to spend a week. The researcher has to accept the limits of five minute samples and then to find the best possible use of that kind of opportunity.

Third, it assumes research will remain as close as possible to the kinds of resources normally available to 'natural' observers. Incidentally, this may not imply 'simplicity' of technique since many practitioners can now obtain access to videotaped close-circuit television but may find even small scale testing or survey programmes beyond their scope.

In SAFARI we are attempting to make some progress towards the realization of such a form of research. We are making case studies of four curriculum projects but we are also undertaking a number of related small scale and exploratory exercises. We are, for example, making recordings (tape-slide) of whole days in the life of local advisors as they travel from school to school, in order through coupled interviews to try and elicit the kinds of criteria they use in making judgements on the basis of observation. One key to the kind of research we have described would seem to be for us to know more about how practitioners operate as observers.

We are experimenting with fieldwork procedures and forms of reporting which make feasible the idea of one week school case studies. The notion of 'condensed fieldwork' described in the case study paper is designed as a device for collapsing the normal time scale of participant observation studies of schools to a length that is more like that used in 'natural' observation.

We are attempting to extend the notion of case study as we have developed it into the study and portrayal, not just of institutions, but also of events and ideas. We have for example tried to study curriculum project training conferences and an historical idea ('The Nuffield Approach' to science teaching).

Another facet of the case study idea we have explored is the collection of life histories. We are currently working on a set of 17 life histories, of teachers who have been involved with Nuffield Science.

Each of these case study exercises relates to our overall aim of trying to study the impact of curriculum innovation, and of trying to do this in a way that helps practitioners take the next step intelligently.

In an attempt to relate our studies of four major curriculum projects more directly to current practice we are engaged in a major case study of one local authority. In this one area we hope to inter-relate the separate studies we have described. Our hope is that in this way we will be able to make direct and indirect connections between what happens inside the classroom and what happens outside. This means relating the actions and decisions of curriculum development teams to the actions and decisions of local authority officers, and to the action and decisions of teachers, in and out of the classrooms. We do not pretend this will be easy, technically, intellectually or politically. What we are suggesting is a new form for educational research, and perhaps one that demands a new ethic for the researcher. We believe there is a need for a form of practice-related research of the kind we are suggesting, but if we are to achieve it, it will almost certainly require us to re-negotiate our relationship, as researchers, to those engaged in educational practice at all levels of the system.

## References

FORD TEACHING PROJECT. *Meanings and a derived schema.* (mimeo) CARE (1973).

HENRY, J. (1966). *Culture against Man.* London: Tavistock, Social Science Paperbacks.

JACKSON, P. W. (1966). *The Way Teaching Is.* Association for Curriculum Development and the NEA.

SAFARI, proposal (1971). 'Making curriculum innovation work.' Written by BARRY MACDONALD. In: SAFARI (1974). *Innovation, Evaluation, Research and the Problem of Control.* Norwich: CARE, UEA.

SAFARI, (1974). 'The conduct of educational case study: ethics, theory and practice.' Included in the collection of papers *Innovation, Evaluation, Research and the Problem of Control.* Available from SAFARI, CARE, University of East Anglia, Norwich.

SAFARI, (1971). *The Nuffield Approach.* Norwich: CARE, University of East Anglia.

STAKE, R. 'Voices.' In: *The Measuring of Education.* McCutchan Publishing Company. (in press).

WALLER, W. (1932). *The Sociology of Teaching.* New York: Dover.

# CHAPTER 13

# Teaching and Talking: A Sociolinguistic Approach to Classroom Interaction

*Michael Stubbs, Department of English Studies, University of Nottingham.*

This paper illustrates what a 'sociolinguistic' approach might offer educational researchers interested in classroom interaction. I will develop three main points:

1. Much research has treated classroom talk in strange isolation from other types of social interaction. A sociolinguistic analysis can relate classroom talk to cultural norms of speech behaviour and investigate culture-specific assumptions concerning the relationship between education and learning. This part of the argument will be by reference to one aspect of Flanders' (1970) Interaction Analysis Categories (FIAC) for studying classroom talk.

2. Studies of classroom interaction have typically ignored the intrinsic linguistic organization of classroom talk as a type of discourse in its own right. Again this is illustrated from FIAC. This develops point 1 at the micro-level of the details of discourse structure.

3. An analysis of discourse structure can show how general cultural norms of speech behaviour are displayed in the fine details of talk. Here I will discuss extracts of teacher-pupil talk to show how the kind of concept I propose can be closely related to data. This will develop the link between points 1 and 2.

The argument will be, then, that sociolinguistic concepts, at both micro- and macro-levels, can enrich the analysis of the values, attitudes and assumptions which are inevitably conveyed when teachers and pupils talk to each other. It is merely for convenience that my examples are taken from Flanders' approach to classroom interaction analysis. In this way I can both be specific, and also refer to an approach already familiar to readers from other papers in this book. However, the points to be made are relevant to research on classroom interaction in general.

## 1.  What is sociolinguistics?

The term 'sociolinguistics' covers a wide range of studies which are not always obviously related. It refers to studies of how language is *used* in *social contexts*. The main focus is on language variation. Language changes in form and function across different cultures and across different social situations within one culture. The aim, of course, is to find system within the variation. 'Sociolinguistics' is used here to refer both to studies of spoken interaction in face-to-face conversation and also to more general studies of norms and conventions for speech behaviour in different cultures.

Paradoxically, there are very few studies of classroom life which use sociolinguistic concepts to analyse teacher-pupil talk[1] – 'paradoxically' because classroom life is a prime example of language use in social contexts. Only a few studies of verbal interaction in the classroom have used any descriptive concepts apart from predetermined category systems (such as FIAC or the many related systems).[2]

## 2.  The classroom as a speech situation

Much of the research on teacher-pupil talk treats classroom interaction in strange isolation from other speech events. Sociolinguistics uses the term 'speech event' to refer to such intuitively recognizable social occasions as a conversation, an argument, a lecture, a tête-à-tête and so on. For some purposes it is useful to regard a school lesson as just one more type of speech event with its own characteristic norms and rules.[3] I will illustrate this point with

[1]For educational readers, a useful short book on this topic is Labov (1970), which is a summary of important sociolinguistic principles and their relevance to educational research.

[2]Studies of classroom talk which do develop sociolinguistic concepts are Gumperz and Herasimchuk (1972), Cazden *et al.* (1972) and Sinclair *et al.* (1972). Gumperz and Herasimchuk provide perceptive commentary on tape-recorded teacher-pupil talk, relating social assumptions about teaching to conversational strategies. Many of the papers in Cazden *et al.* are very general, but Mishler (1972) similarly relates teaching strategies to the fine grain of teachers' talk. Papers by Philips and Dumont (in Cazden *et al.*) and by Sinclar *et al.* are mentioned below.

[3]'School lesson' is, of course, merely a commonsense label. FIAC, and most of my discussion in this paper, are primarily applicable to relatively formal 'chalk and talk' lessons. Other types of lesson (e.g. 'class discussion') have different but equally definable rules.

one specific example from Flanders' work, to show that a sociolinguistic perspective can place classroom interaction in a more meaningful context of cultural norms of behaviour.

Consider, then, one assumption as to what 'teaching' consists of, which underlies FIAC. Flanders' coding categories are: teacher talk: (1) accepts feeling, (2) praises or encourages, (3) accepts or uses ideas of pupils, (4) asks questions, (5) lecturing, (6) giving directions, (7) criticizing or justifying authority; and pupil talk: (8) response, (9) initiation; and (10) silence or confusion (Flanders, 1970, p. 34). There are many assumptions implicit in this coding scheme (and many of them are elsewhere explicitly recogized by Flanders) about the significant things which teachers and pupils do. For example, there are seven categories for teacher talk and only two categories for pupil talk. A first assumption is, then, that 'teaching' consists of teachers talking more and in more varied ways than pupils. As it stands this is a trivial observation. But the point is that FIAC has been found adequate for coding what participants *do* in the kind of relatively formal 'chalk and talk' teaching situations for which the scheme is intended. The assumption inherent in the scheme has been corroborated by observational data on hundreds of teachers. It has been found for example that teachers tend, on average, to talk for about 70 per cent of the time in the classroom.

This strong empirical evidence for a rule or norm of speech behaviour (that, in our culture, teachers appropriately talk for about two-thirds of classroom time) is not related to a wider sociolinguistic framework. Yet this 'two-thirds rule' would be a normal kind of constraint to expect. For there are many other conventions of sociolinguistic behaviour concerned simply with the amount of speech or silence considered appropriate in different social situations. Many of these rules are embodied in proverbs and cliches: 'Children should be seen and not heard', 'speak when you're spoken to', 'she could talk the hind legs off a donkey', 'he talks nineteen to the dozen', 'speech is silver, silence is golden'. Short silences at dinner parties are often embarrassing; on the telephone they are disruptive. Babbling babies are considered cute; the 'strong, silent type' used to be an ideal. Hymes (1967) provides data on the interpretation of silence in other cultures. He mentions the Paliyan of south India who regard verbal persons as abnormal and who tend to speak less and less as they grow older, lapsing into almost complete silence by about the age of forty. Clearly the Paliyan attribute very different values to silence than our culture does.

I might continue indefinitely with other observations and (for us) odd facts and cultural attitudes to speech and silence. But my first point is simply that an important part of our communicative competence involves knowing when to speak and when to hold our peace. Flanders' 'two-thirds' rule means little until we know *what values attach to speech versus silence in our culture*, and until we can see the place of the 'two-thirds' rule in a set of related sociolinguistic conventions.

We can take this point further than simply illustrating a loose link between a finding of Flanders and a miscellaneous, if extensive, range of related sociolinguistic rules. One of Flanders' express aims in teacher training is to get teachers to raise the amount of pupils' contributions to lessons. Flanders is concerned with quality as well as quantity, but there is a clear assumption in his work which equates 'learning' with 'talking': an assumption that talk is the main channel for learning and that pupils learn by composing talk in real time in front of an audience. Whether this is a valuable educational belief is not at present at issue. What I am concerned with here is that, again, comparative sociolinguistic data can set this assumption in a more meaningful context by showing how this equation of education with talking is a highly culture-specific assumption. In two papers on American Indian children, Philips (1972) and Dumont (1972) discuss the problem that such children pose in the classroom. The 'problem', as expressed by white teachers, is that such children 'won't talk' in the classroom although they are observed to be highly verbal in other situations. Philips and Dumont explain the children's behaviour by showing how the Indian groups in question (Sioux and Cherokee) have very different sociolinguistic norms for speech and silence from their white teachers. The Indians regard learning as a process which occurs through observation, supervised participation and self-initiated testing. Speech is minimal in this process.

In this section, then, I have argued that an analysis of classroom interaction can be enriched by taking account of its relationship to other speech events in the culture. Only in this way can we begin to see the *values* attached to different kinds of speech behaviour in the classroom. The aim of the sections which follow is to relate this general notion of a culture-specific assumption about teaching to data in the form of transcripts of teacher-pupil talk, and thereby to show how such assumptions about teaching methods are reflected in discourse structure.

## 3. The organization of discourse

Linguists maintain that language is *used* for different *purposes* in different social *contexts*. But it is fair to say that a specifically linguistic approach to language is concerned first and foremost with the inherent organization of language as a self-contained system. The organization of the language system itself is characteristically ignored by many studies of classroom interaction. For convenience this point can also be illustrated from FIAC.

FIAC requires utterances to be coded *directly* as pedagogical acts (e.g. 'lecturing', 'praises or encourages') which are of immediate interest to the educationalist. These acts are then further taken as immediately transparent instances of 'direct' or 'indirect' influence in teaching ('direct' and 'indirect' teaching styles being computed from the simple addition and division of items in various coding categories – Flanders, 1970, p. 102). Thus utterances are further categorized, without any intervening argument, as evidence of teaching style and, by implication, of the teacher's social role (e.g. 'democratic' versus 'authoritarian'). This procedure thus completely bypasses any inherent organization which the talk itself has. Language has its own organization – or, more accurately, it has various levels of organization which are closely interrelated but which can, and should, be studied in their own right.[1] At each partly autonomous level of linguistic organization there are constraints on possible or appropriate sequences of units. Just as not all sequences of words are grammatical (e.g. 'Mat the cat on the sat'), so there are constraints on discourse sequences. One does not find, for example, sequences such as: 'Excuse me. My name's Mike Stubbs. Can you tell me the way to the station?' (I have borrowed this example from Labov.) That is, in our culture, the sequence is

$$\begin{matrix} \text{interrupting} \\ \text{stranger} \end{matrix} + \begin{matrix} \text{introducing} \\ \text{oneself} \end{matrix} + \begin{matrix} \text{asking for a} \\ \text{small service} \end{matrix}$$

'ungrammatical discourse' ('undiscoursical'?). There is nothing wrong with the sentence grammar, but there is something odd about

[1]Traditional levels of linguistic organization include phonology, morphology, syntax, and semantics. Discourse is now being studied as another set of interrelated levels of linguistic organization. (cf note on page 238.)

J

these conversational acts occurring in that sequence. There are also strong constraints on other aspects of discourse: for example, constraints on stylistic shifts (unless for humorous effect), or constraints on discussing certain topics with certain people. As yet, relatively little is known about such constraints, but it is clear that discourse is a partly autonomous level of linguistic organization (or, more accurately again, a series of interrelated levels).[1] Conversation is in no sense a random or unordered string of utterances.

It is necessary therefore to study the organization of teacher-pupil talk at the level of discourse. Confronted with an utterance one should first ask: what is its function in the interaction? This involves questions such as: what utterances does it follow and precede? what is its status as a discourse act (e.g. a response, question, etc.)?[2] Only after that can one then ask: what is its pedagogical function? or what is its function in sustaining a social role?

This point can be made in a slightly different way. A list of the types of utterances categorized by FIAC can be extended indefinitely. As well as 'lectures', 'gives directions', 'asks questions' and so on, one might have: explains, drills, reads, gives an example, draws an inference, reaches a conclusion, etc. These are all intuitively recognizable pedagogical acts. The only way to prevent such a meaningless proliferation and ever more subtle subdivision of categories is to relate the categories within structural statements, i.e. to define utterances in terms of meaningful selections at different positions in a sequence of discourse. In other words, utterances gain

---

[1]Sinclair *et al.* (1972) is the only attempt so far to propose possible levels of discourse organization. One model of sentence grammar proposes a hierarchically ordered series of ranks: morpheme, word, group, clause, sentence. Analogously, Sinclair *et al.* (1972, and work in progress) propose for discourse the ranks: act, move, exchange, sequence, transaction. The three-part discourse structure discussed below would be at exchange rank.

[2]Flanders (1970, p. 35) uses the terms 'initiation' and 'response' only in a very weak sense. They refer to the initiation of amorphous topics in the lesson – not to the kind of structurally related category of discourse acts which I discuss below. To respond means 'to react to *ideas*' (p. 35, emphasis added). Thus despite Flanders' claim to study 'the chain of small events' (p. 2) in classroom interaction, FIAC cannot be used to study discourse structure. This is simply because an 'event' is defined (p. 4) in arbitrary terms as 'the shortest possible act that a trained observer can identify and record'. Thus the 'chain of events' has nothing to do with the autonomous organization of the talk itself. Further 'patterns' of events are defined in terms of frequency of occurrence of short chains of events, i.e. 'pattern' is a statistical, not a structural, notion. It is clear, however, that we require to know *where* events occur in discourse *structure*, *before* we can be sure what kind of events they are.

an important part of their meaning from where they occur. To study this meaning we must study the intrinsic organization of teacher-pupil discourse itself.

A specifically socio*linguistic* criticism of coding schemes such as FIAC is therefore that the description jumps directly from isolated utterances to teaching methods, as though the talk had no other organization. Schemes which 'code' interactive behaviour have been accused of an extreme form of reductionism, in that they ignore the context of the behaviour, in that they are necessarily concerned only with observable behaviour, in that they reduce a continuum of behaviour to discrete categories, and so on. These objections are well-known. Note however that it is no solution to reductionism simply to remain closer to the observed behaviour, to capture more varied aspects of it, or to 'triangulate' on the situation by combining different types of data. In other words, it is no solution merely to fight shy of abstraction, for any scientific description necessarily involves abstraction, idealization, categories, and so on – otherwise no generalities can be stated. A non-reductionist explanation of social behaviour is rather to be achieved by seeking the *longest* path from the behavioural data to explanatory categories.[1] In the present case this involves passing the data through interrelated levels of discourse organization, and *not* regarding teacher-pupil talk as *direct* evidence of pedagogical strategies or social role. One way of avoiding shallow, and ultimately naive, behaviourist accounts of social behaviour, is therefore to handle the data in terms of as many levels of organization as possible. Other levels of organization, which I will not discuss here, include kinesics (body motion and gesture) and proxemics (body position). These aspects of social interaction likewise have their own inherent organization and do not *directly* reflect sociological categories any more than language does. 'Triangulation' must therefore involve combining different descriptive statements and not merely different kinds of data.

## 4. The discourse structure of teacher-pupil talk

So far I have discussed some general norms associated with speaking and teaching and have made some general theoretical points about discourse structure. It remains now to relate these points more closely by discussing an aspect of the discourse structure

[1] This point is nicely developed in Ashby and Coulthard (1974). I am grateful to the authors for discussion of this concept with them.

of extracts of teacher-pupil talk. Sociolinguistic statements can only be precise if notions such as culture-specific assumptions about speech behaviour can be related to the underlying linguistic organization of what people actually say to each other.

The first extract is from a lesson in which a native English-speaking teacher is teaching English to French pupils. The lesson is about different varieties of English and the teacher is explaining the expression 'telling off':

TEACHER:    . . . but how would you be speaking – to a person you were telling off – Renaud – about time I heard your voice this morning – so wake up – it's not very difficult Renaud this – for even you – come on Renaud – show some sparks of life (1)* s'pose I am telling you off – how would I be speaking to you (5) do you understand or have you been lost by the wayside somewhere – do you understand what I am saying – well then come on (7) we're all waiting Renaud (2) it's not very difficult this (5) well for example would I be speaking to you very very sweetly – if I were telling you off – in a very very friendly way (4) what – pardon

PUPIL:      no

TEACHER:    well speak up – don't speak to your hand – your hand is not very interested in this – we are – again

PUPIL:      no

TEACHER:    no well how would I be speaking then (7) how would I be speaking – if I were telling you off (4) which I'm going to do in about two minutes if you don't wake up – all right Richard (Richard has his hand up)

PUPIL 2:    eh first when you are telling someone off you are angry

TEACHER:    to tell someone off

PUPIL 2:    to tell someone off you are angry

TEACHER:    angry right good – ok stop – . . .

There are three possible ways of relating specific features of this transcript to the kind of issues that I have been discussing.

One way of studying the talk would be to focus on particular isolated utterances. For example, in trying to get the pupil to speak,

*Numbers in brackets represent pauses in seconds

the teacher says, 'about time I heard your voice this morning'. Suppose we take this fragment literally. The teacher seems to be saying something like: just hearing a pupil's voice is a good thing in itself; it is better to talk than to remain silent when nominated by the teacher; and public talk in the classroom should be the norm – he later tells the pupil to 'speak up – don't speak to your hand'. This instance of talk seems to provide a *direct* illustration of my first point above (in section 2). It relates something said to a culture-specific assumption about teaching and talking, by equating learning with public pupil-talk. However, this type of description proceeds *directly* from the literal meaning of the teacher's words to a generalization about teaching. Clearly we cannot proceed by this kind of commentary on each particular utterance the teacher makes. There would be, in principle, no end to the description: it would be open-ended, always open to *ad hoc* additions, and not in any way systematic.

As a second and less *ad hoc* procedure of analysing the transcript we might look instead at some of the discourse functions that the teacher's talk serves. One thing the teacher is trying to do here is to extract talk from the pupil by performing discourse acts that we might label *eliciting, prompting, giving a clue, nominating* (a pupil to speak), *evaluating* (the pupil's answer), and *checking on understanding*.[1] Almost the whole of the extract consists of a string of such acts. Note, again, one crucial distinction between such discourse acts and the type of category in FIAC. The types of act listed here function to control the discourse within which they occur (I am considering their function in organizing the talk, and not jumping immediately to their pedagogical function). Although such acts form a relatively coherent set, however, such a list could still be indefinitely extended, subdivided into subtler categories and so on. On this score, it is open to the same objection as FIAC.

A third, and still more adequate, procedure for analysing the data would be to look at utterances not as isolated instances of acts but as exponents (realizations) of categories of discourse act occurring in definable sequences, i.e. as exponents of an underlying discourse structure. Suppose we begin by looking at the end of the extract and considering the sequence of acts which occur when the teacher does elicit some talk from a pupil. If we label the transcript with the kind of discourse acts I listed above, we have:

[1]See Stubbs (1972, 1974) for discussion of such discourse acts in more detail.

| | | |
|---|---|---|
| TEACHER: | . . . how would you be speaking if | |
| | I were telling you off (4) | *elicit* |
| | which I'm going to do in about two | |
| | minutes if you don't wake up – | *prompt* |
| | all right Richard | *nomination* |
| PUPIL 2: | eh first when you are telling some- | |
| | one off you are angry | *response* |
| TEACHER: | to tell someone off | *correction*( ?) |
| PUPIL 2: | to tell someone off you are angry | *response* |
| TEACHER: | angry right good | *evaluation* |

The basic sequence is: (1) the teacher's eliciting questions, (2) the pupil's responses to the questions, and (3) the teacher's acceptance and evaluation of the pupil's responses. It is not difficult to find data which exemplify this three-part eliciting-responding evaluating structure more closely.[1] This extract is from later in the same lesson:

| | | |
|---|---|---|
| TEACHER: | well how do you speak to someone if | |
| | you're angry . . . | |
| | Richard | *elicit* |
| PUPIL: | you lose control of what you say | *response* |
| TEACHER: | yes – good you shout you lose control | *evaluation* |
| | Daniel | *elicit* |
| PUPIL: | you promise her a big punishment | *response* |
| TEACHER: | yes – you promise people a punishment – | *evaluation* |
| | anything else (3) anything else you | |
| | want to add | |
| | Colin | *elicit* |
| PUPIL: | make sure that you get it into her | *response* |
| TEACHER: | yes you would be very insistent – you | |
| | would make sure that the person had | |
| | understood what you say (6) good | *evaluation* |

One final brief example of the immediate implications of handling discourse in this way: suppose we have a fragment of teacher-pupil talk which goes as follows (from the same lesson again):

[1]It is in this section that my argument owes most to the work of Professor John McH. Sinclair and his colleagues. My argument is in no sense, however, a fair summary of this work. I have taken the concept of a three-part exchange structure which is proposed in Sinclair *et al.* (1972) and adapted it for my own purposes. In Sinclair *et al.* this concept is only one part of a hierarchical model of classroom discourse.

TEACHER : what is a lecture (1)
PUPIL : it's a kind of a lesson where you've got
a professor or somebody important
teaching you about – science or
geography or something like that (2)
TEACHER : well about any subject really it's when
one person takes a lesson and where . . . (3)
(continues with more detailed explanation)

Outside the classroom (1) could be a 'genuine' question, in the sense of a request for information, and after the explanation at (2) the first speaker might give a response such as 'oh I see'. But inside the classroom we know that (1) is a 'pseudo question', in the sense that Teacher already knows the answer and is requesting Pupil to talk and to display his knowledge. This becomes explicit at (3), but we and the pupil had correctly interpreted Teacher's intention before this. If utterances are studied in isolation, (1) provides a 'coding problem' (how do we know that it is not 'really' a question?). But if the talk is studied in terms of its underlying assumptions, and how these assumptions are displayed in its discourse structures, we have a more adequate explanation of how (1) can be understood as a request to display knowledge. In other words we can get some leverage on the question of how talk is interpreted. It should be clear, then, that a discourse structure such as elicit-response-evaluate is not a 'pattern' which has been induced from the data. On the contrary, it formulates part of our communicative competence: something we all know about teacher-pupil talk, and a piece of tacit knowledge on which we draw in hearing and interpreting talk.

This type of description is no longer, therefore, open-ended and indefinitely expandable. The description of this one aspect of the talk consists of a structural statement which specifies that a fixed number of units occur in a fixed sequence. Clearly not all classroom talk confirms to this three-part structure, with or without variations. This is one structure amongst others.

This type of description would require to be worked out in much greater detail. In particular, it would have to specify the exponents of the various categories. For example, for the data in the second extract, one could specify that the evaluation category is realised by the teacher saying 'yes' or 'yes good' and/or by repeating what the pupil has just said.

But I hope I have taken the argument far enough to illustrate my point. To summarize: FIAC forces us to proceed directly from isolated utterances to pedagogical acts to teaching style, as though language had no organization of its own. A linguistic approach to discourse would study how utterances fit together into organized sequences at the level of discourse itself. The sequence of description would be from utterances to discourse acts to discourse structures to broader underlying assumptions. (Note that this is the sequence in the final descriptive statement. It is *not* the sequence in the research procedure. The discovery of categories and structures will proceed simultaneously at all levels.)

### 5. Some implications

Educational researchers are clearly not interested in linguistic description for its own sake. But I have tried to show how this type of description can be related to underlying values, attitudes and assumptions conveyed by the talk. The whole point of this type of approach to classroom interaction is to provide a way of specifying the detailed conversational mechanisms which convey such messages.

Having identified one particular conversational mechanism, a three-part eliciting structure, one might speculate further on what values it conveys. Here are a couple of starters. The three-part structure (elicit-response-evaluation) provides a formal model of one type of teacher-control, i.e. it specifies one conversational device for keeping other speakers in their conversational place. To relinquish this control, a teacher might have to change to a two-part structure. But a two-part elicit-response structure would still be rather different from the structure of casual conversation between social equals. Another way of putting this is that a three-part structure reveals this type of teacher-pupil talk as pseudo-dialogue: it is effectively monologue with the pupils supplying talk when the structure demands it. One might also consider in what other situations, and by what conversational mechanisms, interactional control is exercised by one speaker over another. For example, Speier (1971) discusses how parents exercise interactional control over their children by talking on their behalf, preventing their talking to certain people and so on. Flanders points out (1970, p.102) that simply 'monopolizing talking time is one way to dominate and to express one's will'. Again comparative data from other speech situations is required before we can say what values are conveyed by the specific kind of interactional control that teachers exercise.

Other questions will occur to readers. A structural analysis of the type I have proposed provides a powerful tool for investigating how such underlying values may be conveyed by talk.

## 6. Concluding remarks

Verbal interaction has in recent years been approached from various research directions: psychological, social-psychological, sociological and linguistic. Each discipline has something different to offer. As a linguist I have a particular interest in how language itself works, but I do not put forward my discipline as the only way to look at classroom interaction.[1] I have argued here, however, that such a study can provide a more powerful tool for an 'applied' analysis of language in use.

I have not tried to argue that language is somehow a privileged source of data on social life (although I will admit to a warm feeling that this is, in fact, so). I have argued that if language *is* to be used as data for the analysis of social life, the analysis can be enriched by taking account of how language itself works; and that if this level of organization is ignored then the description is inevitably reductionist. I hope that my examples in this paper have indicated the type of specific finding which sociolinguistics might have to offer classroom research, without implying that my discussion necessarily relates to 'teaching' in general.

The pun in the paper's title, 'Teaching and Talking', should now be clear. Classroom talk is, in one sense, just talk, and is therefore data for descriptive sociolinguistics. But our culture assumes that teaching and learning are somehow inherently related to talk as a medium. This culture-specific assumption is, in turn, revealed in the underlying discourse structure of the classroom talk itself.

## Acknowledgements

This paper owes much to the work of Professor John McH. Sinclair and his colleagues at the University of Birmingham on classroom language (Sinclair *et al.* 1972). I have however adapted

[1] I do not intend this statement as a conventional genuflexion to researchers in other disciplines. In Stubbs and Delamont, (eds.), (in press) we argue precisely the case for combining different but related disciplinary perspectives on the classrooms.

this work in ways with which the authors might not agree. I have also learned much from working with Professor Sinclair and others on a related project on discourse analysis. The work reported here was funded by the SSRC.

## References

ASHBY, M. C. and COULTHARD, R. M. (1974). 'A linguistic description of doctor-patient interviews', University of Birmingham, mimeo. (To appear in WADSWORTH, M. (ed.) *Everday Medical Life*, Dent, forthcoming.)

CAZDEN, C., JOHN, V. and HYMES, D. (eds.) (1972). *Functions of Language in the Classroom*. New York: Teachers' College Press.

DUMONT, R. (1972) 'Learning English and how to be silent: studies in Sioux and Cherokee classrooms.' In: CAZDEN et al. (eds.) 1972.

FLANDERS, N. (1970). *Analyzing Teaching Behaviour*. London: Addison-Wesley.

GUMPERZ, J. and HERNANDCHUK, E. (1972). 'The conversational analysis of social meaning: a study of classroom interaction.' In. SUVY, P. (ed.) (1972). *Sociolinguistics: Current Trends and Prospects*. Georgetown: Monograph Series on Language and Linguistics, 25.

HYMES, D. (1967). 'Models of the interaction of language and social setting', *J. Social Issues*, 23, 2, *Problems of Bilingualism*.

LABOV, W. (1970). *The Study of Nonstandard English*. Illinois: National Council of Teachers of English.

MISHLER, E. (1972). 'Implications of teacher-strategies for language and cognition: observations in first-grade classrooms.' In: CAZDEN et al. (eds.) 1972.

PHILIPS, S. (1972). 'Participant structures and communicative competence: Warm Springs children in community and classroom.' In: CAZDEN et al. (eds.) 1972.

SINCLAIR, J. MCH. et al. (1972). *The English Used by Teachers and Pupils*. Dept of English, University of Birmingham, mimeo, Report to SSRC. (Revised version published as *Towards an Analysis of Discourse*, Oxford University Press, 1974.)

SPEIER, M. (1971). 'The everyday world of the child.' In: DOUGLAS, J. (ed.) *Understanding Everyday Life*. London: Routledge and Kegan Paul.

STUBBS, M. (1972). 'Keeping in touch: some functions of teacher-talk.' Occasional Paper 10, Centre for Research in the Educational Sciences, University of Edinburgh. (Revised version in STUBBS and DELAMONT, (eds.), in press.)

STUBBS, M. (1974). 'Organizing talk in the classroom', Dept of English, University of Birmingham, mimeo. (To appear in German translation in *Thema Curriculum*.)

STUBBS, M. and DELAMONT, S. (eds.) (in press) *Explorations in Classroom Observation*. London: Wiley.

# CHAPTER 14

# The Classroom Setting as a Unit of Analysis in Observation Studies

*Pamela K. Poppleton, Division of Education, University of Sheffield*

The aim of this article is to explore some of the problems connected with the unit of analysis in classroom observation studies and to suggest a framework which would be helpful in generalizing results so that they may be more readily interpreted. It arose from the experience of observing child behaviour in an open-plan junior school where there are frequent changes of activity and where children may be found working on different activities under a variety of conditions at any one time. In such circumstances there are no set lesson periods and the changes of activity are not always signalled by the teacher.

In recording the behaviour of the children it was found essential to distinguish between periods when the teacher was instructing the whole class, other activities in which all the children were involved such as discussion or drama, periods when the children were working individually on assigned work or projects of their own choice and periods when they were working co-operatively in pairs or small groups. The unit of analysis chosen was therefore the activity or *setting*, this term being used to indicate that the teacher had previously made a decision about the range and variety of activities which would occupy the day. In this sense, all settings were teacher-controlled, though not necessarily teacher-directed in that they required continuous intervention or supervision. In fact, the range and variety of the settings employed may be taken as a good indication of the teacher's role flexibility and teaching style (Gibson, 1970).

The use of the term 'setting' is not new. Reference is made in the literature to naturalistic settings (Brandt, 1972, McIntyre, 1974) and educational settings (Rosenshine and Furst, 1973). Within the classroom framework Kounin (1970) distinguished between recitation and seatwork settings and Spaulding (1970) employed the concepts of teacher-directed and non-directed settings. Perkins (1964, 1965) differentiated more finely between group discussion, class recitation, individual work or project, seatwork, small groups and committee work and oral reports. These all have much in common with the *phenomenal units* defined by Barker (1968) as natural breaks in the stream of classroom processes which may be recognized by all participants and with Gump's (1967) *Segments*. They have not however, been widely applied in the study of classroom interaction, and Biddle (1967) considers that such units are too gross to tell us much about interactive processes. In fact, they define the kinds of interaction which are likely to occur. Co-operative work cannot occur when the teacher is instructing the whole class, and social contacts between peers differ in their frequency and nature when children are working individually on assignments as against projects of craft work using shared materials.

The defining characteristics of a setting are, therefore, those of the interaction process itself which determines who communicates with whom and for what purpose. The classroom setting is not so gross a unit as to encompass large numbers of children working in disparate tasks, nor so small that it does not accurately represent classroom activities. It may be added that settings need not relate only to classroom events but also to play and out-of-school activities. Within each setting the observer may sample and categorize behaviours according to any objective scheme. The nature and significance of classroom settings may be demonstrated by some data collected in the course of two investigations.[1] One was concerned with recording child behaviour and the other, patterns of teacher/pupil interaction.

In a study of children's behaviour in an open-plan junior school, the observation instrument chosen was Spaulding's (1970) CASES, the Coping Analysis Schedule for Educational Settings. It has proved to be a reliable and well-validated instrument in the USA and contains 13 categories some of which are subdivided into task appropriate and task inappropriate sections to give a total of 19 categories in all. After first establishing a satisfactory level of inter-observer agreement (81 per cent over all categories) two observers recorded

[1]A. Stevens, *Pupil Behaviour in an Open-plan Junior School*, and D. Ransom, *Classroom Observation of Mathematics Teaching in Mixed Ability Classes* (11-12 year olds). Unpublished MED dissertations, University of Sheffield, 1974.

the behaviour of each child in each of two classes (N=27 and 35) every 10 seconds during two 7 minute periods, one in the morning and one in the afternoon over a period of 3-4 weeks.

Although Spaulding distinguishes between settings which are teacher-directed and those which are not, these two were found to be quite inadequate in a flexible situation. Accordingly, the following settings were defined as being meaningful to both teachers and observers: Teacher instructs the whole class (TIC) or a small group (TIG); Teacher organizes activitity for the whole class (TOC) or for a small group (TOG); Children work individually on assignments (IA) or projects (IP); Children work in pairs or small groups on assignments (GA) or projects (GP). Actual observations were carried out in three settings only (IA, IP and GP) as these were the most frequently used, and from the records it was possible to derive four major categories of behaviours which were individual or social in character and task or non-task related.

When children were working on projects, they interacted freely with peers for approximately 25 per cent of the time in both conditions IP and GP. Some of these interactions were task related and some not. Taking them separately however, there was a significantly higher level of task related behaviour ($p < \cdot 05$) when the children were working together under condition GP than under condition IP. The same freedom of interaction was noted under condition IA and so the behaviour of the same children was compared under conditions IA and IP. Here, no differences were found in individual task-related behaviours but in the social/task category the children showed a significantly higher level of work involvement under IP than IA ($p < \cdot 05$).

These are two findings which would not have emerged by collapsing the data over different settings; and in the midst of controversies about the learning behaviour of children in the flexible environment of open-plan schools, the high level of task involvement in co-operative work and project work is something which requires further exploration and confirmation. It should be added that the general level of all task related behaviour recorded in this school was very high; out of 14 minutes on average, 12 would be spent 'on task' though this ignores wide individual differences.

The teachers were surprised by this finding, and it was clear that their estimates of task attention did not correspond to the observations made, but it is unlikely that a teacher can observe individuals accurately under the high pressure of managerial tasks which has been well documented by Hilsum and Cane (1971) and Jackson (1968). Also, there was evidence that their impressions were strongly coloured by other information they possessed. Previously, both teachers had rated each child on the behaviours represented by each of the CASES categories (observing the conventions necessary to overcome 'halo' effects as far as possible). These were correlated with the observational data and with a measure of reading attainment on the Widespan Reading Test (Brimer, 1972). For both teachers, all ratings correlated significantly with reading attainment, particularly in the category 'pays attention' (0·77 and 0·86, p<·01) and with 'wandering attention' (−0·62 and −0·46, p<·01), categories which are appropriate to class instruction settings and were hardly used in the settings observed. Correlations between observations and teachers' ratings reached significance only in the area of social task behaviour (0·39 and 0·37, p<·05), and partialling out the variable of reading attainment made little difference.

Apart from revealing a constant source of bias in the teachers' judgments it is clear that if comparisons of observations and ratings are to have any meaning, both must be related to the same settings. Garner (1972), in his study of infant school classes, recognizes that the explanation of variations in children's task attention may well be accounted for by the ways in which activities tend to be organized and how these reflect and define teacher style.

Turning now to studies of pupil/teacher interaction, two studies in particular have investigated inequalities of teacher/pupil contacts (Jackson and Lahaderne, 1967; Garner and Bing, 1973). In order to reduce the observational data to orderly dimensions, both chose to concentrate on teacher contacts with individual pupils only and to report their findings in terms of the number of contacts per hour to indicate a rate of interaction. Contacts were categorized as instructional, managerial or prohibitory (disciplinary) and a distinction made as to whether they were teacher or pupil initiated. Jackson and Lahaderne examined the interaction pattern in American high school classes, Garner and Bing in British primary schools. It is apparent from the data given that the former were much more teacher controlled than the latter; what is less clear is the way in which classes were organized, though Garner and Bing indicate that their classes were organized on a mixture of class instruction and seatwork settings. Whenever wide variations in teacher/pupil initiation are reported they are most likely to reflect the varying proportions of the time devoted to the different settings.

This may be demonstrated by an exploratory study in which nine mathematics lessons given to 11-12 year olds were observed in each of four schools (36 lessons in all). On average, the teacher initiated twice as many contacts with individual pupils when teaching the class as a whole as during workshop periods, when the initiated contacts were mainly from pupils. Thus all class instruction settings were teacher-dominated as one might expect, though there were quite large individual differences. Of all teacher-initiated contacts during such periods, 84 per cent were instructional and 16 per cent managerial, compared with 58 and 42 per cent respectively during the workshop periods (significant at $p < \cdot 01$).

Thus to report all findings in terms of a rate per hour and draw conclusions about teacher control is misleading. The high degree of verbal control by the teacher is much more characteristic of the class instruction setting whatever the age group, and the high managerial demands noted by Garner & Bing are more likely to occur in seatwork settings.

The findings presented above have three major implications for observational studies.

### 1. *The size and nature of the unit*

Biddle (1967) raises several issues in his discussion of the unit of analysis which can be summarised as those of size (molar *v* molecular) and nature (analytic *v* phenomenal).

On the issue of size, the investigator has to choose between taking large sequences of events or action as the basic unit (the molar level) and the smallest element which can reliably be observed (the molecular level). The first approach has been adopted by the ecological school (Barker & Wright, 1955) and the latter by the ethologists (e.g. Hutt & Hutt, 1970). For both, the identification and measurement of significant sequences of acts has proved an intractable problem.

Classroom settings are fundamentally molar in character in that they are based upon sequences, but they are sequences which have coherence arising from a unity of task and purpose. In terms of time, any single sequence may occupy a few minutes or an hour or longer. In the constantly changing settings of early education, the investigator must take care to observe an adequate sample of behaviours in each setting for results to have meaning. Time, as Nuthall and Church (1973) have shown, is a basic though neglected, variable in process/product research, and for results to be comparable the sequences of time should be comparable also.

Settings are also phenomenal units. Although Biddle regards these as unacceptable when analysing social processes, for the reasons quoted earlier, it would appear that under methods of flexible organization they are indispensable in describing the framework of classroom events. There is no reason why an investigator *within* this framework should not adopt analytic units to suit his particular conceptual stance (i.e. units such as cycles, episodes and moves which have a specific theoretical base).

### 2. *Settings and the teacher's role*

It has been argued (Hargreaves, 1972, 1974) that studies of class room interaction with their emphasis upon objective measurement, can reveal little about the meaning of events to the participants or about the ways in which they negotiate their respective roles. But the large variety of roles assumed by the teacher can be defined operationally by the range and variety of settings which are employed. The teacher who seeks to establish a controlling role will establish constraints on the possibility of interaction with individual pupils (Adams & Biddle, 1970); similarly, the teacher who sees himself in an advisory role will manipulate settings in order to maximize the spontaneous learning and problem-solving behaviour of the children. Thus Anderson, Brewer and Reed (1945) in their early studies of child behaviour found that teachers worked to cut the 'vicious circle' of dominative behaviour by seeking opportunities for more integrative contacts with individuals. However, a teacher may still act in an authoritarian way in relatively open settings and in an integrative way in periods of class instruction. It is only by examining the pattern of interaction *within* the setting that the relationship between intention and action can be revealed, e.g. Carnegie (1972) suggested that a high incidence of contacts under the pressure of time produced more authoritarian explanations, and thus reduced the levels of cognition used in the classroom. It would appear that the relationship between time and the teacher's choice of settings would be a particular source of interest in circumstances where primary schools are in the transition stage between more traditional and open-plan working. Freedom from the traditional constraints of time and space pose new problems of learning for teachers in handling the pattern of contacts to the best advantage. Terms used to describe teaching, such as authoritarian/democratic, dominative/integrative, direct/indirect, are a vast oversimplification. It is only by examining the teacher's use of settings and the pattern of contacts within them that relationships between the classroom environment and behaviour can be spelled out. In Biddle's words: the 'structure and functional properties of the classroom constitute the enfolding environment which enables and is affected by teacher-pupil interaction'.

3. *The generalization of findings*

McIntyre (1974) argues that systematic observation in natural classroom settings is necessary to produce valid information about classroom activities, and that in order to be able to generalize from one naturalistic setting to another, researchers must identify their sample of classes in terms of pupil, task, architecture and organizational activities. The organizational and task variables may clearly be represented by classroom settings, and generalization will be impossible unless the structural characteristics of different classroom environments are given a clear conceptual definition. A tentative framework has been suggested, and there is little doubt that the adoption of these or similar units would do much to clarify the findings of investigators in this area.

## References

ANDERSON, H. H., BREWER, J. E. and REED, M. F. (1945). 'Studies of teacher's classroom personalities', *Appl. Psychology Monographs*, Stanford Univ. Press.

ADAMS, R. S. and BIDDLE, B. J. (1970). *Realities of teaching: explorations with videotape*. New York: Holt, Rinehart & Winston.

BARKER, R. G. (1968). *Ecological Psychology*. Stanford, Cal: Stanford Univ. Press.

BARKER, R. G. and WRIGHT, H. F. (1955). *Midwest and its Children*. Evanston, Ill.: Row, Peterson & Co.

BIDDLE, B. J. (1967). 'Methods and concepts in classroom research', *Rev. Educ. Res.* **37,** 337–57.

BRANDT, R. M. (1972). *Studying Behaviour in Natural Settings*. New York: Holt, Rinehart & Winston.

BRIMER, M. A. (1972). *Widespan Reading Test*. London: Nelson.

CARNEGIE, V. (1972). *A Study of Teachers' Explanations*. Unpub. MA thesis. Univ. of Lancaster.

GARNER, J. and BING, M., (1973). 'Inequalities of teacher-pupil contacts', *Brit. J. Educ. Psychol*, **43,** 3 234–243.

GIBSON, D. R. (1970). 'The role of the primary and secondary school teacher', *Ed. Res.* **13,** 20–29.

GUMP, P. V. (1967). *Setting Variables and the Prediction of Teacher Behaviour.* Paper presented to the AERA New York.

HARGREAVES, D. H. (1972). *Interpersonal Relations and Education.* London: Routledge & Kegan Paul.

HARGREAVES, D. H. (1974). *Symbolic Interactionist Perspective on Classroom Studies:* a brief note. Paper presented to Inaugural Meeting of British Educational Research Association, University of Birmingham.

HILSUM, S. and CANE, B. S. (1971). *The Teacher's Day.* Slough: NFER

HUTT, S. J. and HUTT, C. (1970). *Direct Observation and Measurement of Behaviour.* Springfield, Illinois: Charles C. Thomas.

JACKSON, P. W. (1968). *Life in Classrooms.* New York: Holt Rinehart & Winston.

JACKSON, P. W. and LAHADERNE, H. M. (1967). 'Inequalities of teacher-pupil contacts', *Psychology in the Schools,* **4,** 204–11.

KOUNIN, J. S. (1970). *Discipline and group management in classrooms.* New York: Holt, Rinehart & Winston.

MCINTYRE, D. (1974). *Systematic Observation in Naturalistic Research.* Paper presented at Inaugural Meeting of the British Educational Research Association. Univ. of Birmingham.

PERKINS, HUGH V. (1964). 'A procedure for assessing the classroom behaviour of students and teachers', *Am. Ed. Res. Journal,* **1,** 49–60

PERKINS, HUGH V. (1965). 'Classroom behaviour and underachievement, *Am. Ed. Res. Journal,* **2,** 1–12.

ROSENSHINE, B. and FURST, N. (1973). 'The use of direct observation to study teaching.' In: TRAVERS, R. M. W. (ed.) *Second Handbook of Research on Teaching.* Chicago: Rand McNally, 122-183.

SPAULDING, R. L. (1970). *Classroom Behaviour Analysis and Treatment.* San José State College: Author.

# CHAPTER 15

# A Scottish Alternative to Interaction Analysis

*John L. Powell, Scottish Council for Research in Education*

When one starts to talk about any theme prefixed by the words 'alternatives to', there is an obvious risk of seeming to imply that one is seeking to substitute for an old and inefficient system some bright new panacea. I wish, therefore, to make it explicit that I have no wish to attack interaction analysis or its proponents. To do so would, in my view, be to criticize screwdrivers for not being efficient chisels. My subject here is a newly devised, relatively high inference system designed to serve a function different from, although related to, that of interaction analysis. By high inference I mean a system in which some reliance is placed on the observer's interpretation of what is happening.

Low inference measures permit one to look intensively, and with a high degree of objectivity, at a *small sub-set* of the complex set of behaviours exhibited by an individual (or perhaps a group of individuals) interacting with another individual or group. Usually a single aspect of the interaction is highlighted. The view of the classroom situation is a partial one. What is discovered may, for example, permit a detailed examination of one or more aspects of teaching technique, such as type of questioning employed, but ignore all other aspects. It may provide, at best, very limited contextualization of those chosen aspects. Moreover, since the output is typically in the form of frequency counts of discrete actions or sequences of actions, added interpretation is required.

Many of us, while grateful for such revelations as the microscope of interaction analysis may be able to provide, yearn for a more global approach. Of course, as soon as one attempts to look at many aspects of how a teacher is teaching, one finds it impracticable to use such methods. A higher level of inference is required. The whole process of observation has, therefore, inevitably to become more subjective, *at least at the time of the observation*. (Since, however, the output of interaction analysis normally requires interpretation, it is usually not itself wholly free of subjectivity.) Where subjectivity cannot be eliminated, it must as far as possible be controlled. How such control may be attempted is illustrated in the work described below.

In October 1973 The Scottish Council for Research in Education began a project which has come to be known as *Teaching Strategies in the Primary School*. The principal undertaking so far has been the production, by Mabel Scrimgeour and myself, of a classroom observation schedule which we have called SCOTS (System for Classroom Observation of Teaching Strategies). Limited trials of this schedule were carried out during the period of construction and development, and these led to substantial revisions. The schedule is being used during the 1974-75 school session when it will be used in recording observations of some 140 Scottish teachers. It may later be modified and published. The schedule is intended for use only in the middle and upper forms of the primary schools.

The term 'teaching strategies' is intended to cover all aspects of a teacher's teaching and classroom management with the exception of 'methods' in the narrowest sense. Thus, for example, it is not concerned with whether a teacher uses phonic or non-phonic methods of teaching reading, but it is concerned with those aspects of teaching practice that cut across these methods and probably influence the ways in which they are employed.

The SCOTS schedule in its current form makes assessments of 55 aspects of a teacher's strategy, each one relating to what has been judged to be a unitary dimension of teaching behaviour. The selection of these dimensions has, to some degree, been an arbitrary process. It was based on judgements made during unstructured or partially-structured observations of more than 40 teachers in the city of Dundee. Those aspects of behaviour noted during these observations and judged to be of potential significance were analysed to determine whether the observed variation lay on a unitary dimension or was the product of concurrent but independent variation on more than one *behavioural* dimension. Each dimension was then defined, special attention being paid to the extreme positions to ensure covering the full range of variation that might be encountered. These extreme positions were then arbitrarily designated 1 and 5, and intermediate positions – 2, 3, and 4 – defined so as to divide the range up reasonably evenly. Where necessary zero was used to indicate non-applicability to a specific case. The result is something looking very like the questions of a multiple-choice test of reading comprehension (see Table 1). It is, however, the observer who has to pick whichever option best describes what he has seen.

**Table 1:** Excerpts from 'System for classroom observation of teaching strategies (SCOTS)' by John L. Powell and Mabel N. G. Scrimgeour.*

**(I) Items requiring both information from Teacher and Observation****

| | T | | | |
|---|---|---|---|---|
| (1) *Visible differentiation by ability/achievement*<br>    (1) Pupils seated in rank order in accordance with test results or teacher's current assessment of each pupil's relative merit. | T | | | |
| (2) Pupils work for most of the time in ability groups whose composition does not change from subject to subject. | | | | |
| (3) Pupils work for most of the time in ability groups, but with numbership of groups varied according to subject. | | | | |
| (4) Work undertaken in ability groups *either* for one or two subjects *or* by some children only (e.g. the least and most able). | | | | |
| (5) No intentional correspondence between seating position and ability/achievement *and* no regular work undertaken in groups of identifiable ability level. | | | | |
| (2) *Flexibility/rigidity of locations*<br>    (1) No changing of pupils' seating positions permitted except when required by teacher. | T | | | |
| (2) For some subjects no changing of pupils' seating positions except as required by teacher; at other times pupils may change positions after consulting the teacher (who normally consents†). | | | | |
| † If the teacher refuses more than half of the requests made, code as 1. | | | | |

\* © The Scottish Council for Research in Education, 1974, whose permission to reproduce these extracts is gratefully acknowledged.

\*\* Columns marked 'T' indicate the observation at the end of which inquiries should be addressed to the teacher. Wherever possible the observer should clarify/confirm the teacher's statements by recalling for discussion relevant instances that have been observed.

*continued on next page*

| | T | | | | |
|---|---|---|---|---|---|

(3) At most times pupils may change positions after consulting the teacher (who normally consents*).

(4) For some subjects no changing of pupil's seating positions, but at other times free to change at will.

(5) Almost always pupils may change seating positions at will.

\* If the teacher refuses more than half the requests made, code as 2, though if more than 90 per cent refused, code as 1.

*Note:* If very few changes in fact occur such that there is doubt as to which coding applies, choose the lowest of the codings with which the evidence is consistent.

## (II) Items requiring observations only

(20) *Nature of teacher contacts with individual pupils*
 (1) All contacts of minimal duration and concerned only with answering simple questions, giving instructions, or making comments.

 (2) Contacts short and confined to clarifications or reminders of previous teaching or to suggesting new applications of existing knowledge.

 (3) Contacts short but devoted to either short periods of individual instruction or to guiding children to explore more widely aspects of ongoing work.

 (4) Contacts include, from time to time, individual instruction in depth (and therefore of some duration).

 (5) Contacts regularly include individual instruction in depth (and therefore of some duration).

(21) *Feedback to pupils*
 (1) Virtually no feedback: neither written correction nor oral response nor self-correcting materials to assist pupils in correcting errors or overcoming misunderstandings.

*continued on next page*

(2) Limited feedback provided, but not at a relevant time (e.g. corrections undertaken or marked work returned later than the day on which it has been done* *and* no attempt made by teacher to recall for the pupils the problems that were experienced at the time).

(3) Limited feedback provided at a relevant time (e.g. correction undertaken immediately or at least on the same day* *or*, if not on the same day, teacher makes effort to recall for pupil the problems that were experienced at the time).

(4) Feedback provided promptly and to a degree that appears to satisfy a substantial proportion of pupils' needs; limited facilities for pupil-correction of own work possibly available.

(5) A very full and well-organized system of feedback provided such that it is not impaired by over-involvement of teacher, (e.g. means of self-correction generally available such that the teacher can devote whole effort to providing assistance with major difficulties experienced by pupils).

* If the volume of correction is too great for completion within the day – e.g. extended written composition – or if the work is undertaken very near the end of a day's session, due allowance should be made.

*Note:* *Feedback* connotes any method by which a child is given assessment and/or correction of work undertaken.

*Note:* Items 20 and 21 come from the section of the schedule relating to Teaching and Learning.

It is necessary firstly to discuss the general validity of using a schedule of this sort. I have already mentioned the problems of controlling observer subjectivity. Control can best be achieved by requiring observers to rate separately relatively large numbers o aspects of behaviour that are not only carefully delineated, but fairly narrow in scope. To ask an observer to rate, say, 'teaching effectiveness' would, of course, be to invite disaster since the ratings would be likely to reflect the observer's own opinions of what constitutes good teaching. If, however, narrow dimensions of teaching behaviour can be defined and behavioural markers indicated, the risks of bias *in trained observers* can be reduced to negligible proportions. The markers of different levels on a dimension of teaching behaviour can be extremely variable and in some cases it is not possible to do more than indicate typical markers. Other manifestations have to be matched to these by the observer. This is not, however, necessarily a disadvantage. Indeed, the very purpose of employing a higher inference schedule is to make maximum use of the trained observer's ability to observe and interpret a large number of behavioural clues, and in particular to take cognizance of any 'counter-indications' that may be present.

This last point is particularly important because closely similar teaching behaviours can 'mean' quite different things according to the contexts in which they occur. One depends on the observer to distinguish between the superficial and the fundamental, between the essential and the inessential, between the appearance and the reality. To interpret what is occurring the human observer can take into account *whatever* evidence there is available to enable him to make as reliable a judgement as is possible on each of the dimensions of behaviour he is assessing. The global view which it is the purpose of the schedule to provide comes from the combination of all these assessments. The observer is, in effect, classifying each teaching strategy in more than fifty ways. (If making so many assessments seems a lot, it should be noted that trained observers find the task manageable. By no means all the assessments are difficult to make and there is adequate time to make them.)

The items in the SCOTS schedule have for convenience been arranged in seven groups: (1) those relating to practices about which the teacher is questioned to supplement what may be observed (7 items); (2) those relating to the direction or control of work (5 items); (3) those relating to teaching or learning (9 items); (4) those relating to motivation, class control, and discipline (11 items); (5) those relating to underemployment of pupils (4 items); (6) those relating to teacher personality and relationships with pupils (5 items); (7) miscellaneous (mode of performing administrative functions, pupil talk, etc.) (13 items).

The items reproduced in Table 1 have been selected on the basis that they are less of a 'security risk' than many of the other items. It is obviously necessary to treat a schedule such as this as analogues to a 'secure' test, since teachers familiar with it might when under observation modify their teaching in whatever direction they supposed the observers might judge favourably.

Item 1 is a particularly straightforward example. It seeks to cover the sort of ability grouping that, if it exists, will be readily apparent to the pupils concerned, though it implies no judgement on whether such knowledge has an adverse effect on the pupils. It happens to be also one of the items for which information is obtained from the teacher. The reason for asking the teacher about this matter is of course that it is often impossible for the observer to deduce the basis on which the most visible of groupings have been made. It is equally necessary to ask the teacher about item 2, since it relates to something that, even during five quarter-day observations of a single teacher (the period we intend to use), may be quite inadequately observed. The necessary questions are, it should be noted, posed in a very informal way at the end of an observation. The two inquiries already mentioned are made at the end of the *initial* observation. Others, where there is more risk of the teacher's being unintentionally influenced, are left to the end of the third or fourth observation. On such later occasions it is possible to recall to the teacher specific incidents that have occurred. This is advantageous since the teacher may be less likely to give an explanation divorced from the reality of his/her practice.

Item 20 is a good example of one way in which scots differs from a lower inference schedule – and not least so because this item is one of the very few in the scots schedule that does lend itself to a low-inference type of recording. Had it been found feasible for the observers to combine high and low inference recording, the latter might well have been adopted in this case. It can be seen to be at once a less accurate measure and yet one capable of making useful quasi-qualitative discriminations.

In the case of most items, the recordings made during each successive observation can be regarded as progressively closer approximations to the 'truth'. Very tentative entries are gradually replaced by ones about which the observer feels reasonably confident. This can, however, be true only of stable features of a teacher's classroom behaviour. Though there appear to be large numbers of such stable features, some features do vary from lesson to lesson, perhaps in response to the nature of the activity. Such variation is obviously more difficult to summate, though there may be no difficulty within any single observation. In some cases some sort of approximate 'averaging' at the end of the five observations makes sense, but more often it does not. Two 5's, two 2's and a 1 may be very poorly represented by a 3 as an average; the 3 may be simply wrong about all the occasions. For this reason in a number of cases – of which item 20 is one – a separate 'summative' version has had to be produced. In some cases this involves recording the extent of the variation; in others the most 'extreme' occurrence (at one end of the spectrum) is taken as the most significant feature.

Item 21, which has one of the most complex sets of behavioural markers of any item in the schedule, illustrates how carefully the schedule attempts to discriminate amongst cases. It would have been very easy to treat all feedback as equally valid functionally. Yet it is obvious that this is not so. It is a commonplace experience that guidance on a problem the nature of which one has forgotten is of little value. If feedback is to have any chance of being useful to pupils it has either to be immediate or to be accompanied by some form of recall of the original problem. Item 21 attempts to define as relevant feedback only that satisfying one of these criteria. (As a result the observer has to take pains to gather a good deal of data, partly from marked written work, before assigning a case to any category.)

At this point it may be helpful to state briefly a number of characteristics of the scots schedule:

(1) Though the schedule operates at a behavioural level, many of the behaviours are likely to be markers of more fundamental, and probably more important, characteristics. Thus, for example, though one item describes how responsibilities are allocated (if at all) amongst pupils, its main aim is to reveal whether the teacher regards responsibility as an important experience for all pupils (and particularly the least able) or whether the giving of responsibilities is no more than a way of relieving the teacher of some work. Similarly another item, while recording the relative prominence of competition or cooperation in respect of work, serves indirectly to record how far situations arise where the successful pupil is likely to find his success underlined and the less successful pupil his failure. Yet again, where an item ostensibly describes a range of ways of eliciting answers to questions in the cognitive domain, it in fact is seeking to reveal the *function* being served by the questioning – whether, at the one extreme, it is a scarcely disguised form of teacher statement, or whether, at the other, it is a means of getting pupils to arrive at answers by means of reasoning.

(2) The schedule is intended to be value-free, despite the fact that almost all the behaviours described in it are ones about which teachers and others commonly make value judgments. The point to bear in mind is that not everyone making a value judgment will agree on which of the five behaviours defined in an item is the 'best'. The range of an item is *not* from good to bad but from one extreme to the other. It is open to the individual to value any extreme or any intermediate position the most highly. The function of the observer is to record accurately and perceptively. If he makes value judgments, they are private, and irrelevant to his task.

(3) The schedule can record teacher-centred and pupil-centred teaching with equal facility. The fact that, though it uses the spoken word as evidence, it uses actions no less, is clearly important here. It should be noted that often interaction analysis systems suit only teacher-centred situations and that most are highly dependent on verbal interchange.

(4) The risk of misinterpreting what happens in a classroom is much diminished by the fact that the observer both has time to follow occurrences through before assessing them and may take into account anything he has observed that may lead to the making of a more valid judgment.

Construction of a schedule of this nature gives rise to considerable technical difficulties. For instance items have to be uni-dimensional since if there is more than one variant each operating independently the observer is likely to be faced on some occasions with contradictory indications. Examples A, B and C in Table 2 illustrate these points. Even given a dimension, the problem of ordering the items in a defensible sequence can be formidable. Good examples of the sort of areas where it may be difficult to find dimensions are paralinguistic signals and 'slowdowns'. Paralinguistic signals can relate to almost any dimension of behaviour and cannot be isolated. They have therefore to be treated by the observer as simply one of many sources of evidence for arriving at his assessments of dimensions of behaviour. Rather similarly, teachers slow down for many different reasons. Slowing down in itself means nothing. One may be able to incorporate specific instances of slowing down in different items in the schedule, but it is not a dimension in its own right.

**TABLE 2: Examples of unsuitable items**

---

### A

Example of an item unsuitable because of the lack of a dimension of variability.

*Diversion of pupil attention*

(1) Pupil's attention diverted by interruption of other pupils.
(2) Group of pupils diverted by teacher calling some pupils to another task.
(3) Pupils diverted by listening in to work of another group.
(4) Pupils diverted by teacher using loud voice when working with group of individual children.
(5) Pupils' attention diverted by incidents outside room.

*Note:*   *Degree of diversion is apparently approximately constant. Type of interruption does not fall on any continuum. There is thus no dimension of variation.*

### B

Example of more than one variable within an item.

*Organizational information*

(1) Teacher proceeds without cueing pupils.
(2) Inappropriate, ill-thought out and probably confusing instructions.
(3) Instructions appropriate but lacking in precision.
(4) Instructions clear and precise *but no questions allowed.*
(5) Instructions clear and precise. *Individual queries answered.*

*Note:*   (1)   *The italicized phrases constitute a second independent dimension of variation.*
(2)   *There are insufficient behavioural indications.*
(3)   *With the omission of the italicized phrases and the adding of additional matter this item became suitable for inclusion in the schedule.*

### C

Example of lack of a unitary dimension.

*Organization: uniform/diverse activity*

(1) All pupils work at same subject task.
(2) All pupils work in same subject area but two clearly separate tasks allocated.
(3) All pupils work in the same subject area but there are more groups involved in different tasks.
(4) Tasks and subject areas vary between groups.
(5) Individuals work at own task.

*Note:*   *The variants include (a) difficulty levels, (b) subject areas, (c) number of groups. It is essential to decide which is the variant to be taken. If more than one is to be taken, more than one item must be constructed.*

---

A behavioural schedule clearly requires definition in behavioural terms. In practice, however, the variety of manifestations of essentially similar behaviours is so great that defining for the observer all possible behaviours would yield a schedule of unmanageable proportions. Frequently the observer can only be given examples of the type of behaviours that should be taken as good indicators. He has to assess for himself what other behaviours should be regarded as equivalent. Nonetheless it should be stressed that behavioural indications should be given as fully as is reasonable.

Using a schedule such as SCOTS clearly requires a good deal of training. Not only has the observer to become familiar with it but he has to learn the ways in which many of the descriptive terms used are operationally defined. No less important is experience of the range of behaviours likely to be found. Inexperienced observers tend to use too extreme ratings – say a 5 when only a 4 is justified – simply because they have never experienced anything more extreme than what they are looking at. The observer who knows the full range has no difficulty. In short, placing a teacher on any of the dimensions does involve some relative assessment as well as matching to the behavioural descriptions. The behavioural descriptions often cannot be exhaustive enough to avoid some dependence on assessment of 'level'.

This last point may give rise to doubts about observer reliability using the SCOTS schedule. Data on inter-observer agreement is in the process of being gathered, and experience so far suggests that acceptable levels are attainable.

It is hoped that, by the use of various forms of cluster analysis, we shall be able to isolate groups of teachers each having what may reasonably be termed a common teaching strategy. Thereafter we aim to try to establish associations between the employment of these strategies and patterns of pupil outcomes in the cognitive and affective domains. This will be a formidable task, but it is essential to attempt to provide teachers with some indications of the effects of some of the most basic elements of their teaching techniques, elements that may well be far more significant than any teaching 'method' that may be adopted to teach a specific subject or skill. The variables we are attempting to measure are no doubt in most cases themselves only surrogates, but it is in terms of these surrogates that a teacher commonly thinks when deciding what to do. What the surrogates stand for may not be clear and may not matter in practi-

cal terms. Whether we have included in the schedule all the elements
of teaching behaviour that we should is of course an open question.
There can be little doubt that some of our dimensions will prove
irrelevant and that they will constitute only 'noise' in the analysis.
Identifying which these are will no doubt be a major difficulty. It may
be argued that our coverage would have been better had we based
the schedule on some theoretical framework. Our view is that the
'state of the art' does not permit this. Various, possibly overlapping,
subsets of the items relate to various possible theoretical frameworks.
It is our hope that the eclectic approach of the scots schedule will
help in the identification of the most useful frameworks.